POLITICAL CHANGE IN
JAPAN

D1121314

 **COMPARATIVE STUDIES OF POLITICAL LIFE**

SERIES EDITOR: **Martin O. Heisler**

POLITICAL CHANGE IN
JAPAN
RESPONSE TO POSTINDUSTRIAL CHALLENGE

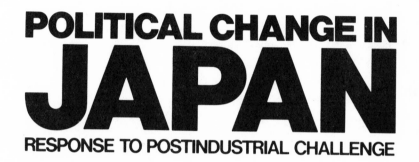

TAKETSUGU TSURUTANI

Washington State University

Longman

New York & London

Political Change in Japan:
Response to Postindustrial Challenge

COPYRIGHT © 1977 BY LONGMAN INC.

All rights reserved, including the right to reproduce
this book, or parts thereof, in any form, except for
the inclusion of brief quotations in a review.

Library of Congress Cataloging in Publication Data

Tsurutani, Taketsugu.
  Political change in Japan.

  (Comparative studies of political life)
  Bibliography: p.
  Includes index.
  1. Japan—Politics and government—1945-
2. Political parties—Japan. 3. Political participa-
tion—Japan. I. Title. II. Series:
Comparative studies of political life (New York)
JQ1681.T75   1980   320.952   80-10282
ISBN 0-582-28183-0 pbk.

MANUFACTURED IN THE UNITED STATES OF AMERICA
9 8 7 6 5 4 3 2

To Gabu

Preface

In preparing this volume, I incurred many unrepayable debts. Special thanks go to Terrence Cook, Charles Sheldon, Andrea Weber, and the publisher's anonymous reviewer for their thorough, detailed, and most helpful criticisms of the first draft of the manuscript. Errors and other shortcomings that still remain are entirely mine. I am grateful also to Donald Hoisington, Grace Loftin, and Jose Peer, who spared time to read and comment on the manuscript. Last but not least, I offer my appreciation to Joyce Lynd, who typed both the first and the revised drafts of the manuscript with her unfailing cheerfulness, concern, and dispatch.

Each scholar has different motives for writing a book. I wrote this volume partly because I wanted to impress my young daughter that I knew something about one of her two homelands. In the years to come, she might say "Daddy, you were all wrong!"

But, then, I would at least have the satisfaction that she understood what I was talking about. It is to her that this book is dedicated.

Tokyo
July 1976

Contents

Part ▌

JAPAN AS A
POSTINDUSTRIAL SOCIETY

1

Introduction

This is a book about politics in Japan. It is written from a perspective that differs significantly from the one that is common among recent scholarly books on Japanese politics. Those books compare Japanese politics with Western—or, perhaps more precisely, Anglo-American—politics. Either explicitly or implicitly, Western politics serve as a model against which Japanese politics are studied and, more often than not, evaluated. From this conventional perspective, Japan is a highly industrialized and affluent society (that is to say, much like the advanced Western nations) whose politics are not quite modern or sophisticated (unlike those Western nations). In short, Japan is industrially very modern but sociopolitically neither as modern nor as developed. Interestingly enough, this conventional view is shared not only among Western students of Japanese politics but also among Japanese scholars themselves. Thus, "Japan is an open society made up of closed components."[1] Her politics is that curious amalgam of parochial interpersonal and social relationship and procedural pluralism called a "patron-client democracy,"[2] and her society is still not only highly stratified but also characterized by mutually exclusive group loyalties that inhibit genuine social integration.[3] The Western model of modernity gives us the picture of a highly industrialized society where the political process is open, rational, and highly competitive, and where the major criterion for social and political mobility, recruitment, and advancement is ability and achievement. The sample remarks quoted above obviously indicate that Japan is a bit short of satisfying this model.

I am not saying that those remarks about Japanese politics are incorrect. To a considerable extent, they are accurate, or, we might begin to say that they *were* accurate. Much of what they describe still persists in Japan. The purpose of this book, however, is neither to challenge their accuracy nor to dispute the value of comparing Japanese politics against any national or cultural model, whether derived from Western politics or not. It is rather to suggest another method of studying and evaluating Japanese politics, from a perspective that is different both conceptually and analytically from the one most books on Japanese politics have employed. The reason for employing this new perspective is my conviction that this different approach will significantly enhance our knowledge and understanding of Japanese politics in a number of important ways that the conventional approach cannot. The conventional approach has served its purpose (mainly of showing how different Japan is from other nations), and it may still be useful to many. But a new approach will add new dimensions to the scholarship on Japanese politics.

The perspective from which this book is written, then, focuses on the transition of a society from industrialism to postindustrialism. It arises out of a recognition that changes take place beyond the stage of modernity and development that the

1. Robert Scalapino and Junnosuke Masume, *Parties and Politics in Contemporary Japan* (Berkeley and Los Angeles: University of California Press, 1961), p. 154.

2. Nobutaka Ike, *Japanese Politics: Patron-Client Democracy* (New York: Knopf, 1972).

3. Chie Nakane, *Japanese Society* (Berkeley and Los Angeles: University of California Press, 1970).

conventional Western model of political development prescribes and that some things are in fact already happening beyond this stage. In the *lingua franca* of political science, the whole spectrum of the development of society has been divided into three stages: traditional, transitional, and modern (or, alternatively, underdeveloped, developing, and developed). And a varying set of properties or features has been posited in each of these stages.

Briefly summarized: The traditional stage of society is characterized by subsistence agrarian economy, monopoly of power by the few whose rule is legitimized by tradition (secular or religious), a low level of education and social integration, and a very parochial political culture, among others. The modern society, on the other hand, is a highly industrialized and integrated one where people are sophisticated and active participants in the political process, through interest groups at one level and political parties and elections at another, in ways to hold formal political decision makers accountable to them; where the individual's worth is judged on the basis of ability and achievement; and where stability is sustained by an enlightened "civic" political culture.[4] The transitional stage of development falls in between these two types of society or phases of development. Both traditional and modern societies are said to be characterized by stability, while the transitional period manifests varying degrees of instability and unpredictability precisely because it is transitional. Thus, during the transitional stage, society, depending upon its particular predicament, frequently suffers from regression and digression, or what Huntington termed "political decay."[5] Accordingly, most nations of the world before, say, 1850 were traditional, as were such countries as Ethiopia, Afghanistan, Bhutan, and Sikkim until only a few years ago. Most of the Third World nations (and Japan, to some observers) are at various points of the "transitional" or "developing" stage, some perhaps more modern than transitional while others are barely developing. Northwestern European nations and Anglo-American countries are presumably modern or developed. Or so we are given to understand. Apart from any

4. Gabriel A. Almond and Sidney Verba, *The Civic Culture: Political Attitudes and Democracy in Five Nations* (Boston and Toronto: Little, Brown, 1965).

5. Samuel P. Huntington, "Political Development and Political Decay," *World Politics* 17 (April 1965).

legitimate quibbles about semantics[6] and the obvious ethnocentrism of this prevailing perspective of political development and change, one could reasonably ask: "Is the so-called developed or modern stage as posited in this model the end of political change?" It is out of this query that the perspective on which this book is based arises.

POSTINDUSTRIALISM AS A FORMATIVE CONCEPT

My approach derives from a division of developmental process or spectrum of political change that is considerably different from the conventional one mentioned above. It is, of course, just as arbitrary a construct as its conventional counterpart, but it may help us see political change in ways that the other perspective does not. We divide the developmental spectrum into three stages: preindustrial, industrial, and postindustrial. The reader may say, "Well, that's still three stages, like the other one!" But there is a very important difference. Our perspective, as will become clear in subsequent chapters, specifically focuses on fundamental political change as arising out of certain critical shifts in the nature and character as well as process of politics from one stage to another, while the conventional model concerns itself largely with the twin process of political integration and industrialization up to the stage assumed to have been achieved by certain Western industrial nations. The conventional developmental spectrum thus contains only the preindustrial (i.e., agrarian) and the industrial periods in terms of the nature, character, and process of politics; it does not, as we shall find shortly, include the postindustrial stage. The transitional or developing stage on this spectrum is a varying mix of preindustrialism and industrialism both in economy and politics, while the modern or developed stage is presumed to be wholly industrial in both dimensions. Our spectrum, in contrast, contains an additional stage, the postindustrial stage, which I believe manifests a very important change in the nature, character, and process of politics from that posited or assumed in the modern or developed stage in the conventional model.

To digress a bit: The term "postindustrial" is no longer

6. For an interesting discussion of ideas of progress and change, see, for example, Robin G. Collingwood, *The Idea of History* (New York: Oxford University Press, 1967), esp. pp. 144–46 and 321–34.

novel, though its use by political scientists is fairly recent. The term was first coined, rather casually, it seems, by David Riesman in 1958[7] but it was not until the mid-1960s that this concept began to be studied seriously by certain sociologists, such as Daniel Bell and Alain Touraine.[8] The initial concept that grew out of scholarly perceptions of certain novel social and economic phenomena of advanced industrial society such as the United States has at the same time also given rise to a wide variety of terms either basically the same or at least similar in meaning, such as "temporary society,"[9] "technological society,"[10] "post-modern society,"[11] "post-welfare state,"[12] and so on.[13] Today, the concept "postindustrial," depending upon who is using it, subsumes under its rubric a variety of considerations and indices relating to levels of technological development, theoretical knowledge, industrial structure, economic conditions, social relationships, and the like. It is, however, still a very loose, if complex, concept, and considerable debate and controversy continue over it. Again, briefly summarized: the major features of postindustrial society that emerge from these various works include, among others, the majority of labor employment to be found in the so-called service sector, the service sector generating a larger share of the gross national product (GNP) than the agricultural and manufacturing sectors combined, a high level of affluence and mass material well-being, the national economy becoming "knowledge-intensive" in contrast to "capital-intensive" and

7. "Leisure and Work in Post-Industrial Society," in *Mass Leisure*, ed. E. Larrabee and R. Meyersohn (New York: Free Press, 1958).

8. See, for example, "Notes on the Post-Industrial Society (1)," *Public Interest* 6 (Winter 1967); "Notes on the Post-Industrial Society (2)," *Public Interest* 7 (Spring 1967); and Alain Touraine, *The Post-Industrial Society*, trans. Leonard F. X. Mayhew (New York: Random House, 1971); among others.

9. Warren G. Bennis and Philip E. Slater, *The Temporary Society* (New York: Harper & Row, 1968).

10. Jacques Ellul, *The Technological Society* (New York: Vintage Book, 1964).

11. Amitai Etzioni, *The Active Society* (New York: Free Press, 1968).

12. M. Donald Hancock and Gideon Sjoberg, eds., *Politics in the Post-Welfare State* (New York and London: Columbia University Press, 1972).

13. For other terms or titles describing essentially the same phenomenon, see, for example, Daniel Bell, *The Coming of Postindustrial Society: A Venture in Social Forecasting* (New York: Basic Books, 1973), chap. 1.

"labor-intensive," and a decline of "work ethic" and "materialist values."

All these features are interesting, but there is one important feature of postindustrial society that has not been subjected to as much scrutiny as these features and other considerations, and that is the explicitly political dimension. Political scientists have been rather tardy in paying close attention to postindustrialism, with the result that, thus far, the most interesting and best-known works regarding postindustrial society have been produced by sociologists, economists,[14] social critics,[15] and futurologists.[16] A relatively small number of political scientists have been devoting some of their attention to postindustrialism,[17] and college courses in comparative politics are still conducted according to the conventional approach. In a way, therefore, our effort to study Japanese politics within the context of transition from indus-trialism to postindustrialism is among the early efforts by political scientists to focus on political consequences of postindustrialism. And I hope we can make some sense in our endeavor.

Now, back to our developmental spectrum of political change. We all recognize that a model is a model, not the precise and faithful reproduction of any real society or developmental stage. A model is an intellectual construct designed to provide a new view of the subject of inquiry, to suggest a different way of looking at it, so that we may become aware of phenomena that

14. For example, John K. Galbraith, *The New Industrial State* (Boston: Houghton Mifflin, 1967).

15. Two of the more prominent among them are Charles Reich, *The Greening of America* (New York: Random House, 1971); and Theodore Roszak, *Where the Wasteland Ends: Politics and Transcendence in Post-industrial Society* (New York: Doubleday, 1972).

16. See Herman Kahn and Anthony Wiener, *The Year 2,000: A Frame-work for Speculation on the Next Thirty-Three Years* (New York: Mac-millan, 1967); Alvin Toffler, *Future Shock* (New York: Bantam Books, 1970); and others.

17. See Zbigniew Brzezinski, *Between Two Ages: America's Role in the Technetronic Era* (New York: Viking Press, 1970); Samuel P. Hunting-ton, "Postindustrial Politics: How Benign Will It Be?" *Comparative Politics* 6 (January 1974); Leon N. Lindberg, ed., *Politics and the Future of Industrial Society* (New York: David McKay, 1976); Leon N. Lindberg, ed., *Stress and Contradiction in Modern Capitalism: Public Policy and the Theory of the State* (Lexington, Mass.: Lexington Press, 1976); Martin O. Heisler, ed., *Politics in Europe: Structures and Processes in Some Postindustrial Democracies* (New York: David McKay, 1974); and Hancock and Sjoberg, *Politics in the Post-Welfare State*.

might otherwise remain invisible or unclear, and explain them, to make sense of them. Thus, while conceptually distinguishable, there are in reality no pure "postindustrial" societies, at least as yet. Instead, what we can find are societies that are relatively more postindustrial than others. For this reason we shall employ in this volume what is called a scalar conceptualization, according to which we may be able to say that society X is more postindustrial than, say, society Y, and so on. At the same time, we should be able to find a certain configuration of phenomena that sets a given society apart from other societies. The features of post-industrial society we cited above, features suggested by a series of works by sociologists and others as elements of postindustrial economic and social conditions, themselves would help us identify any number of societies that might be viewed as postindustrial, however arbitrary the selection of those features may be. Presumably, we may find some societies that manifest all those features (though some of the criteria are hard to operationalize, or at least more difficult to apply than others because of the nature of data involved), while, most likely, more societies satisfy only some criteria. Hence the scalar conceptualization.

The perspective to be employed in this book is based on the idea that economic conditions, some of which are relatively easy to ascertain (notice that the term "industrial" is included in the description of all three stages of change), generate certain distinct political phenomena. One need not be a Marxist to say this, and I do not subscribe to either Marxism as such or any perspective that might be considered Marxian. What I am suggesting here (and we shall examine Japanese politics as a case study in this volume) is that the particular kind of configuration of economic conditions found in each of those three stages of change on our developmental spectrum can largely determine (or ascertainably influence, if "determine" is too strong a word) the nature, the character, the process, and the objective of political conflict. In particular, I suggest that the politics of the postindustrial stage differs significantly and ascertainably from the politics in the so-called modern, open, industrial society that, after all, has served as the model for other nations to emulate.

JAPAN AS A CASE STUDY

The reader may wonder why Japan, which the conventional perspective has regarded as less than fully modern or developed politically, can serve as a useful case study of emerging post-industrial politics. There are three reasons. The most obvious one is that I regard Japan as postindustrial on the basis of three fairly clear and cross-nationally applicable economic criteria (see p. 12).

The second reason is that the developmental process can be telescoped in many different ways, and this is true whether we use our developmental spectrum or the conventional one. That Japan is less developed politically than, say, the United States in terms of the conventional notion of political change does not in itself mean that Japan must always remain behind the United States in her political change. In the past, Japan has, in more senses than one, telescoped the developmental process. While Britain and America, for example, took over a century to evolve from a basically agrarian condition to indus-trialization, Japan accomplished the task in less than sixty years. While feudalism expired in Britain more than five centuries ago, Japan was a feudal, insulated island nation until little more than a hundred years ago, but her political development from feudalism to a parliamentary system with universal manhood suffrage spanned less than sixty years. In short, Japan's develop-ment, both industrially and politically, was highly abbreviated. Japan, of course, is not the only extant nation to perform this rather amazing feat; the rise and development of Germany followed a similar pattern. Both nations, we might say, "skipped" certain steps in their evolution to modernity. These historical experiences seem to argue that it is possible for some societies to dispense with certain points in the modern or industrial period and advance into what we call the postindustrial stage. As the following chapters indicate, Japan is doing exactly that. Which brings us to the third reason for studying Japan.

Japan, I submit, is relatively free from a number of significant institutional constraints by which some nations that, together with Japan, may be considered postindustrial, according to the three cross-nationally applicable *economic* criteria, seem to be variously handicapped in *politically* evolving into the post-industrial period. These constraints are what would otherwise be regarded as strengths if we were talking simply about "modern" or "developed" society according to the conventional develop-mental perspective.

For example, the so-called democratic political organizations (such as parties, the process of participation, interest groups) are not only highly developed but also deeply entrenched in the whole process of politics in such modern, open industrial nations as the United States, and they are properly credited with having promoted and helped maintain general domestic stability and well-being over the past hundred years. These organizations and arrangements, of course, have not remained static in those years; they in fact have undergone important qualitative, quantitative, and incremental modifications together with the gradual advance and consolidation of modern industrial society. In short, they have in the past demonstrated varying degrees of adaptability to the changing socioeconomic environment. This is actually the primary reason for the conventional developmental spectrum constructed by political scientists.

In Japan, on the other hand, those "modern" political organizations and arrangements are relatively new—they are at best only thirty years old. Moreover, they were imposed on Japan by the victorious Americans during their military occupation of the country after World War II. Their degree of entrenchment (or institutionalization, to use political sciencese) in Japanese society, therefore, is not very great. In an important sense, they may still be viewed as fragile. It is precisely for this reason that many scholars and observers, Japanese and foreign alike, regard the viability of democracy (as it exists today) in Japan with varying degrees of uncertainty and apprehension and that many political scientists feel Japan is not yet fully developed or modern in her politics.

Notice, however, that those organizations and arrangements, wherever they are entrenched, came into being and/or evolved in industrial society during the industrial stage of our developmental spectrum. Why? Because, as we will find in later chapters, they emerged or were created in a crucial sense in response to the requirements and needs of industrial society. They are therefore deeply embedded in such a society. Now, if we are right in arguing that postindustrial society faces significantly different economic conditions and hence is becoming different politically as well from industrial society, it stands to reason that those organizations and arrangements, wedded as they are to the requirements and needs of industrial society and tied as they are to its values, goals, and preferences, would have difficulty meeting the new requirements and needs of postindustrial society. The level of difficulty or infirmity they would face would be commensurate with the degree to which they are entrenched and habituated or, parodoxically enough, with the degree to which they have proved to be successful in the past.[18] When an organization or an arrangement becomes deeply entrenched, it can lose its ability to adapt itself to new circumstances. Lowi observes this phenomenon as the "tendency of all organizations to maintain themselves at the expense of needed change and innovation," and terms it "the iron law of decadence."[19]

And this is the reason for my thinking that, since those political organizations and arrangements typical of modern industrial society are relatively new, hence less entrenched, in Japan, the country is less constrained in its evolutionary development into the postindustrial period than some other highly industrial nations (such as the United States) where those organizations are deeply entrenched, and that this fact helps Japan manifest more readily many phenomena that we might associate with postindustrial politics. In an important sense, I am venturing to say that in certain important respects, postindustrial politics is emerging in Japan much earlier than in the United States. To study political change in Japan from our particular perspective, therefore, is a very useful exercise not only because we may understand Japanese politics and society better, but also because, by so doing, we may be able (though we will not in this volume make any explicit attempt) to generate a number of hypotheses and considerations that could be applied to studies of other nations that may be viewed as postindustrial.

JAPAN AS A POSTINDUSTRIAL SOCIETY

We are interested in studying political change in Japan as she undergoes transition from her period of industrialism to that of postindustrialism. We shall begin, therefore, with a set of relatively simple economic criteria in order to identify Japan as a postindustrial society. In the study of complex problems, it is helpful sometimes to start with a simple definition of the subject of inquiry in order to ascertain its more complex dimensions. In

18. See, for example, Mark Kesselman, "Overinstitutionalization and Political Constraints: The Case of France," *Comparative Politics* 3 (October 1970).

19. Theodore Lowi, *The Politics of Disorder* (New York and London: Basic Books, 1971), p. 5. Also consider "dynamic conservatism" as discussed by Donald A. Schon, *Beyond The Stable State* (New York: Norton, 1971), p. 32.

short, we commence with the simple and work our way to the complex.

In an attempt to identify Japan as postindustrial, we shall use three simple, cross-nationally applicable material criteria. They are: (1) the proportion of labor force employed in the so-called service sector of national economy; (2) the output by this sector as a percentage of the gross national product (GNP); and (3) the level of capital accumulation.

A nation's economy is generally divided into three sectors. The primary sector consists of agriculture, fishery, and forestry. The secondary (also called manufacturing) sector comprehends mining, construction, and all other endeavors for conversion of raw materials into finished or semifinished products. The tertiary (or service) sector provides services but does not produce material goods in the sense that a factory does. While the primary sector produces rice, corn, wheat, vegetables, lumber, and fish, for example, and the secondary sector turns out steel, coal, cars, machinery, canned goods, and a whole range of both consumer and capital goods, the tertiary sector provides such services as repair work, transportation and communication, utilities, sanitation, government service, education, entertainment, medical care, legal counsel, sales, banking and real estate, postal service, and so forth.

Every society has a different mix of these three economic sectors, and different societies can be categorized according to the extent to which each of the three economic sectors predominates. A society is "postindustrial," according to a generally accepted or acquiesced notion among interested scholars, if its tertiary economic sector employs the majority of its labor force.[20] Likewise, society can be classified as "industrial" when the secondary sector employs the largest number of workers, and as clearly "preindustrial" if an overwhelming majority of the population is engaged in agriculture. In this regard, Japan today is clearly

20. A postindustrial society is "one in which more than half of the economic activity is devoted to services, whether measured by value of product or by distribution of the labor force." Eleanor Sheldon and Wilbert Moore, "Monitoring Social Change in American Society," in *Indicators of Social Change*, ed. Sheldon and Moore (New York: Russell Sage Foundation, 1968), p. 13. Although most students of postindustrial society tend to take the 50%-plus as a handy delineation in terms of labor distribution, others use different points of demarcation. For example, one author suggests not a mere 50%-plus but a minimum of 70%. See James J. Heaphy, *Spatial Dimensions of Developmental Administration* (Durham, N.C.: Duke University Press, 1971).

TABLE 1.1. GROSS DOMESTIC CAPITAL FORMATION

(in billion yen)				
1955	**1960**	**1965**	**1970**	**1972**
3,613.4	6,639.2	14,714.4	32,389.2	44,162.2

Source: *Nihon Tokei Nenkan Showa 48–49 Nen*, p. 489.

postindustrial. In 1973, according to statistical information provided by the Japanese government, 54.6 percent of the labor force was in the tertiary sector.[21] Another source even indicates that she was postindustrial as early as in 1968 (53 percent).[22] In this respect, Japan is one of at least nine economically highly advanced nations that can be viewed as postindustrial.[23] (See table 1.2.)

The output by the tertiary sector as a proportion of Japan's GNP, which is a second measure used here for identifying post-industrial society, has been above 50 percent since 1963.[24] As of 1972, there were thirteen other countries whose tertiary sectors produced more than 50 percent of their GNP (the United States, Great Britain, Canada, Australia, Sweden, New Zealand, Israel, Holland, Denmark, Norway, Argentina, Finland, and Belgium).[25] The level of capital accumulation in Japan has risen at a phenomenal rate in the past twenty years, as we can readily see in table 1.1 To use another, more comprehensive index, the total capital accumulation (excluding that of financial and in-surance firms) in 1960 was 6.7 trillion yen. By 1969, it increased to 25 trillion yen.[26] All these figures may be interesting, but how high should the level of capital accumulation be in order for a society to be postindustrial? I do not think anybody is quite

21. *Nihon Tokei Nenkan Showa 48–49 Nen* (Tokyo: Sorifu Tokei Kyoku, 1974), pp. 50–51.

22. Ryuken Ohashi, *Nihon no Kaikyu Kosei* (Tokyo: Iwanami, 1972), p. 132.

23. *Kokusai Tokei Yoran 1975* (Tokyo: Sorifu Tokei Kyoku, 1975), p. 29.

24. Computed from data in *Asahi Nenkan 1975* (Tokyo: Asahi Shimbum Sha, 1975), p. 303. The figure was 51.3% in 1963 and increased to 56.5% by 1973.

25. *Kokusai Tokei Yoran 1975*, pp. 185–86.

26. Ohashi, *Nihon no Kaikyu Kosei*, pp. 96–97.

certain, for it is like asking "how wealthy does one have to be in order to be wealthy?" A rule of thumb suggested by one student of postindustrialism, however, is that the level of capital accumulation should be such that "scarcity is no longer a major *social* problem."[27] What this means is simply that the level of capital accumulation reflected in various relevant and interrelated indices such as domestic capital formation, per capita national income, and so on, is such that, objectively speaking, poverty is no longer an insoluble economic problem and that there is an amount of income for society to support everybody in a decent standard of living. Given the fact of the insatiability of human desires, we should of course anticipate that the more everybody gets, the more he is likely to want. Madison Avenue would see to that.

In any event, the mere fact that a nation generates the level of income that would provide a high standard of living for its citizenry does not mean that poverty is nonexistent. Indeed, there are many pockets of poverty and affluence in Japan, as in other postindustrial societies. Those pockets of poverty exist, however, because there are defects in the existing policies and mechanisms of income and wealth distribution and because there is strong resistance against instituting policies and mechanisms to implement a more equitable distribution of income and wealth. Poverty, therefore, is no longer an economic problem. It is a serious political problem calling not for further economic growth but for political action and solution. By 1972, for example, Japan's per capita income had risen well above $2,500[28] and there was no reason why everybody could not live comfortably in that prosperous society. The fact that not everybody could was a serious political, and not economic, problem, and the problem persists.

In industrialized nations, the level of annual per capita income closely reflects that of capital accumulation (unlike suddenly rich nations, of which we know a few). The accumulated capital, in the form of factories, machinery, distribution and sales networks, raw material inventories, combined with modern technology and skilled manpower, produces the income.

27. Christopher Lasch, "Toward a Theory of Post-Industrial Society," in *Politics in the Post-Welfare State,* ed. M. Donald Hancock and Gideon Sjoberg (New York and London: Columbia University Press, 1972), p. 36. Emphasis mine.

28. *Asahi Nenkan 1975,* p. 298.

Hence the close correlation between capital accumulation and per capita income. Let us take an annual per capita income of $2,500 as the minimum for identifying postindustrial societies in this dimension and see in table 1.2 which major open industrial nations satisfy this criterion as well as the preceding two dimensions. The figures in table 1.2 are approximations by the very nature of statistics. On the basis of the three cross-nationally applicable economic criteria, then, Japan is one of eight "post-industrial" countries. The remaining seven are not far behind: West Germany, New Zealand, Holland, and Norway satisfy two of the three criteria while Argentina, Finland, and France meet at least one, and all but Argentina enjoyed high capital accumulation judging from per capita income. Within the composite context of these three criteria, even among the "postindustrial" group of nations, some are more postindustrial than others; of the other six, one could say some are closer to being postindustrial than others. By the time this book meets the reader's eye, all the nations in the table, with the possible exception of Argentina, will most likely be postindustrial and ranked differently in terms of their respective degrees of postindustrialism.

TABLE 1.2. POSTINDUSTRIAL SOCIETIES, 1970–72

	Tertiary Sector Employment as % of Total	Tertiary Sector Output as % of GNP	Per Capita Annual Income (U.S.$)
Argentina	46	52	1,100
Australia	58	54	3,400
Belgium	53	56	3,300
Britain	52	60	2,500
Canada	63	65	4,300
Denmark	59	57	3,800
Finland	46	48	2,600
France	48	48	3,400
Holland	48	55	3,100
Japan	54	56	2,600
New Zealand	52	49	2,700
Norway	45	60	3,100
Sweden	63	52	4,700
United States	63	63	5,000
West Germany	44	56	3,700

Sources: *Kokusai Tokei Yoran*, pp. 181–82, 185–86; *1972 Year Book of Labour Statistics* (Geneva: International Labour Office, 1973), pp. 44–277; *Yearbook of National Accounts Statistics 1974* (N.Y.: United Nations, 1975), 1:16 and 63, 2:520–21.

So Japan is postindustrial. But what does that mean politically? I said earlier that postindustrialism (identified in economic terms) induces political change. We are yet to see how. Now, while that is the whole purpose of this book, it may not be altogether unprofitable to take a brief look at how such postindustrialism is affecting the Japanese society at large. The next chapter examines some of the more significant socioeconomic changes that have taken place in Japan in recent years and also some elements of continuity from the past in order to provide an empirical background to discussions in the subsequent chapters.

2

Socioeconomic Change and Continuity

SOCIOECONOMIC CHANGE

That Japan today is significantly different, in some respects radically different, from, say, even the 1960s seems obvious. Simple statistics tell the story. Consider the increases in the GNP and national income: In 1955 the GNP was 8.9 trillion yen; ten years later, it was 32.8 trillion yen; and by 1972, it had grown to 95.6 trillion yen. The net national income in the meantime had grown from 7.3 trillion yen in 1955 to 26.1 trillion yen in 1965 to 76.2 trillion yen in 1972. During the same period, the *net* annual growth rate of GNP averaged well over 10 percent.[1] Labor productivity in the secondary (i.e., manufacturing) sector during the ten-year period between 1959 and 1969 nearly tripled and so did the wages in that crucial sector.[2] Indeed, Japan's

1. *Nihon Tokei Nenkan Showa 48–49 Nen,* pp. 389 and 487.

2. Charles F. Gallagher, *Prosperity, Pollution, Prestige* (American University Field Staff Report, *Asia* 17, no. 3 [July 1971]), p. 11.

TABLE 2.1. AVAILABILITY OF MEDICAL FACILITIES

	Hospitals	Beds	Population	Population per Bed
Japan (1971)	8,026	1,082,647	105,006,000	97
United States (1969)	7,135	1,649,663	203,210,000	123
Britain (1969)	2,490	461,126	48,830,000	106

Source: *Showa 48 Nen Ban Kosei Hakusho*, p. 176.

economic advances were so rapid that, today, at least one-fifth of the world's 500 largest corporations are Japanese.[3]

In the meantime, the distribution of rising prosperity became more equitable and the compensation of employees as a share of the national income steadily rose, reflecting this new egalitarian trend: it rose from 50 percent in 1960 to 58 percent in 1972.[4] Another indication of the spreading egalitarianism is a significant decline in the number of welfare recipients. In 1955, there were 1,930,000 persons on the welfare roll, but this number, despite increases in the population, dropped to 1,350,000 individuals in 1972, and this in the face of the fact that the government had in the meantime become more committed to welfare.[5] Yet another index of rising well-being of the Japanese masses is availability of medical facilities. In this regard, table 2.1 may be informative.

There is really nothing miraculous about the rapid economic growth and the rising affluence in Japan in the past twenty some years. They would have been less spectacular had it not been for the Japanese propensity to save and, hence, to invest for larger future returns. One source indicates the annual Japanese domestic savings rate between 1956 and 1963 was 34.2 percent of the GNP. This figure was nearly twice that of the United States (18.0 percent) and Britain (16.9 percent) during the same period and well ahead of Norway, which showed the second highest savings rate (27.8 percent) among industrialized nations.[6] Of all Japanese households, 96.8 percent are said to

3. Robert Shaplen, "Letter from Tokyo," *New Yorker*, 20 May 1974, p. 110.

4. *Nihon Tokei Nenkan Showa 48–49 Nen*, pp. 487–90.

5. *Showa 48 Nen Ban Kosei Hakusho* (Tokyo: Kosei Sho, 1973), p. 81.

6. Tsunehiro Yui, "The Japanese Propensity for Saving," *Japan Interpreter* 8 (Winter 1974): 479. 34.2% of the GNP equaled 25% of the net national income.

have savings in the form of stocks, bonds, shares, and various savings accounts, and they averaged 1.6 million yen per household in 1973 (over $6,000 at the then prevailing exchange rate).[7] This propensity to save, which many economists have noted as a characteristic of modern Japanese society, is shared commonly by single persons, and their average savings were estimated at 260,000 yen per capita in 1970.[8]

The characteristic propensity to save, however, has done nothing to inhibit the rise and expansion of a consumer economy that verges on the fabulous. By early-1970s, a good third of all Japanese households owned automobiles. Virtually all households had acquired refrigerators, color TV sets, and washing machines and over 80 percent of them had telephones.[9] The traditionally wide gap between white-collar and blue-collar incomes was narrowed: in 1954, white-collar income was 50 percent higher than blue-collar income, but by 1969 the differential had been almost halved to 27 percent.[10] If there had ever been a serious class struggle between the haves and the have-nots in Japanese society, as Marxists would argue there was (and still is), surely its intensity must have declined considerably.[11]

Economic growth and prosperity, and all that it has entailed, such as expansion and penetration of mass communications media, especially TV and the growing ease of mobility, have significantly narrowed the traditional difference between rural and urban Japan in consumption pattern, life style, culture, and general well-being. The famous "Village Japan"[12] is still there, physically and geographically, but its parochialism and traditionalism have ascertainably declined. Farmers and city folk watch the same TV programs, laugh at the same jokes, eat the same foods, drink the same beverages, drive the same makes of cars, listen to the same music over the radio and stereo and

7. *Asahi Nenkan 1973*, pp. 507–8.

8. *Asahi Shimbun*, 2 January 1971, p. 1.

9. See Don Oberdorfer, "Japan: The Risen Sun," *Washington Post*, 5 August 1975, p. A-10.

10. Ohashi, *Nihon no Kaikyu Kosei*, p. 140.

11. Ronald Segal discusses this phenomenon in West Germany. See his *The Struggle Against History* (London: Weidenfeld & Nicolson, 1971), p. 9.

12. Richard K. Beardsley, John W. Hall, and Robert E. Ward, *Village Japan* (Chicago: University of Chicago Press, 1959).

cassettes, read the same newspapers and magazines, and commonly contemplate the inanity of politics with a declining equanimity. Not only has the farming family income risen year after year, but agriculture as the primary source of income has declined at the same time; today, approximately two-thirds of the agricultural family income is derived from nonagricultural sources such as industry and service, thereby helping further reduce the rural-urban dichotomy that was once quite pronounced in Japan.[13]

One interesting consequence of the leveling effect produced by economic growth and prosperity upon the traditional gaps between rural and urban sectors and between rich and poor is that, as years went by, more and more Japanese came to consider themselves middle class. In 1962, well into the era of prosperity and affluence, 76 percent of the people did so; by 1969, the figure increased to 90 percent.[14]

Economic advances and prosperity have also spilled over into the realms of demography, education, and culture. Urbanization as an index of modernization or industrialism took place with great rapidity from the early 1950s through the decade of the 1960s; today, Japan is basically not an urban but more like a metropolitan society where 63 percent of the people live in only 15 percent of the habitable space, mostly on the narrow coastal belts extending from Chiba on the eastern side of Tokyo Bay through the Tokyo-Kawasaki-Yokohama industrial megalopolis through Nagoya and from Kyoto through Osaka and Kobe on the mainland of Honshu down to Fukuoka on the northern part of the southern island of Kyushu. The Japanese are not only 100 percent literate but also highly educated. The most significant aspect of growth of education is the rise in college and university enrollments. In 1950 the size of such enrollment in institutions

13. The average farming family's income in 1972 was over 1.8 million yen, but only a small minority of farmers engaged solely in agriculture. For most of the Japanese farmers, agriculture is a part-time job. See, for example, *Information Bulletin 1973* (Tokyo: Ministry of Foreign Affairs, 1973), pp. 214–17; and Ohashi, *Nihon no Kaikyu Kosei*, p. 116. Between 1960 and 1971, the agricultural population in Japan was halved. Nobutaka Ike, *Japan: The New Superstate* (San Francisco: Freeman, 1974), p. 64. Also see Kiyoshi Oshima, "Nihon Nogyo wa korede yoinoka," *Sekai*, November 1971, p. 249.

14. *Kokumin Seikatsu Hakusho 1970* (Tokyo: Keizai Kikaku Cho, 1971), p. 44.

of higher learning (excluding junior college enrollment) was less than a quarter of a million (225,000); by 1974 it had risen to over one and a half million (1,659,000).[15] And educational personnel as a proportion of the labor force in Japan is the second highest in the world (after the United States).[16] Pervasiveness of mass culture in Japan is apparent everywhere. One can hardly find a household that does not subscribe to at least one of the three major Tokyo-based newspapers and not read at least two or three weekly and/or monthly magazines that cover virtually everything from art to politics and from crime to international relations. Theaters and cinemas are almost always crowded; concerts, museums, and public lectures find few, if any, vacant spaces left. In proportion to her population, Japan perhaps has the largest number of bookstores in the world. One gets the impression that Japanese society is materially and culturally saturated.

Valuationally and attitudinally, too, there has been significant, though not as readily visible, change in recent decades. Perhaps the most important aspect of such change is reflected in the generational gap between those who were born and raised in prewar Japan and those who were born and/or grew up after the war. Ike, a Stanford expert on Japanese politics and society, found that the younger generation is less trusting toward formal authority (e.g., the government), less concerned or preoccupied with material acquisition, and more democratically predisposed.[17] Other scholars have reported that younger Japanese are less ideological than their elders,[18] giving credence, in effect, to the

15. *Nihon Tokei Nenkan Showa 48–49 Nen*, p. 556; and *Asahi Shimbun*, 13 February 1975, p. 3.

16. William K. Cummings, "Japan's Educational Revolution" (Paper presented at the Mid-West Japan Seminar, Toronto, Canada, 17 April 1973, and at the Association for Asian Studies Annual Meeting, Chicago, 30 March 1973).

17. Nobutaka Ike, "Economic Growth and Intergenerational Change in Japan," *American Political Science Review* 67 (December 1973).

18. E.g., Herbert Passin, "The Sources of Protest in Japan," *American Political Science Review* 56 (June 1962): 402; Robert E. Cole, "Japanese Workers, Unions and the Marxist Appeal," *Japan Interpreter* 6 (Summer 1970): 115; Gerald Curtis, "The 1969 General Election in Japan," *Asian Survey* 10 (October 1970): 868; and Ellis S. Krauss, *Japanese Radicals Revisited: Student Protest in Post-war Japan* (Berkeley, Los Angeles, London: University of California Press, 1974), pp. 152–54.

oft-repeated observation that economic growth and prosperity induce the waning of ideological conflict and intensity.[19]

We could go on virtually ad infinitum citing aspects of change that indicate the rapid transformation of Japanese society in recent decades. It would be tedious and unnecessary to do so. The samples of change presented above give us a fair picture, fleeting though it might be, of Japanese society today. They are also the types of change that, as we shall see, cumulatively generate an important impact upon the emergence of postindustrial politics in Japan.

CONTINUITY OF TRADITION

Extensive and significant though the elements of change may be, some aspects of Japanese society have changed relatively little. In other words, there is a powerful continuity in that increasingly fluid society. Many attitudes and practices have been carried into the 1970s from the past, and they persist with varying degrees of tenacity. Tradition, as I think we are aware, is not inevitably inimical to progress. Indeed, many elements of tradition can and should be mobilized in the service of social change and political progress. In the case of modern Japan, her rapid development and modernization, as many historians and political scientists have noted, were greatly facilitated and economized by selective and discretionary mobilization and exploitation of many elements of tradition, while numerous other nations, in their impatience for quick modernization and development, have forcibly destroyed them in the name of modernity and/or revolution and thus sown seeds of instability and decay.[20]

On the other hand, elements of tradition constrain or critically inhibit social change and political progress, and it is in part for this reason that a great majority of nations have been

19. For discussions on the decline of ideology, compare, e.g., Daniel Bell, *The End of Ideology* (Glencoe, Ill.: Free Press, 1960), and Seymour Martin Lipset, *Political Man: The Social Bases of Politics* (Garden City, N.Y.: Doubleday, 1960), chap. 13.

20. For the importance and utility of tradition, see Taketsugu Tsurutani, *The Politics of National Development: Political Leadership in Transitional Societies* (New York: Chandler, 1973), chap. 6; and, especially regarding Japan, the same author's "Political Leadership: Some Tentative Thoughts from Early Meiji Japan," *Journal of Political and Military Sociology* 1 (Fall 1973).

stagnating at barely developing stages. The same problem may accompany political change from industrial society to postindustrial society. It is axiomatic, therefore, that any society in transition experiences a cross-pressure between an impulse toward change and a powerful resistance against it. Japan is no exception. Indeed, these two contradictory forces, existing side by side, give rise to volatility and tension at both the conscious and subconscious levels of her national psyche and affect the process of her transition to postindustrial society.

A Dual Economy

The notion of "Japan, Inc."—the sobriquet that for some years has been bandied about regarding Japan in envy as well as in derision—tends to conjure a picture of Japanese economy as highly advanced, aggressive, competitive, and sophisticated. This impression is largely accurate but does not tell the whole story. The reality of Japanese economy is a bit different. The Japanese economy, powerful and dynamic as it obviously is, is still a dual economy to a surprising extent. By dual economy here is meant an economic system that is sharply bifurcated between a highly modern, capital-intensive sector on the one hand and a much less advanced, more labor-intensive, small-scale sector on the other. When foreigners think of "Japan, Inc." or the spectacular advances of Japanese economy, they are in fact thinking only of the former sector, consisting, as it does, of such giant, ultramodern enterprises and conglomerates as Nissan Motors, Mitsubishi Heavy Industries, New Japan Steel, Hitachi, Toyota, Sony, Toshiba, Matsushita Electric, and so forth. But these corporations are but the top layer of a more complex, schizophrenic economic structure.

In numerical terms, the great majority of enterprises in Japan are small. For example, as late as 1972, 37 percent of nonagricultural employment took place in enterprises employing 30 or fewer workers. Another 16 percent was hired by firms employing between 31 and 40 employees.[21] A clear majority of Japanese workers, therefore, toiled for either small or marginal business establishments. At the same time, the 100 largest

21. *Nihon Rodo Nenkan* (Tokyo: Ohara Shakai Kenkyujo, Hosei Daigaku, 1974), iii. Also see K. Bieda, *The Structure and Operation of the Japanese Economy* (Sidney: John Wiley & Sons Australasia Pty., 1970).

corporations possessed one-half of the nation's entire corporate capital in the mid-1960s,[22] or, to use another figure, a minuscule 0.08 percent of the total number of business and industrial firms (excluding banking and insurance businesses) monopolized 52 percent of the total corporate capital accumulation in the country in 1969.[23] At an expanded level, 0.5 percent of all those firms represented 75 percent of the total corporate capital funds by the middle of the last decade.[24] These various figures clearly suggest that Japan's economic structure is not only mixed but also quite lopsided, to say the least.

This structural peculiarity (not limited to Japan, of course) of the national economy that evolved during the period of industrialization, growth, and prosperity has in the meantime produced some significant socioeconomic problems that are likely to be aggravated unless some effective curative measures are taken. For example, there is a considerable difference between those two layers of the economy not only in terms of capital and enterprise size, but also in wages and salaries, fringe benefits, and labor condition. Employees of large modern corporations are a labor elite, with good salaries and wages, powerful union organizations, large semiannual bonuses, and other fringe benefits such as company-subsidized medical and health care, housing, and recreation and vacation facilities. In contrast, the majority of Japanese workers, who are employed by numerous medium to small enterprises, are paid lower salaries and wages and more modest bonuses, do not belong to powerful unions (which means their compensations do not rise as much as they would if they were effectively unionized), and generally cannot enjoy many of the fringe benefits that their brethren in big enterprises take for granted. And there are ascertainable gaps in attitude and value orientation between these two groups of workers.[25] These gaps

22. Marshall E. Dimock, *The Japanese Technocracy* (New York and Tokyo: Walker-Weatherhill, 1968), p. 24.

23. Ohashi, *Nihon no Kaikyu Kosei*, pp. 96–97.

24. Masao Takahashi, *Modern Japanese Economy* (Tokyo: Kokusai Bunka Shinko Kai, 1968), p. 161.

25. For an inside observation of these differences in value and attitude, at once informative and illuminating, see Robert E. Cole, *Japanese Blue Collar: The Changing Tradition* (Berkeley, Los Angeles, and London: University of California Press, 1971). It should perhaps be noted here that Cole, in preparation for his book, worked for both a small factory and a large modern plant in Japan.

are likely to become politically salient as the pace of economic growth has now been drastically tempered by the changing world economic situation. Relatively disadvantaged workers are likely to acquiesce in, or at least not vociferously attack, the existing inequality as long as they more or less confidently perceive the prospect of continuing improvement in their lot relative to their more fortunate counterparts. Once such an optimistic perception is critically eroded, however, their disaffection with their condition would multiply and could lead to overt behavioral manifestations. If this happens, then the transition toward postindustrial politics may well be constrained, since the disaffection and its behavioral manifestations would revive an issue that, as we shall see in the next chapter, is typical of politics in industrial society.

Seniority System

Personnel administration in a modern society or a modern sector of society is presumably based on a rational universalistic criterion: ability and achievement, though it is never exclusive of other considerations, such as personality. In each of the various categories of personnel in the United States, we find younger or newer persons holding positions of authority over older or more veteran colleagues within one organization or institution, such as a university, a business firm, or a government department. One rarely encounters a comparable phenomenon in Japan. For the tradition of seniority system (*nenko joretsu*) persists there. A person is not promoted to the next step of the promotional ladder until a man senior to him is elevated to the next higher step or level. It is normally unthinkable for a man to be promoted *over* another who is senior to him. And all this regardless of his ability or achievement. The reader may think this practice frustrating to ambitious and capable men and women. In Japanese organizations, however, personal ambition, aggressiveness, or competitiveness regarding promotion and reward is eschewed, and this eschewal is internalized in most people. It is regarded as bad form, within any organization or institution, to be personally ambitious and aggressive and to compete for promotion with one's peers. Ambition, aggressiveness, and competitiveness are properties of intergroup or interorganizational relationship. The seniority system is really consistent with, in fact integral to, the Japanese tradition of intragroup and interpersonal relations. It is viewed as preventive of personal conflict and generative of group harmony. In actuality, this tradition can be considered to produce some desirable effect on Japanese workers. For example, one recent cross-national study indicated that Japanese workers are far more relaxed than American or European workers because they feel little if any competitive pressure in their work.[26] A survey of higher civil servants showed that, while they complained about and are critical of many aspects of the civil service (such as red tape, mandatory early retirement, inadequate compensation, periodic transfer, legalistic attitude), competition or competitiveness was not even once mentioned, and fewer than 3 percent of respondents cited personnel.[27] In an important sense, Japanese workers may be said to be much less harried than their Western counterparts, with fewer ulcers and lower blood pressures.

The seniority system has thus served a very useful purpose in the past of restraining or obviating one important potential source of social conflict in modern or industrial society, and it continues to serve the same purpose. Nevertheless, its inherent virtue is now coming to be seriously challenged by the changing environment, especially in some of the more critical sectors of society, such as the bureaucracy, parties, and universities. These are the institutions responsible for steering society in its difficult transitional travail. They must demonstrate the critical ability to adapt themselves to the requirements of this transition. In short, they must abandon the business-as-usual attitude. The seniority system, however, tends, for obvious reasons, to resist daring experimentation and creative imagination. It discourages deviations from the existing values and goals. And, to varying extents, these institutions, as we shall see in later chapters, are being handicapped by these ramifications of the seniority system.

Institutional Elitism

Another continuing tradition or custom in Japan is what is called "university cliques" (*gakubatsu*). The Japanese are very ranking or rating conscious. Schools as well as business and industrial firms are ranked in the minds of people according to their presumed or actual qualities (in the case of the former),

26. Tamotsu Sengoku and Atsuko Toyama, *Hikaku Nihon-jin Ron* (Tokyo: Shogakukan, 1973), p. 121.

27. See Yasuo Watanabe, "Kokyu Komu-in no Ishiki," in *Gendai Gyosei to Kanryosei,* ed. Ken Taniuchi et al. (Tokyo: Tokyo University Press, 1974), 2:432.

prestige (in both cases), or size (in the case of the latter). When asked about his occupation, the Japanese does not say, "I am a salesman," or, "I am a computer specialist" or, "I am an engineer." Instead, he is likely to answer, "I work for Ajinomoto" or, "I am with Toyota," indicating his deep-seated propensity to identify himself not with his skill or profession but with the establishment that employs him.[28] Only if he works for an obscure or third-rate firm will he answer the query by identifying himself with his skill or occupational category. Thus, every school graduate (high school or university) wishes to be employed by a prestigious firm or the government (the civil service is viewed not only as occupationally secure but as traditionally highly prestigious). But, in order successfully to seek employment by a first-rate corporate firm or the civil service, one has to be a graduate of a first-rate university, especially Tokyo University, which has always been the most prestigious institution of higher learning in Japan. Educational credentials do not mean one's academic record but rather the credentials or prestige of one's school, and topmost positions in government as well as corporate bureaucracies have been virtually monopolized by graduates of Tokyo University. These people constitute the Tokyo clique. This clique perpetuates itself because, each year, new graduates of this university naturally gravitate toward those prestigious firms and government ministries where their school seniors occupy responsible positions.

The predominance of the Tokyo clique may be glimpsed in these two examples: There are 169 positions above the rank of bureau chief up to that of administrative vice minister (the posts of minister and parliamentary vice minister are held by MPs of the ruling party) in the ministerial headquarters in Tokyo (there are 21 ministries and cabinet-rank agencies), and fully 83 percent (141) of them, circa 1974, were occupied by Tokyo graduates. In the corporate world, of the 303 giant firms with the capital of 5 billion yen or more each, 124 (41 percent) were presided over by graduates of the same university.[29] Political parties, including the Communists, are controlled and run by Tokyo graduates (see chapters 4 and 5). The Tokyo graduate can thus begin his career with a considerable head start over graduates of other schools.

28. Chie Nakane, *Japanese Society* (Berkeley and Los Angeles: University of California Press, 1970), chap. 3.

29. "Naze Tokyo Daigaku ka?" *Sande Mainichi*, 7 April 1974, p. 19.

There are other university cliques—graduates of other prominent institutions of higher learning such as four other former "Imperial universities" (Kyoto, Tohoku, Hokkaido, and Kyushu) and other top-notch government universities (especially Hitotsubashi in Tokyo) and private Keio and Waseda universities —and each has an influential niche in the whole structure of society. (For example, graduates of Kyoto and Tohoku universities are a second major—though far smaller than Tokyo— source of higher civil service recruitment. The press refers to Tokyo, Kyoto, and Tohoku as the Big Three—*gosanke*—for civil service recruitment.) This is not without serious problems.

For example, the crucial importance of the prestige of his alma mater and his old-school tie in his life (employment and, understandably, marriage) creates a rather special predicament for Japan's youngster. In order to have a desirable career, he must graduate from a top-flight university. In order to pass his entrance examination to such a university, he must be educated in a first-rate high school. But to enter such a high school, he must be graduated from an equally top-notch junior high, and to get into such a junior high, he must have done very well in its entrance examination, and so on and so forth. These days, even kindergartens have become part of this chain of upward pre-career educational struggle and competition. Thus, since his early school days, the life of Japan's youngster becomes a series of recurrent "examination hell" (*shiken jigoku*). Between examinations, he must constantly study and, more often than not, he spends a couple of evenings each week at a tutorial session given by free-enterprising teachers and former teachers. As he moves from the grade school to the junior high and so on, he will have less time for play if he wants to make it to the top. He is constantly prodded by his anxious parents, especially his mother (who is commonly called *kyoiku mama*—an education-obsessed mother), who would spare no effort to help him succeed (or, perhaps more accurately, force him to succeed). And, at the level of university entrance examinations, a phenomenon un-known in America is observed: if he fails in the entrance examination to the school of his first choice, Japan's youngster, instead of going to the school of his second or third choice, often waits for next year's entrance examination to the same school. (A similar phenomenon is developing at the high school level.) During the forced or self-imposed interim, he spends full-time, with redoubled efforts and determination, preparing for the second try, usually attending one of those numerous privately owned "preparation academies" that cater to him and his like. A year later, he may fail again. It is not unusual in Japan to find a youth who has repeated this attempt more than twice. But it is better to graduate from a first-rate university late than to graduate from a less prestigious school on time.

But, then, the axiom applies only to those who sooner or later get into the first-rate school. What about those who don't? A great majority of those who seek higher education, of course, resign themselves to going to second- and third-rate schools (in terms of prestige) where they may get just as good an education as they would at top-flight schools. For them, however, the gates to the civil service or blue-ribbon corporations are massively resistant and forbidding. A greater tragedy sometimes befalls the unsuccessful aspirants for admission to top schools: instances of suicide are not very rare.

In an important sense, the structure of Japanese society is basically elitist.[30] This in itself might not be undesirable. The fact that elites are maintained in effect by institutional credentials and a prematurely and narrowly determined meritocracy rather than by genuine, socially demonstrated ability and accomplishment, however, poses considerable obstacles on the path of society's evolution toward postindustrialism. It is, for example, clearly inconsistent with the egalitarian ethos that seems to be emerging in society, especially among postwar generations. Educational credentials have been one of the significant authority referents (another is seniority) in society, but people are gradually discovering that there is no consistent positive relationship between it and performance. And, clearly, there is blatant inequity in this conventional elitism: one's relevant merit to be considered in obtaining an employment is the presumed merit of the school he graduates from; likewise, one's most important social merit in a career is not so much the quality of one's work as the prestige of the institution or organization of which he is a member. Chances for late bloomers are severely curtailed.

Yet another problem of this particular brand of elitism is the danger of the predominance of certain bureaucratic culture in society. This needs a bit of explaining, and an explanation is offered in chapter 4. Suffice, at this point, to say that higher civil servants, who are in most cases Tokyo graduates or graduates of

---

30. For this aspect of Japanese tradition, see, for example, Ko Takeuchi, "Chugoku no Kindai to Nihon no Kindai" in *Nihon no Nashonarizumu,* ed. Shumpei Uehara (Tokyo: Tokuma Shoten, 1966), pp. 256–90.

the Big Three, move into party and corporate leadership structures. Former bureaucrats dominate both parties and giant
corporations. In short, there is this Tokyo University–civil servant
syndrome in the crucial leadership sectors of both politics and
economy. On the surface, this phenomenon may not suggest
anything undesirable or insidious. After all, one might argue, the
best and the brightest rule, and that is good. But is it? After all,
it is they—dominant as they have been in both government and
economy—that are largely responsible, not only for bringing
about the consolidation of modern industrialism, but, more and
more important these days, also for allowing serious consequences to arise from it. Is this elitism-by-institutional-creden-
tials sufficiently capable of adapting itself to the fast-changing
postindustrial environment? Or is it culture-bound to industrialism and its imperatives? There is a growing unease about
this problem, especially pronounced, as discussed in chapter 7,
at the grass-roots level. The enormous power that this elite wields
at the crucial nerve centers of society and its deep entrenchment
in modern industrial society may hinder, rather than promote,
society's political change from industrialism to postindustrialism.

Other Traditional Features

Other elements of continuity of tradition may variously
inhibit the ongoing political transition. Behavioral inhibitions
resulting from such traditional if not peculiarly Japanese properties of interpersonal relationships as *giri* (personal obligation),
on (Benedict called it a passively incurred obligation), and *kankei*
(personal connections) could negatively affect the process of
transition,[31] precisely because they are the qualities that have
characterized these relationships during the long period of social
stratification and mutual group insulation. The dynamics of
postindustrialism, some of which were variously hinted at earlier,
seem increasingly incompatible with these qualities. On the one
hand, rapid urbanization and rising demographic mobility, for
example, are perforce eroding those traditional qualities, and

31. For functions of these and other properties of interpersonal and
social relationship in Japanese society, see, for example, Ruth Benedict,
The Chrysanthemum and the Sword (Boston: Houghton Mifflin, 1946);
Nakane, *Japanese Society;* and Robert Smith and Richard K. Beardsley,
eds., *Japanese Culture: Its Development and Characteristics* (Chicago:
Aldine, 1962). Takeo Doi, *Amae no Kozo* (Tokyo: Kobundo, 1971).

degrees of their erosion are ascertainable (see chapter 6).[32] On the other hand, those qualities are still potent enough variously to frustrate needed change in individual and group behavior at critical junctures in the whole process of politics at different levels of society.

With all the outward changes, and some inward ones as well, that have taken place in postwar Japan, therefore, many forces are countering further evolution of society. In more senses than one, many political phenomena in Japan today are symptomatic of this underlying conflict between an impulse toward change and resistance against it.

32. See, for example, Kokuminsei Chosa Iinkai, Tokei Suri Kenkyujo, *Nihonjin no Kokuminsei* (Tokyo: Shiseido, 1973), 2: 75–77.

3

The Rise of New Issues
and Problems

One of the many fascinating phenomena in the evolution of society is that the nature and the type of issues that are politically relevant change from one period to the next. This, of course, is not to say that all the problems that are objects of political conflict in one period completely disappear in the next. As with the different distributions of labor employment we discussed in chapter 1, what we actually see in each society or period in terms of politically relevant issues or problems is a different "mix." As with patterns of labor distribution, however, the kind of mix we see or, more precisely, the type of issue that tends to rise in importance conceptually characterizes each period of society's evolution.

Consider the United States: pollution, abortion, divorce, affirmative action, busing of school children, energy crisis, stagflation, urban renewal, et al. Only twenty years ago, let alone forty or seventy years ago, none of these pressing issues of today was significant or important. Few Americans contemplated them. At the same time, it is equally obvious that many of the problems that were objects of public controversy thirty or fifty or a hundred years ago are no longer relevant politically today, e.g., the right of workers to unionize, strike, or collectively bargain with management; the federal income tax; social security; child labor; government subsidies to education. Perhaps we can put these differences in a more systematic way.

SOCIETY AND ITS PROBLEMS

In preindustrial society, politically relevant issues have generally (though not exclusively) to do with conflicts among regions (e.g., east vs. west, lowland vs. upland), racial, religious, ethnic or communal groups (e.g., Catholics vs. Protestants, Christians vs. Moslems, Malays vs. Chinese), among dynasties (the House of York vs. the House of Lancaster), or between the ruling aristocracy and the aspirant bourgeoisie (e.g., France in the 1780s). The object of this type of conflict is political power that is presumed to inhere in office (or officeholding). The political actors (and their supporting casts) all vie for political power or formal office. Thus the War of the Roses and the Glorious Revolution in England, the Revolution of 1789 in France, and the War of Independence in the North American colonies of the British Empire, to cite but a few historic examples. These historic instances, all taking place in what we in the previous chapter defined as "preindustrial" societies, had one central issue or decisive ingredient of conflict in common: office. The struggle in the political arena, therefore, centered around the issue of who or what group should rule or participate in ruling. The objective was pure and simple: the political power that officeholding (or, more broadly, political participation) was considered to provide. Economic programs and social reforms were *not* primary: they were at best ancillary or peripheral matters, and, normally, they had little if anything to do with the basic issue of political struggle, as long as the existing social relationship and pattern of distribution of goods and services were left more or less intact. Social and economic problems arose in the realm of politics only when the equilibrium of this traditional relationship and distribution pattern was upset by natural disaster, ravages of war, caprice of kings, or negligence of lords.

In industrial society (or in the industrial period of society's evolution), politically relevant issues are largely economic in both origin and character. Put differently, they have to do not with office or political participation as such, as in the preindustrial period, but with the distribution of income and wealth. If Locke and Rousseau are two of the most prominent spokesmen of the preindustrial politics, then we can safely say that Marx is the most controversial ideologist of the industrial politics.

The issue of office or political participation, which is central to the politics of preindustrial society, loses the intensity and magnitude that characterized it during the earlier period because it is gradually resolved through, for instance, the expansion of suffrage and introduction of variously representative government. (We admit that, in some industrial societies, this traditional, basically preindustrial issue involving racial or other ascriptive cleavages still persists—as in Northern Ireland, Lebanon, Malaysia, Belgium, and, to some extent, even the United States— and that, even in a more generally open democratic society, there is the problem of genuinely effective participation on the part of, say, women, youth, and so forth. These problems however, tend, in a majority of cases, to be incidental or peripheral in terms of central features of the politics of industrial society and they at times are camouflage for economic struggle and/or compound economic struggle.) Instead, the central issue in industrial society is the distribution of income and wealth which industrialism and technological progress constantly generate in increasing quantities and varieties. Stated a bit differently, the central political issue now is about who or which group/class should get how big a share of the rising national income and wealth when, why, and how. For this reason we witness an important shift in the character of ideological conflict in industrial society from that in preindustrial society. In preindustrial society, the conflict is between ideologies of political justice (e.g., those of the *philosophes* in France; Locke, Jefferson, and Paine in the English-speaking world; all variously arguing for popular political participation and the democratization of decision-making processes) and ideologies of political justification (e.g., Filmer and Burke, who respectively argued against radical change in favor of the status quo). In industrial society, however, where the object of political struggle is different, the verbal war is engaged in by ideologies of economic justice (socialism, communism, syndicalism) on the one hand and ideologies of economic justification (capitalism and a variety of social Darwinism, for example) on the other, with the former stridently demanding democracy not so much in politics as in economic well-being or economic egalitarianism and the latter recalcitrantly defending and justifying the existing inequality in the distribution of income and wealth. It is significant that, while ideologies of political justice assume that justice in economic conditions would more or less naturally ensue once justice in political relations is established, ideologies of economic justice are founded on the proposition that genuine political democracy is possible only when justice in economic relations has been achieved.

There is also some significant structural change in society that reflects the basic shift in the nature of politically relevant issues from the preindustrial to the industrial period. In the preindustrial period, society is likely to be vertically fragmented, for example geographically or dynastically or communally. A horizontal division may also obtain, sometimes submerging the vertical as a politically more significant division, especially toward the end of the preindustrial era or, perhaps more accurately, in those preindustrial societies where feudalism has long declined and been replaced by a more unified nation-state, as in eighteenth-century France and in Britain long before then. In those post-feudal cases of preindustrial society, the more relevant division is between the traditional ruling class (the aristocracy *cum* monarchy) and the rising bourgeoisie.

In the industrial period, the most significant division of society is no longer along the dynastic or regional or communal lines, though, as stated, these lines of division, especially communal or racial, may persist in some cases. The division far more characteristic of industrial society is in terms of common interests peculiar to economic and occupational differences. On the surface, the most visible, and hence most talked-about, division of society is one between the haves and the have-nots, between the rich and the poor, between the bourgeoisie and the proletariat. The preindustrial struggle between the aristocracy and the bourgeoisie, for instance, over office is now transformed into a struggle between the bourgeoisie and the proletariat over income and wealth.

This apparent division in industrial society, however, conceals the more important fact of segmentation especially within the proletariat. The proposition or fact that workers are variously exploited by their socioeconomic superiors does not lead to the conclusion that they are united or unitable (as in "The workers of the world, unite! You have nothing to lose but your chains!"). In fact, they are not. The main reason for this is that workers, grouped in terms of income and occupational differences, are engaged in competition among themselves as much as in struggle against their common "enemies," i.e., the haves. It is often assumed, as in a zero-sum game, that if one group gets more, another group gets less. It is at least in part for this reason that there has never been a genuinely cohesive, internally harmonious nationwide workers' organization, except in those authoritarian countries where such nationwide organizations of "workers" and "peasants" are created by fiat. What we see in a typical open industrial society, instead, is a proliferation of groups (organized across preindustrial cleavages) each of which is organized on the basis of a certain specific occupation, enterprise, or craft, in order to maximize its share of the income and wealth that industrialism generates, and it does so in competition against every other group. Each group seeks its interest first, last, and in between. Interests of groups are frequently mutually exclusive or are so perceived by those groups.

A similar phenomenon of segmentation is observed within the so-called bourgeoisie. There is little operative unity within various segments of this class beyond their common antipathy toward the actual or potential influence of the working class and their unstated desire to minimize the share of income and wealth they are willing, or forced, to grant the workers. This class, too, organizes itself into a variety of groups on the basis of certain specific types of economic interest which are more often than not mutually exclusive. And these "have" groups, too, all want to get as much of the income and wealth generated by industrialism as they possibly can in competition against one another and against the workers. The politics of industrial society, therefore, is characterized by conflict and, insofar as the political arrangement is open and democratic, bargaining and compromise among these various groups of both the working class and the haves concerning the distribution of income and wealth.

CHANGE IN JAPAN FROM PREINDUSTRIAL TO INDUSTRIAL POLITICS

Japan's case closely followed this highly generalized version of transition from preindustrial to industrial society. In her preindustrial period, the basic conflict characterizing it was among competing dynasties or would-be dynasties up to the early seventeenth century when the House of Tokugawa succeeded in establishing its undisputed hegemony and its shogunate; then between the pro-Tokugawa feudal lords (*daimyo*) and anti-Tokugawa feudatories latently during most of the shogunate and openly toward its end; then regional between the famous four southwestern clans of Satsuma, Choshu, Tosa, and Hizen on the one hand and their rivals on the other during the first years of the Meiji Restoration; and, later, between the Satsuma-Choshu dominance of the central government and their disgruntled rivals on the other well into the decade of the 1880s. Some Japanese scholars argue that the most significant political struggle during the early Meiji period was over the rights of the people, but actually it was a cover for the rivalry among regional elites or, more precisely, between those elites that were in power and those that were out. But even if it had indeed been a struggle over people's rights, the fundamental nature of political conflict would have remained the same. All this is not to say, of course, that there were no other politically relevant issues in preindustrial Japan. I only mean that, in Japan, too, preindustrial politics was characterized most prominently by a certain conceptually specific type of issue, which corresponds to its counterparts elsewhere.

In her industrial period (beginning, say, some time early in this century), Japan witnessed different kinds of politically relevant issues dominating her political arena, and they were in the main economic in origin and character. This, of course, is not to suggest that as of, say, 1890 the type of issues that is characteristic of the preindustrial period suddenly disappeared. There is always what we might call a time lag in the decline of preindustrial politics in the industrial period. Certain issues and behavior patterns that are more characteristic of one period linger or persist on into the next. Structural change and behavioral change almost never occur simultaneously. We term this phenomenon "residual behavior." I have explained it elsewhere as:

> Various institutions in society as well as groups and individuals, long accustomed to thinking and behaving in certain ways, tend to persist in behaving in the same way even when circumstances have changed. There is always a gap between the rate of change in the environment and the rate of change in thought and behavior, and the greater the gap, the more strain society experiences.[1]

In any event, the reader, if familiar with modern Japanese history, will readily recognize that certain of the preindustrial political conflict, namely the issue of office or political participation, lingered on in Japan until at least the promulgation of

---

1. Taketsugu Tsurutani, "Japan as a Postindustrial Society" in *Politics and the Future of Industrial Society*, ed. Leon N. Lindberg (New York: David McKay, 1976), p. 102.

universal manhood suffrage in 1925 and that, even after that, because of restrictive laws regarding political activities enacted by the relatively hidebound (an instance of residual behavior?) powers that be, its persistence was much longer than it might otherwise have been. The point, however, is that issues of economic character, pertaining, as discussed, to the distribution of income and wealth, became the main feature of the politics as Japan entered her period of industrialism, overshadowing and eventually submerging the preindustrial issue of political participation.

Among those new issues of economic character were disjunctions of interest between landlord and tenant, between labor and management, between the rich and the poor. As Hannah Arendt notes, industrial society is characterized by the politicization of poverty.[2] This is another way of saying that industrial society politicizes the distribution of income and wealth. Predictably, therefore, labor agitation and organizations emerged during this period. Haves, too, began to organize into various associations and groups in order to counter and combat the rising economic demands of various have-not groups and to exert influence upon political decision makers concerning how wealth and income were to be distributed. Equally predictably, this economic conflict quickly came to be compounded by the emergence of a struggle between such ideologies of economic justice as communism and socialism on the one hand and, on the other, ideologies of economic justification such as conservatism and imperialism, thus, in the process, enhancing further the political salience of the basically economic conflict. And the major function of authoritative decision making became one of allocating economic benefits to competing classes and groups as they were differentially capable of inducing it to give.

We might note parenthetically at this point that there is some important, though not fundamental (i.e., within the context of our discussion here), difference between prewar and postwar Japanese politics. The difference has to do not with the fundamental character of politics of an industrial society but rather with the degree of relative equality on the basis of which both the haves and the have-nots are allowed to engage in this industrial political competition. Because of the basically authoritarian nature of the prewar political arrangement, the have-nots were forced to operate at great disadvantage vis-à-vis the haves. Thus

2. *On Revolution* (New York: Viking, 1965), p. 225.

the so-called progressive political forces, e.g. labor, socialists, communists, even "liberals," were constantly suppressed and to that extent the have-nots and their sympathizers were effectively deprived of organizational weapons with which to combat and compete with the haves. After the war, with fundamental political and institutional reforms imposed upon her by the victorious Americans, Japan did away with the unfair handicaps under which the have-nots in general had been forced to operate. Thus, the artificial and residual shackles were removed from the political arena, enabling the have-nots to participate freely in the political process. The fundamental nature of political conflict, however, remained the same.

Thus, during the postwar industrial period in Japan, political cleavages followed economic cleavages, and they in turn generated certain ascertainable coalitions and alignments among groups and between them and political parties, much in the same way and for the same reasons as in other industrial societies. Big business and industry became powerful supporters (or, as some would say, sponsors) of the conservative parties that in 1955 merged into the current Liberal Democratic party (LDP). So did most of the nation's agrarian interests. These sectors, though their interests are not always mutually harmonious, are said to be conservative in virtually all industrial nations, opposed, for instance, to heavy public spending on education, health, and welfare but not at all opposed to such spending on themselves in the form of price supports for agriculture, monetary and fiscal policies favorable to business and industry, and, in the case of Japan, gradual modification of Occupation reforms in their favor. And they have varying numbers of allies in the party. In terms of haves and have-nots, it is generally thought that the haves, e.g., managerial and entrepreneurial groups, favor the LDP. It is obvious from past electoral records, however, that the LDP has commanded a much wider support than could be provided only by the haves, in order to maintain its semipermanent control of government. Indeed, the party has enjoyed consistent, though discernibly declining, support from all sectors of society in the past, from groups who compete among themselves for shares of income and wealth. And the reason for this fact is simple and straightforward: most Japanese are conservative in the sense that, instead of seeking a change of the ruling class or the existing political arrangement in order to achieve a new system of distribution of income and wealth, they have sought as much benefit as possible within the existing system. They have not been noted for strong ideological proclivities.[3] Haves and have-nots alike viewed the LDP as more capable than any other party of promoting economic growth and prosperity, and of generating larger incomes and more wealth for every group. They were aware that the party consisted of more experienced politicians, former high government officials, and business executives rather than labor unionists with no experience in management and government and ideologues with rhetorical brilliance but no practical experience in public and business affairs. In short, many members of various groups in society—entrepreneurial and laboring alike—thought the party had something to offer them.

The Japan Socialist party (JSP), the second largest of the parties, was and still is closely aligned with the General Council of Trade Unions (*Sohyo*), the largest and avowedly Marxist sector of organized labor. They were mutually aligned on the basis of their common advocacy of an ideology of economic justice, though they both eschew violent overthrow of the existing political system. A considerable proportion of the so-called intelligentsia also supported the JSP, as its counterparts support various parties pursuing economic justice in other industrial societies.

The Japan Communist party (JCP), now the third largest party in the Parliament (Diet) for reasons that will become clear later, was theoretically the vanguard of the proletariat but in reality managed to receive electoral support from little more than a fraction of the working class because the party was viewed by them as philosophically alien to their culture and society and incapable of bringing benefits to them. During the industrial period, therefore, the party at times hovered on the verge of electoral extinction. The Democratic Socialist party (DSP), after its secession from the JSP in 1960, attracted much of the anti- or non-Marxist segment of labor and was openly aligned with the moderate Japan Confederation of Labor (*Domei*) in particular. It also commanded electoral support from those sectors of the middle class that had become disenchanted with the ruling LDP but could not embrace the vocally Marxist JSP, let alone the JCP. These voters supported the DSP in their belief that the party was committed to a more equitable distribution of income and wealth than the LDP but resistant to the kind of radical political change advocated by the JSP, which they feared.

3. Yasushi Haga, *Gendai Seiji no Choryu* (Tokyo: Ningen no Kagaku Sha, 1975), pp. 34–35.

The Clean Government party (CGP), now larger than the DSP in the Diet, cultivated the support of those groups whose socio-economic conditions in the period of rapid industrial growth were in more senses than one marginal, hence particularly insecure, e.g., lower-middle-class people such as small merchants, shopkeepers, and nonunion laborers, who felt neglected by both the ruling LDP and the opposition JSP and bypassed by the rising prosperity and affluence. It was for this reason that the party's rise in the 1960s was very rapid.

Until recently, therefore, the politics in Japan was indeed the politics of industrial society in which partisan alignments, as one aspect of it, were determined largely by economic interests perceived by each group or aggregate of voters concerned. Issues that dominated the political arena were economic. Perhaps it is for this reason that no single party gained any electoral mileage out of, for instance, foreign policy issues.

POSTWAR NATIONAL PREOCCUPATION AND ITS CONSEQUENCES

Toward the end of the 1960s, however, a gradual but nevertheless ascertainable change began to occur, signaling, I might venture to suggest, the beginning of the end of the politics of industrial society in Japan. The initial and most readily observable cause for this change was the emergence of a rather novel phenomenon: the rise of issues, or rather the rise in salience of issues that cut across the conventional (i.e., conventional to the industrial period) socioeconomic and ideological cleavages. This new phenomenon was and is clearly related to Japan's emergence as a postindustrial society as we tentatively defined it in chapter 1. As we discussed at the outset of the present chapter, different periods in the evolution and development of society generate political problems of different nature and type, and it seems that the entry of society into its postindustrial period engenders the kind of political issue that is conceptually and contextually different from its counterpart in the industrial period. In the briefest manner of speaking, the phenomenon of issues that cut across conventional cleavages has been engendered by certain dynamics in the development and advance of modern industrialism.

Industrialism is historically predicated upon the assumption that man's ingenuity to devise and invent technology for exploiting nature and for producing material wealth and comfort is boundless. Preindustrial society is philosophically based on the belief (unless corrupted by another nation or nations that are already industrial) in the static nature of society, that is, the notion that, in terms of material growth and well-being, today is much like yesterday and tomorrow is not going to be very different from today, barring, of course, the conquest and plunder of foreign countries or territories. In the word of a recent scholar, preindustrial economy is rooted in the "constant pie" orientation.[4] There is little, if any, technological innovation, and so the economic productivity would increase little or not at all, in any event making no perceptively significant change in the level of life of the people. The size of the economic pie remains more or less the same, hence "the constant pie."[5]

The Industrial Revolution, however, touched off a series of interrelated events that eventually came to change this preindustrial outlook about the economic life. Man's discovery that his ingenuity and inventiveness are boundless (something he had largely been unaware of during the preindustrial period) also led to another important discovery: through his ingenuity and inventiveness, he could exploit nature and manipulate his fellow men in order to produce more and more wealth in greater and greater varieties. It was thus that what Weber calls the "expanding pie" orientation came into being, replacing once and for all the preindustrial "constant pie" outlook.[6] Hence the subsequent economic development and the realization of a level of comfort and wealth undreamed of in preindustrial society.

The "expanding pie" orientation, while providing ever-increasing dynamism to societal life, contained one serious flaw: a callous disregard for or neglect of potential consequences of technological and industrial expansion and their intangible ramifications. For example, we know today how serious that inherent flaw of the "expanding pie" philosophy has turned out to be, the philosophy that generated what a recent study of the problem calls the "grow-forever policy."[7]

In Japan, the "expanding pie" outlook became a national obsession in the postwar period. Against the background of

4. Andrea Weber, "The Politics of Postindustrialism: A Comparative Inquiry" (Ph.D. dissertation, Washington State University, 1974), p. 86.

5. Ibid.

6. Ibid., pp. 86–92.

7. Donella H. Meadows et al., *The Limits to Growth: A Report for the Club of Rome's Project on the Predicament of Mankind* (New York: New American Library, 1972), p. 157.

austerity in the age of relative scarcity before the war, and the deprivation and hardship to which the nation had been subjected during the war and for several years after the war, government and people, bourgeois and proletarian alike, were united in their common desire to make the country materially comfortable and abundant. They became engaged in the singleminded pursuit of economic recovery, growth, and prosperity with uncritical mass devotion and national unity. This collective pursuit was appropriately typified by the policy of "high economic growth" (*kodo keizai seicho*) that, especially since the mid-1950s, prominently characterized the national policy of the ruling Liberal Democratic party. Insofar as this general national commitment was concerned, there was unanimity among otherwise disparate political, economic, and ideological alignments and groupings. Corporate executives and blue-collar workers, conservatives and socialists, farmers and bureaucrats were intent upon as rapid an economic growth and prosperity as possible and upon maximizing material benefits for all concerned. With their characteristic penchant for being "first rate" in any endeavor they commit themselves to undertaking, the Japanese were anxious to catch up with, even overtake, the most advanced and prosperous of the Western nations. It is largely for this general unanimity of commitment and purpose that the business-aligned LDP was returned to power election after election, thus promoting continuously rising prosperity and a steadily declining political drama for the people.

This policy based upon the expanding-pie philosophy was never seriously questioned either in terms of its basic orientation or its simplistic thrust, or in terms of the general manner of its implementation and reinforcement. Opposition parties of course sniped at certain minor or ancillary aspects or technical problems, but more by way of parliamentary political ritual than substantive debate, and they never meaningfully challenged its crude thrust and blatantly materialistic objectives and potential ramifications for the future of the nation. Every prime minister was a Guizot, and "*Enrichissez-vous!*" was the unstated slogan of the entirely suprapartisan national endeavor supported by all. The LDP was the political engine of this endeavor, and while conflict among various groups over distribution of income and wealth never abated, its otherwise volatile intensity was greatly tempered by the unanimity of the collective endeavor and by the fact that the economic pie continued rapidly to expand year after year. By the beginning of the 1970s, the fruits of the high-economic-growth policy penetrated into every corner of the country, if not into every household, in the form of an unprecedentedly high per capita income surpassing that of Britain, and an amazingly wide range of amenities of the affluent society such as color TV sets, electric appliances, nutritious and varied diet, fashionable clothing, shiny automobiles, mass culture, and extravagant consumer economy. In the meantime, the policy of high economic growth catapulted the nation as a foremost industrial power in the world next only to the United States and the Soviet Union, prompting some foreign observers to predict that we were entering, in fact if not in name, a "Japanese century" in which Japan would become the greatest and most prosperous industrial power in the world.[8]

All this was well and good for the Japanese—for some time, that is. The grumblings of nations that were being overtaken by Japan or whose markets were increasingly saturated with Japanese goods were received by the Japanese with a bit of apprehension combined with a lot of concealed pride. Neither the Japanese themselves nor foreign observers were clearly aware that the obverse side of the coin of the policy of rapid economic growth would turn up. They forgot that there was a price to be paid for every good thing. The price that such a feverishly growth-oriented, prosperity-obsessed, ever-expanding-pie policy devoid of critical concern for potentially negative consequences and ramifications was bound to become manifest. Sooner than later, people were to become acutely aware of the exorbitant price they had to pay for this past neglect. The predicament of the Japanese people is essentially the same as that of people of other industrial nations, except that, in more senses than one, it is much worse in Japan because of her high population density, unbalanced demographic distribution, and the rapidity of her past industrial development. Let us first take a glance at some of the more obvious aspects of the price whose payment has become due, though there are more subtle but equally critical aspects as well.

EFFECTS OF INDUSTRIALISM AND THEIR RISE
IN POLITICAL SALIENCE

That Japan is a small island nation is well known. Less well known is how much smaller its habitable space is. In customary

8. See, for example, Herman Kahn, *The Emerging Japanese Superstate* (Englewood Cliffs, N.J.: Prentice-Hall, 1970); and Norman Macrae, "Pacific Century: 1975–2075?," *Economist*, 4–10 January 1975.

calculation (that is, the total population divided by the total land space), her population density is 280 per square kilometer, roughly comparable to Holland. But that is not a very meaningful comparison. Holland is flat. Japan is extremely mountainous and the space available for residences, factories, and roads is only 3.2 percent of the total land mass, while arable land takes up another 16 percent.[9] Thus the actual population density in the *inhabited* space comes to over 9,000 per square kilometer. And the three largest metropolises—Greater Tokyo, Osaka, and Nagoya—contain 47.3 percent of the national population of 108 million as of 1974.[10] This demographic development, caused by rapid advances in industrialism, has created an enormous range of serious problems such as congestion, housing shortage, inadequate social capital, and pollution, to name but a few examples, prompting an observation by Ken'ichi Tominaga, a Tokyo University sociologist, that Japan's most pressing issues are "urban problems rather than poverty problems."[11]

In an advanced industrial society, congestion inevitably means, among other things, pollution. For Japan, this may be seen in the rapid increases during the recent decade in the amounts, for example, of three major air pollutants emitted by automobiles. The annual amount of carbon monoxide emitted by automobile exhausts in the capital region consisting of Tokyo, Chiba, Kanagawa, and Saitama increased between 1960 and 1970 from 4.5 million tons to 9.5 million tons; hydrocarbon from 790,000 to 2.3 million tons; and nitrogen oxide from 310,000 tons to 1.7 million tons.[12] In a three-year period since 1970, public authorities recorded 105,705 cases of serious photochemical smog affliction of which 90,000 were concentrated in the same capital region.[13] Environmental pollution, of which air pollution is only part, is not limited to burgeoning, overcrowded urban and metropolitan areas. Rivers, streams, lakes, and seashores too became increasingly contaminated, and such contamination increased on the average by over 400 percent be-

9. *Quality of the Environment in Japan* (Tokyo: Environment Agency, 1973), p. 30.

10. *Asahi Shimbun*, 14 March 1974, p. 3.

11. *Social Change in the United States and Japan* (Report of a Wingspread Conference sponsored by Japan Society, Inc. and the Johnson Foundation, November 1972), p. 11.

12. *Quality of Environment in Japan*, p. 85.

13. *Asahi Shimbun*, 29 July 1973, p. 3.

tween 1964 and 1971, caused by indiscriminate discharge of chemical wastes from plants and factories.[14] Not only have these contaminated rivers, streams, and lakes become eyesores, unfit for swimming or fishing, but their increasing contamination has resulted in the appearance of deadly ailments that have since added to the medical lexicon but for which cures are yet to be found. Two of these new diseases are *minamata* disease and *itai-itai* disease. The former involves serious damage to the nervous system caused by the ingestion of fish and shellfish contaminated by mercury contained in the industrial waste discharged into bodies of water; it is named after the area on the southern island of Kyushu where it was first detected on a large scale. *Itai-itai* disease is caused by cadmium poisoning and results in the impairment of kidney function, changes in the endocrine system, and esteomalcia. "Itai itai" is a verbal expression of severe physical pain.[15]

These are but a few samples of the more obvious problems caused by industrial advances and economic growth which indiscriminately affect the people, be they rich or not so rich. And the level of stoicism normally characteristic of the Japanese rapidly evaporates these days when they daily confront urban and traffic congestion, whether they travel by private car or public transportation. There are other critical visible problems: farmers and city folk alike are witness to the denaturing process that has been perpetrated upon their surroundings by giant real estate conglomerates and sharp-eyed, fast-talking developers. Back in 1932, Tokyo, for example, enjoyed greens in the form of forests, woods, parks, and grasslands over more than 80 percent of its premises. In 1960, two-thirds of Tokyo did. Today, less than one-third does.[16] Those formerly green areas are now covered with concrete, steel, aluminum, and glass. Birds, butterflies, crickets, and other charming creatures of nature are harder to find, unless one goes to the suburbs or countryside. Rapid industrialization and economic growth have also deprived many

---

14. Ibid.

15. For the spread of these crippling ailments, see *Quality of Environment in Japan*, part 2, chap. 5; *Information Bulletin 1973* (Tokyo: Public Information Bureau, Ministry of Foreign Affairs, 1973), pp. 89–90; and Donald R. Thurston, "Aftermath in Minamata," *Japan Interpreter* 9 (Spring 1974).

16. *Quality of Environment in Japan*, p. 36; and *Mainichi Shimbun*, 14 July 1972, p. 5.

urban and metropolitan areas of even a minimally adequate park space. Per capita park space today is only 1.2 square meters in Tokyo, 1.4 in Osaka, and 2.9 in Nagoya, for example. In contrast, the figure for London is 22.8 square meters and, for New York, it is 19.2; and these are two of the most crowded cities in the world.[17] Growth and prosperity have consumed so much space for construction of factories, office buildings, housing complexes, warehouses, roads and expressways that they have left little for children's enjoyment of nature and adults' aesthetic gratification. Nor is the countryside free any longer from such massive exploitation in the name of growth, progress, and development. Many picturesque land spaces that used to be tended by the loving care of farmers, changing their colors according to the seasons, have been obliterated by ugly, albeit functional, industrial plants, pollutant-belching smokestacks, monotonously uniform housing projects, and less than taste-fully constructed amusement parks and food emporia. Japan, indeed, is a much less charming, much less attractive country to visit than those travel posters and brochures attempt to induce the reader to believe.

NEW ISSUES AND PROBLEMS

To be sure, those visible problems of which we have cited a few examples did not emerge overnight. They had been there before, albeit with much less gravity or urgency. And many people were aware of their existence. Those problems, however, had been by and large regarded with the kind of stoicism historically typical of the Japanese as inevitable inconveniences accompanying the collective national endeavor for an economic superpowerdom and/or with an optimism equally typical of the Japanese as remediable shortcomings that would be somehow resolved as the nation continued to make spectacular economic advances and technological development. This general popular attitude was clearly indicated by an opinion poll taken in 1966 (which we surmise as still falling in the industrial period). In this poll, the number of respondents who viewed pollution, for example, as "inevitable" far outnumbered those who considered it "unacceptable." In 1971 (which I suggest falls in the category

17. *Asahi Nenkan 1973* (Tokyo: Asahi Shimbun Sha, 1974), p. 538. Municipal park laws specify a minimum of 6 square meters per capita. Goro Hani, *Toshi no Ronri* (Tokyo: Keiso Shobo, 1969), p. 378.

of the postindustrial), however, the number of respondents viewing pollution as "unacceptable" outnumbered by nearly 4 to 1 those who still regarded it as "inevitable."[18] I think this difference is quite revealing. What is inevitable (like a storm or earthquake) is not political because it is a matter of course, an act of God according to the lexicon of insurance policies. What is unacceptable, like injustice or discrimination, is clearly the stuff of politics. In short, during the industrial period, problems of pollution and many other ills emanating from technological advances and economic growth were not the kinds of issues that would arouse public passion and thus become objects of political conflict. In other words, they were politically not relevant or salient, for they were regarded as "inevitable." They became salient, however, once people began to perceive them as "unacceptable," that is, capable of being dealt with, and thus to view them as serious political problems. Change in the nature and type of issues relevant in one period of society to the next is the function of an emergence of new kinds of popular perception.

Other problems have gained in salience in recent years in Japan, and they, too, suggest various consequences of the advanced industrialism that dominated the country in postwar years. Perhaps we should tentatively categorize them, together with the problems already discussed. I would like to put them in the following categories:

1. politicization of costs of modern industrialism
2. status politics
3. expressive politics
4. trivialization of politics

Neither these categories nor the issues and phenomena to be discussed in each of them are by any means exhaustive. They are meant only to be suggestive of the kind of change that I think is taking place in Japan in the nature, character, and type of politics.

Politicization of Costs of Modern Industrialism

In industrial society, whatever its political arrangement and ideological configuration may be, the primary object of general

18. *Quality of the Environment in Japan*, p. 39.

public concern and political struggle is the *benefits* (income and wealth and what they afford), and not the *costs*, of economic advance and industrial growth and how such benefits (i.e., the expanding pie) ought to be distributed. This is not to say that the costs are not incurred. They are indeed incurred in both tangible and intangible ways; hence they exist, for example, in terms of the psychic dislocation and discontinuity suffered by those who migrate from countryside to city in search of allegedly or actually more profitable jobs, discontinuities in certain of the fabric of society, proletarianization of masses of people, and inevitable environmental destruction for purposes of building factories, hydroelectric dams, strip-mining, and so on. Consider the plight of working-class people as depicted in the novels by Emile Zola and Charles Dickens and the famous historical work by Edmund Wilson. In these works we can readily see both the physical and psychological damages perpetrated by industrialism in its early stages. Costs, therefore, exist. But, then, they do not themselves become salient political issues, except in isolated instances for certain limited groups such as the Luddites in England in the nineteenth century. As we saw earlier, industrialism (that is, industrial society) is growth-oriented, and growth is equated with progress, and progress is universally regarded as desirable for man and society. Those who resist progress are considered backward, parochial, unenlightened, or sometimes even dangerous.

Quite unlike the distribution of *benefits* of industrialism, which in the nature of things is perforce selective, discretionary, and differential, owing, quite simply, to different degrees of influence or pressure contending groups are respectively capable of bringing upon decision makers, be they corporate or governmental, the *costs* of industrialism in the form, for example, of increasingly apparent negative material impact tend to be egalitarian, catholic, indiscriminate, hence cross-stratal in nature. This does not necessarily mean, of course, that all groups are equally affected. There is, after all, the phenomenon of differential impact: an event, a problem, or a policy affects different groups differently, i.e., some worse than others (or benefits some more than others, as the case may be). For example, inflation affects people with fixed incomes far worse than others; a sales tax is more disadvantageous to lower-income people than to higher-income groups; a typhoon (an annual phenomenon in

Japan) is more dreadful to people living in certain areas or in certain kinds of dwelling than to others. Better-situated people (in terms of income, location, and the like) can tolerate a given phenomenon or problem with greater equanimity than the less fortunate. This is true with those material *costs* of industrialism, be they pollution or an unabatable inflation. But only to a certain extent.

There are two reasons that help explain why the negative material impact is cross-stratal. One is that a wide enough range of groups of people begin to view these problems as no longer "inevitable" but as "intolerable." These problems may still be "less" intolerable to some than to others, but they are intolerable all the same. Indeed, petrochemical smog, for instance, does not know the difference between upper-middle-class children and working-class children, whose respiratory systems are equally affected on the school playground. Traffic congestion is the same. The rich and the not-so-rich alike love fish in Japan, but fish, in all too many cases, are poisoned by chemical wastes that industrial plants so callously disposed of into all convenient bodies of water. So water pollution becomes as intolerable to the rich as to the not-so-rich. There is another reason why negative material impact is cross-stratal in nature. The growing egalitarian trend in income that obtained during the period of rapid economic growth promoted an increasing equalization of susceptibility to many of those costs of industrialism. As we mentioned in chapter 2, income differentials narrowed in Japan. Most Japanese are paid well, and in proportion to the entire population, the very rich are very small in number, as are the very poor.[19] Thus, the impact of inflation, for instance, is more or less equally felt by most people across conventional socioeconomic and ideological cleavages or strata. It is their perception, not the perception of either the small number of the rich (who can weather inflation with relative insouciance) or the very poor (whose voice has little or no influence in good times or bad), that is politically relevant. Differential or otherwise, therefore, the negative material impact emanating from advanced industrialism is today acutely felt cross-stratally because it has, in the perception of the widening range of sectors and groups in society, become "intolerable."

19. Howard Van Zandt, "Japanese Culture and the Business Boom," *Foreign Affairs* 48 (January 1970): 347–48.

The Spread of "Status Politics"[20]

Status is a value that is conceptually and analytically distinct from material goods, though they frequently go hand in hand. Status is a function of recognition by society as important to its quality and integrity. "Second class" citizenship, for example, suggests lack of status. So everybody, every group or every aggregate of individuals seeks status to gain a sense of self-importance, self-respect. In Japan, the growing egalitarian ethos to which I referred in chapter 2 tends to encourage this phenomenon.

There are many groups of people in Japan who, while legally or constitutionally equal, have been socially unequal or lacking in status. This was so not simply because they were viewed by others as unequal or lacking in status but equally because they regarded themselves as less than full-fledged members of society or felt ambivalent about their roles in society. The lack of status, therefore, was both subjective and objective, imposed as well as self-imposed. Very much like the bourgeoisie in a moribund aristocratic society, these groups begin to perceive a growing disjunction between improvement in their material well-being and lack of corresponding improvement in their status. (Other groups, while enjoying a degree of status, nevertheless want to improve their status relative to others because they feel that their own status has been overtaken by others.) They were generally acquiescent or quiescent during the industrial period but are becoming increasingly aggressive in demanding recognition and status. Among these groups we find *burakumin* (people of special communal hamlets),[21] women, welfare recipients, and senior citizens, to cite a few examples.

20. The term is adopted from Joseph R. Gusfield, *Symbolic Crusade: Status Politics and the American Temperance Movement* (Urbana and London: University of Illinois Press, 1966).

21. *Burakumin*, numbering a few millions and racially not distinct from other Japanese, are descendants of the feudal outcasts of the Tokugawa era who were engaged in such then despised occupations as slaughtering, leather-making and jailers. Since then, they have constituted a group with a distinct subculture and still live in their own self-segregated communities in metropolitan and urban areas and work as physical laborers and other lowly employees. For a good description of their community and life, see George A. DeVos, "Japan's Outcast: The Problem of the Burakumin," in *The Fourth World: Victims of Group Oppression,* ed. Ben Whitaker (New York: Schocken, 1973).

Advanced industrialism seems to have generated a powerful impetus to the rise of status politics. The general egalitarian trend in politics and economy it engendered, the growing acceptance of the notion that to receive public assistance in case of need is a citizen's right, and the decline in a number of traditional behavioral inhibitions regarding social relations, among others, have combined to generate a widespread perception among *burakumin*, women, and welfare recipients that their respective statuses should be raised to a level equal to any other group. They are no longer content with second-class citizenship and with being at the mercy, however benign, of the rest of society. They want to participate in politics as full-fledged citizens.[22]

Nuclearization of families has created a growing body of old people separated from the kind of secure postretirement life their predecessors had taken for granted, i.e., living with their loving children and grandchildren in the psychic and material comfort of the home they had built for themselves and their progeny. Today, as the result of rapid urbanization and rising demographic mobility, families are nuclearized; grandparents more often than not live alone or in retirement homes. They constitute a new social group with its own economic and social interests, and they want to be recognized as such, with an appropriate level of status accorded them.

Degrees of intensity—and subsequent political salience—of "status politics" vary from group to group. The status politics of women is widespread but, perhaps for that reason, diffuse in impact. That of *burakumin*, because of their concentration in a few urban or metropolitan areas, has become intense, so much so that local gubernatorial elections in recent years were seriously affected by it. Welfare recipients have yet to develop their political muscle, but there are signs of growing intensity of their status politics at the local level. The same holds true for senior citizens.

We must note here that the rise of status politics is significant in postindustrial Japan not only because the groups seeking recognition and status are becoming politicized but also because members of "established" groups are politicizing the issue of status-seeking groups. Members of these established groups support, or advocate the interest of, status-seeking groups out of a

---

22. See the concept of "emancipative erruptions" in Heinz Hartman, "Institutional Immobility and Attitudinal Change in West Germany," *Comparative Politics* 2 (July 1970): 585.

variety of motives not all of which are altruistic. One of those reasons—perhaps a major one—is clearly related to some of the political consequences of modern industrialism, as we shall see shortly.

Intensification of "Expressive Politics"[23]

Modern industrialism and one of its concomitants in the form of technology of organizational and institutional management and manipulation has bureaucratized politics and government to the extent that for all but an increasingly narrow range of effective political participants, meaningful, i.e., effective, political input into the decision-making process is felt to be more and more remote or difficult. For most of the citizenry, preoccupied as they are with material pursuit in an increasingly affluent society, this is problematic only intermittently. For some politically highly motivated or committed groups that find themselves increasingly on the periphery of the political arena, this is extremely frustrating. To them, the system is unresponsive, unconcerned, unrepresentative, aloof, remote, and invariably unjust. These groups are fervently committed to their own respective (and often mutually contradictory) visions of what society should be like (e.g., "liberated society," "society of genuine equality," "revolutionary society"). Since whatever specific programs they might formulate for society could not work unless they took power, and since the taking of power is realistically not possible, they are devoid of any realistic proposals of specific nature. The more remote the chances of success of their goal, the more frustrated and committed they become, and the more impelled they are to express their frustration and commitment in a manner that would with maximum impact convey their feeling to the insensitive society at large. Thus they engage in "expressive politics," that is, "political action for the sake of expression rather than for the sake of influencing or controlling" the basic decision making and conduct of society.[24] Various extremist groups in Japan, such as the Red Army, the Wolves, the Scorpions, fall into this class; engaged in expressive politics,

---

23. For the description and discussion of expressive politics as a *genre* of political action, see Gusfield, *Symbolic Crusade*, and Richard Hofstadter, "The Pseudo-Conservative Revolt," in *The New American Right*, ed. Daniel Bell (New York: Criterion, 1955).

24. Gusfield, *Symbolic Crusade*, p. 19.

political actions they normally choose include urban terrorism, skyjackings, assassination attempts, kidnapping, participation in the Palestinian Liberation Organization (PLO). At a less violent level, many student demonstrations allegedly aimed at a government policy or a specific act of a high official (e.g., the premier's visit to the United States) are in their deeper motivation basically expressive (i.e., a display of unarticulated frustration by the participants with something other than the alleged target) rather than instrumental (i.e., designed specifically to prevent the policy or act).

Neither expressive politics nor status politics is entirely absent in industrial society, but in postindustrial Japan both are becoming more pronounced and are assuming a qualitatively different level of magnitude and salience.

Trivialization of Politics

The decline in intensity of political struggle in industrial society over the distribution of income and wealth caused by the increasingly leveling effect of rapidly advancing industrialism and the subsequent popular immunization to radical appeal soon came to produce a sense of ennui and tedium about the continuing rituals and rhetoric of partisan competition on the formal stage of politics. Politics, in short, became boring. Indeed, the politics of the 1960s in Japan demonstrated a growing lack of excitement and drama. There were few issues of genuine moment. Issues germane to industrial society that had not been sufficiently resolved remained largely dormant because of the prospects of their gradual resolution as the nation's economic advance continued unabated.

This political boredom, however, eventually precipitated a search for issues, a desire to energize the slumbering political community, to restore the drama of political conflict. This search for issues was especially strong among politically active members of established groups, and its rise more or less coincided with, at least in part, and was reinforced by, the politicization of costs of industrialism and played no insignificant part in generating status politics. At times, it is difficult to see where the politicization of the costs of industrialism or the status politics ends and the search for political issues begins. In any event, this search for the drama of conflict has in recent years led to the injection into the political arena of many matters that are largely trivial, and the politicization and subsequent confrontation over them tend to render the business of politics increasingly trivial as well as taxing.

Among issues that I think are trivial (that is, trivial to the formal arena of political conflict) are strident demands for totally free medical care for certain age groups without regard to their socioeconomic stations, such as people over sixty-five and infants; free public transportation for those over seventy; free nursing care for the children of all working women; free admission of senior citizens to public bathhouses; removal from electronic and print media of all expressions that are in any sense derogatory of any group (e.g., women, the elderly, the dim-witted, the physically handicapped, the ill, the poor). Some of the disputes precipitated by powerful organized labor are increasingly capricious. And there are issues that suggest their postindustrial character (i.e., pertaining to costs of industrialism) but are nevertheless less than weighty. Among these are demands for new "citizen rights" such as "the right to sunshine" (*nisshoken*), "the right to unobstructed view" (*choboken*), "the right to see and hear" (*shichoken*). The right to sunshine, for example, is the right of each household to receive and enjoy direct sunshine, and this has in recent years become an object of public demand in urban and metropolitan areas. "The right to unobstructed view" is the right of each household not to be deprived of an unobstructed view of the sky and distant fields and mountains that it has enjoyed. "The right to see and hear" is a similar right not to be deprived of the sight and sound of natural phenomena such as the chirping of birds, rustling of leaves of trees and blades of grass, and so on.

Perhaps these issues are individually of some significance and even contain certain aesthetic dimensions. Most, if not all, of them appear, however, variously to be contentious when viewed against the fundamental responsibility and capability of the political system to deal with problems of authentic import. Every problem, insofar as it is viewed as such by any aggregate of citizens, is a problem. But, then, there are different levels of magnitude among various problems and different degrees to which they may or may not warrant or deserve authoritative public resolution. And there is also the question of the political and administrative (that is, conflict resolving) capability of government and society, and whether or not a given issue or problem is deserving of critical exertion by the existing political arrangement must be determined relative to the existing political and administrative capability as well as relative to the magnitude of other problems calling for authoritative resolution. Politicization of problems that could or should be resolved in the private sector or through private or voluntary efforts would not only overload the existing capacity for conflict management and resolution, thus dissipating such critical capacity at the expense of the need for resolution of genuinely important public problems, but also cheapen and trivialize the whole business of politics.

Perhaps there is an additional reason for the trivialization of politics, apart from the boredom of politics in modern industrial society. I am thinking of certain consequences of politics and government in modern industrial society. As industrialism advances and society becomes more complex and interdependent in its structure and operation, the role of government increases by leaps and bounds. It intervenes in the economy with growing penetration and explicitness; its role in group and social relations expands; and it finds itself taking upon its shoulders a widening range of responsibilities for education, material well-being, and the sociocultural ecology of the entire citizenry. All this has positive and useful effects on the stability and well-being of society. Nevertheless, there are unintended results as well. One result is that the people at large and groups or various aggregates of citizens in particular become, in their expectation and disposition, so dependent on government or public decision-making processes that they begin to feel that the government should take care of everything and anything, even the most trivial annoyances. Another unintended albeit inevitable consequence of modern industrialism is the growing impersonalization of social relations with the rapid urbanization of society. Areas in which people can relate with one another and interact with one another in personal ways or with a sense of community become smaller and smaller. People can no longer sit down and reason together to resolve through face-to-face informal negotiations what would be regarded as private disputes in simpler times. Instead, they go to the court, start political agitation, appeal to public authorities for intervention, and otherwise make public issues out of private matters. These two unintended consequences of modern industrialism turn out to be mutually reinforcing.

The four categories of problems thus far discussed as more characteristic of postindustrial Japan are not always neatly separable from one another. In many ways they overlap. And, sometimes, each one overlaps with the conventional issue of the distribution of benefits of industrialism. Status politics is in more senses than one related, at least in part or at times, to the question of material well-being. Some aspects of expressive politics are basically trivial; others are, in their origin if not in their metamorphosis, industrial. And there is much cheap air of the trivia about some of the aspects of status politics. For all these reasons and others, the political arena of postindustrial Japan becomes highly fluid and volatile.

POPULAR AMBIVALENCE: BETWEEN INDUSTRIALISM AND POSTINDUSTRIALISM

The rise of new issues and problems in postindustrial Japan does not in itself signify that the issues and problems more typical of the industrial period have disappeared or ceased to be politically salient. Not everything changes at once or at an equal rate. Affluent masses continue to covet more and more shares of the benefits of modern industrialism while becoming more and more concerned with their visible negative consequences. What we see in Japan today, then, is a rather diffuse kind of popular ambivalence. People perceive the need for some significant modification in priorities and values, and this modification is at least in part being promoted by their own conscious and unselfconscious response or reaction (see pp. 47–48 and chapters 6 and 7) to some consequences of industrialism. At the same time, there is this persistent or continuing desire, born of the industrial period, for more material benefits, especially since the idea of progress and the expanding-pie outlook of the industrial period raised the level of popular expectations and segmental self-interests. What Inglehart called "the materialist value" continues to dominate Japanese society.[25] Thus conventional political competition of industrial society among various groups for what can be gotten persists.

Vastly complicating this basic ambivalence is the new intensity of status politics and expressive politics as well as the growing trend toward trivialization of politics entirely independent of the basic disjunction between the imperatives of an industrial society and those of a postindustrial society. Politics in Japan is becoming extremely vulnerable to a much wider

25. Ronald Inglehart, "The Silent Revolution in Europe: Intergenerational Change in Post-Industrial Societies," *American Political Science Review* 65 (December 1971).

range of forces than was the case during her industrial period. Structurally Japan is perhaps already postindustrial, but culturally and politically her aspects are volatile, even unpredictable.

It is nevertheless significant that the conventional issue of the distribution of the benefits of modern industrialism as such has ceased to be all-encompassing. Not all the new kinds of issues and problems—or their emergence in the political arena—are desirable, of course. The fact remains, however, that they are affecting Japanese politics in many of its dimensions for well or for ill, forcing it to respond to the challenge they cumulatively and singly pose. Indeed, the extent to which these "postindustrial" issues and problems have gained in salience may be variously seen in certain corresponding behavioral manifestations. The party system, which in the postwar years of industrial growth and advance functioned as the fount of the political system, is gradually but perceptively forced to experience some significant modifications in its aspects. Many conventional parameters of political action and process that in the past served well are declining in their congruence and relevance with the changing environment. An increasingly apparent disparity between the existing political arrangement on the one hand and the nature and character of new kinds of problems and issues on the other has already resulted in an acute popular frustration with and an incipient rejection of the party system and party government without, however, any corresponding popular withdrawal from the political arena. Indeed, what we see is a trend toward an increasing popular participation of which there is a wholly novel and unprecedented pattern. As well, there is the appearance of a new breed of politicians, activists, and leaders, who consciously reject conventional political referents and behavioral inhibitions. These growing phenomena, in turn, are beginning to affect the style, the rhetoric, and the content of electoral politics ascertainably. In an important sense, all these phenomena (and the kind of dynamics they respectively generate) seem to be producing a mutually reinforcing effect. And it is to these important dimensions of ongoing political change in Japan that the rest of the present volume addresses itself.

Part II
PARTIES AND PARTY GOVERNMENT

In a broad historical sense, political parties as we know them in modern society are products of industrialism. They arise in response to the emergence of a new environment called industrialism some key features of which we discussed in preceding chapters. They do not necessarily develop in one fashion in all industrial societies, for each society is in an important sense unique, with its own peculiar historical background and cultural tradition. Moreover, parties, depending upon what they do, can affect the environment in response to whose change they appear.[1] But these parties emerge primarily to meet the requirements of political competition and struggle in the new society where the fundamental issue of politics is the distribution of income and wealth, the benefits of industrialism and its expanding pie.

1. Leon D. Epstein, *Political Parties in Western Democracies* (New York: Praeger, 1967), chap. 2.

PARTIES IN PREINDUSTRIAL SOCIETY

Parties, or at least their prototypes, are observable historically in preindustrial society. Party politics existed in ancient Rome, medieval Italy, eighteenth-century England, during the French Revolution, and in the United States immediately after the Philadelphia Convention. But the object of party politics in these preindustrial societies had little to do with the issue of how income and wealth were to be distributed among various social groups. It was concerned rather with office or how office was to be shared or not shared. And this was clearly reflective of the nature and the objective of political conflict in those societies. This fact was reflected also in party organization. In the preindustrial Western context, parties, if they existed, were preeminently those of the influentials and the notables, representing the topmost social strata; masses of people had little or no relations to them in any meaningful sense.

Today the situation is superficially different in preindustrial societies (of which there are many), because contemporary preindustrial societies have political parties fashioned after those that are more characteristic of industrial society in terms of objectives, organization, and activities. This is the function of what we might term "imitative behavior" or "spillover effect." Consider, for example, the phenomenon of the so-called revolution of rising expectations in Third World nations that are largely preindustrial or barely industrializing. "Rising expectations" as such are a more common feature of industrial society in which the "expanding pie" outlook has replaced the traditional "constant pie" orientation concerning material well-being. But they have become a more pronounced feature (and a highly destabilizing one at that) of those Third World nations. This is the result of the exposure, through introduction of modern communication media, of people in those nations to the visions of the rising material well-being and affluence industrialism brought to advanced industrial nations of the First and Second Worlds. People have adopted or imitate the basic value orientation of an industrial society. In other words, the "expanding pie" philosophy of industrialism has "spilled over" into societies that are not industrial. This has caused serious problems. For example, this spillover effect upsets a certain social and cultural equilibrium that has been historically and developmentally characteristic of preindustrial societies, causing people to demand what their society cannot provide, and to expect their government to do what it is unable to do.

The emergence of seemingly "modern" political parties in those societies is also the function of the same "imitative behavior" or "spillover effect" phenomenon. Since there is some structural or systemic disjunction between such "modern" parties and the basic developmental condition of today's preindustrial society, as there is between the "imitated" rising expectations and the material predicament of such a society, political parties, or the party system, these tend to be highly precarious, unstable, and volatile. In short, the party system is not well integrated into such a society at all.

PARTIES IN INDUSTRIAL SOCIETY

With the coming of the industrial period, the nature of political parties gradually shifts because the nature and object of political conflict change. But party organization and its mode of operation, because of old habits, both human and institutional, change much more slowly than the objective environment. There is always this element of time lag or residual behavior in the evolution of various aspects of society. For this reason, parties of influentials or notables, characteristic of preindustrial society, persist into the industrial period; mass parties, deemed unique to industrial society, fail to emerge with dispatch.

As society moves further into the industrial period, two developments are likely to take place in the political arena, if society is relatively open. One is the emergence of leftist parties based philosophically upon what we in the preceding chapter called ideologies of economic justice. Socialist and Communist parties are common among industrial societies, but other parties variously advocate economic justice and adopt different names such as democratic socialist, progressive, farm-labor, labor, and so on. They all emerge, however, to challenge the prevailing patterns of the distribution of income and wealth in industrial societies. Not all these parties are viable, however, and some are unable to, or encounter various obstacles and difficulties in their effort to, develop effective organizational networks. The difference arises, not out of any divergence in the fundamental issue of politics, but rather out of differences in the sociopolitical tradition and cultural history peculiar to each nation. Many parties of economic justice survive to become mass parties because they are either supported by, or seek to appeal to, the wider sector of society that was not politicized in the preindustrial period. They now pose increasingly serious electoral challenge to the parties of the influentials and notables.

In response to this threat by mass parties, the existing parties undergo significant organizational and tactical changes in order to ensure their own survival and retention of power. They attempt to expand both membership and range of appeal in order to solicit support from masses who are increasingly politicized concerning the distribution of the benefits of industrialism.[2] In this manner traditional parties with their original roots in preindustrial politics attempt to adapt themselves to the environment of industrial society and, together with parties of the left, reflect the politicization of the issue of income and wealth distribution. The parties of the right defend the existing pattern of wealth and income distribution while those of the left attack it. Not all the working masses support the parties of the left, however. Many support the parties of the right because, while desirous of bigger slices of the expanding pie, they believe in the benignity of those parties and/or acutely fear (be such fear rational or otherwise) what they view as radical or extreme in the parties of the left. In any event, those who support the parties of the right do so because they think they would benefit more by supporting these parties.

The second important development takes place as society moves further into the industrial period, and it has to do with change in the nature and intensity of conflict between the parties of the right and those of the left. In the early stages of industrialism, the gap in shares of income and wealth between those who control the means of production and those who sell their labor to them is very wide. At first glance, those in control of the means of production receive (or give themselves) a disproportionately large share of the benefits of industrialism, while those who sell their labor receive a disproportionately small amount; this seems terribly unfair, and it is unfair if we think that income and wealth should be more or less fairly distributed. The distribution is unfair or grossly unequal, not basically because "capitalists" or the bourgeoisie are greedy and merciless

2. Consider the concept of "contagion from the left" in Maurice Duverger, *Political Parties*, trans. Barbara and Robert North (New York: Wiley, 1963), p. xxvii.

exploiters of the working masses (though some obviously are), but more because of certain systemic imperatives of industrialism. As we said more than once, the underlying philosophy or outlook of industrial society is that of the expanding pie. The fundamental requirement of industrialism, then, is continuously to raise the material well-being of the individual and society. How can this be done?

The question is a troublesome one, for it causes hardship for many in a society that is becoming industrial. Let me quote one prominent economic historian on this problem:

> If we are to enjoy a greater material well-being . . . we must produce more. . . . Despite all the inequities of distribution which attend the society of serf and lord, capitalist and child-employee, underlying the meanness of the times was one overriding reality; this was scarcity. There was simply not enough to go around, and if somewhat less lopsided distributive arrangements might have lessened the *moral* indignity of the times, they would not have contributed much to a massive improvement in basic economic well-being. Even assuming that the wage of the city laborer and the income of the peasant could have been doubled had the rich been deprived of their share—and this is an extravagant assumption—still, the characteristic of rural and urban life would have been its poverty.[3]

The point here, of course, is that the requirement of the expanding pie calls for a great deal of sacrifice—a high rate of saving—at earlier stages of industrialism. The wealthy do not spend or consume all they receive; what they do not consume is plowed back into investment for further increases in the size of the economic pie. The poor, that massive sector for which the parties of the left speak, would spend, i.e., consume, all they earn or receive. An equitable distribution of income, then, would result in a dwindling or disappearance of savings to be plowed back into further productive enterprises to increase the size of the pie. In short, it is "a hard economic reality that the amount of construction for the future can never exceed the amount of resources and effort which are unused or which can be released for consumption in the present."[4] This is the most basic systemic imperative of industrialism in its early stages in any nation, capitalist or socialist.

In those early stages of industrialism, therefore, conflict

3. Robert L. Heilbroner, *The Making of Economic Society* (Englewood Cliffs, N.J.: Prentice-Hall, 1962), p. 88.

4. Ibid., p. 96.

between the party of the right and the party of the left is fierce, often violent, and contending ideologies are highly intense and intensely committed to by their respective proponents. As industrialism progresses and the expanding pie continues to expand, aided by rising capital accumulation and technological advance, however, there eventually sets in a powerful and irreversible trend toward narrowing the wide gap in the distribution of the benefits of industrialism. To put an actually complex process very simplistically, the viability and further growth of industrialism necessitates a more and more equal distribution of the expanding economic pie. For one thing, the constantly rising output of manufactured goods must be absorbed, that is to say, consumed, so as to ensure further production of those goods as well as capital goods that are used to produce them. This suggests a very interesting shift in the imperative of industrialism from its earlier stages. In those earlier stages, the major concern was how to increase production and productivity (or, on the other side of the same coin, how to squeeze investment capital out of the small economic pie), but it has changed to one of how to maintain a rising level of consumption. This point is arrived at when society has reached the stage of sustained economic growth, i.e., when the need to generate investment capital ceases to be a major technical problem, or, to put the same thing differently, when consumption becomes positively correlated to investment.

A high and rising rate of consumption can be achieved only if the masses are allowed to purchase and consume. This means they should be given larger shares of the benefits of industrialism so that industrialism can produce more benefits. This is one of the imperatives of advanced industrialism. Not only do workers receive increasingly more attractive wages and salaries and fringe benefits, but they also are permitted to organize themselves to demand even more attractive wages, salaries, and the like. When they are unemployed or unable to work because of temporary or permanent infirmities or old age, they are provided with social security, welfare programs, pensions, and other forms of benefits that are designed to enable them to continue to purchase and consume, albeit at a reduced level, so that the institution of industrialism may continue to function. The fundamental motive in this change in the fortune of the masses in advanced industrial society, therefore, is not any humanitarian impulse (though such is not totally absent), but rather the systemic imperatives of industrialism. By these programs industrialism attempts to ensure its own survival and growth. And this results in certain consequences for the nature and intensity of party conflict.

The narrowing of the distributive gap in society and subsequent mass recognition of more and more immediate prospects of further improvement in material well-being cause a gradual decline in intensity of ideological conflict between the erstwhile bourgeoisie and proletariat and, consequently, between the parties of the right and those of the left. This process is further enhanced by the leveling effect that the rising material well-being of the masses produces regarding patterns of consumption and life style between them and their traditional "class enemies." "Proletarians" become more and more committed supporters of the existing political arrangement. In short, they become politically integrated, sharing the same set of basic values with the "bourgeoisie," for the "integrating process which is the chief characteristic of industrial society has now encompassed that class whose inability to integrate into the society was once supposed to destroy that society."[5]

Reflecting the dynamics of advancing industrialism and the subsequent integration of working masses into the fabric of industrial society, parties draw nearer to each other toward the middle of the ideological spectrum. In fact, in many, if not most, advanced industrial societies, they draw so near that they become almost alike. Parties of the right come to accept, albeit grudgingly, progressive income tax, social security, workers' rights to unionize and bargain, and varying degrees of welfare statism, all anathema to their original ideologies of economic justification. Any party that does not accept these things comes to be viewed as "extreme right" or "reactionary." At the same time, "leftists," too, come to accept the undesirability (or infeasibility) of violent class struggle and revolution, incremental rather than radical socioeconomic change, and the existing process of conflict management and decision making. Those who do not become the "radical left." There is, therefore, a convergence of the right and the left toward the middle of the politico-ideological spectrum. Of course, there is a considerable variation of this highly generalized pattern

5. Norman Birnbaum, *The Crisis of Industrial Society* (New York: Oxford University Press, 1969), p. 8. Also see his *Toward a Critical Sociology* (New York: Oxford University Press, 1971), p. 371.

among nations,[6] but the general tendency of major parties of
the right and the left seems to have been more often than not
consistent in industrial societies.

In one sense, this growing convergence of the right and the
left on the middle deprives politics in industrial society of its
earlier sense of drama and moment, for now the difference
between the former parties of the right and those of the left has
ceased to be one of kind and instead become one of degree. As
a Swedish journalist once said, "The only issues are whether the
metal workers should get a nickel more an hour, the price of
milk should be raised, or old-age pensions extended."[7] Indeed,
the major point of conflict between the former right and the
former left now is which can more competently accommodate
the imperatives of industrialism than the other. In other words,
the question is a tactical one of which party can promote the
kind of income and wealth distribution that would best help
industrialism. One argues, for example, that less taxes would
promote growth (while, of course, benefiting the better-off
sectors and groups more than the less-well-off), and the other
counters by saying that a higher level of income redistribution
(through a different set of income and fiscal policies) would be
more appropriate (while obviously benefiting the lower-income
groups much more than the higher-income ones). So, some
differences between the former parties of the right and those of
the left remain, but those differences, while clearly indicating
the persistence of the fundamental issue of industrial politics,
are becoming increasingly less conspicuous because both, now
inseparably integrated into industrial society and embedded in
the values it represents and pursues, act more or less according
to shifting emphases of the systemic imperatives and requirements of industrialism. Old ideological rhetoric, especially
Marxian, persists, for want, one might suppose, of any better
ideas; customary homage is paid to the ideology as well as to its
founders; and certain rituals and mode of disputation are more
often than not honored. They are, however, more an instance of
residual behavior than anything else. They also help former

6. On this development, especially regarding voter behavior, see the
critical comment in Joseph LaPalombara, *Politics Within Nations* (Englewood Cliffs, N.J.: Prentice-Hall, 1974), pp. 451–54.

7. Quoted in Seymour Martin Lipset, *Political Man: The Social Bases of
Politics* (Garden City, N.Y.: Doubleday, 1963), p. 442.

parties of the left maintain their distinct, albeit less and less meaningful, identity in the political arena.[8]

PARTIES IN POSTINDUSTRIAL SOCIETY

We have yet to see how parties will evolve or what kind of party will emerge in postindustrial society. Our discussion in the next two chapters of Japan's political parties is designed to elicit some considerations regarding possible directions or ways in which parties, generally born of and entrenched in industrial society and its requirements, may evolve. Certain other considerations suggest themselves, however, according to the logic of the role and function of parties discussed thus far.

If modern political parties as we know them either emerged in response to, or adapted themselves to, the imperatives and requirements of industrial society and their organization and operation evolved in close conjunction with the advance and entrenchment of modern industrialism, it seems axiomatic that they would have to reorient themselves and restructure their priorities or their operational principles in postindustrial society where the nature, character, and process of politics shift. Industrial society is founded in the belief in the infinite capacity of human ingenuity and creativity. Its god is growth; its prophet, science and technology; its priest, industrial manager; and parties are its political vehicles. And the conflict over income and wealth distribution is the central stuff of industrial politics. Coalition of constituencies or groups for each major party in industrial society, especially in its advanced stage, is relatively easy to form and remains relatively constant; it is also relatively easy for the party to represent, inasmuch as the unifying criteria are economic and the allocation of benefits is discreet and

8. For decline in intensity of ideological conflict, see, for example, Daniel Bell, *The End of Ideology* (Glencoe, Ill.: Free Press, 1960); Ronald Segal, *The Struggle Against History* (London: Weidenfeld & Nicolson, 1971), pp. 9–10; and Ulf Himmelstrand, "Depoliticization and Political Involvement: A Theoretical and Empirical Approach," in *Mass Politics: Studies in Political Sociology*, ed. Erik Allardt and Stein Rokkan (New York: Free Press, 1970). For opposing views, see, for example, Joseph LaPalombara, "Decline of Ideology: A Dissent and an Interpretation," *American Political Science Review* 60 (March 1966); and Giuseppe DiPalma, *The Study of Conflict in Western Society: A Critique of the End of Ideology* (Morristown, N.J.: General Learning Press, 1973).

selective. In other words, issues over which each coalition is formed and maintained and aligned with the party are manageable both in character and in range. Indeed, this manageability of issues for the party is the function of congruence between the organizational and processual character of the party on the one hand and the universality of values the coalition of constituencies seek through its alignment with the party. In postindustrial society, however, this basic pattern of relations between party and constituency may no longer obtain.

In the first place, we noted in chapter 3 that, at least in Japan, new types of issues are in character and range quite different from conventional issues of politics in industrial society. Consider the issue of air pollution. Is it an issue favored by leftists or rightists? Clearly the question is irrelevant; the issue is cross-stratal. Now let us consider the status politics. Is it a right-vs.-left question? It does not seem to be that. In many ways, some former conservatives, e.g., the middle class or white-collar sector, are becoming more liberal than many former proletarians, i.e., blue-collar workers. This sort of conventional class-based distinction suffers further when we separate issues that relate basically to the distribution of income and wealth and those that are clearly political in thrust. The phenomenon of trivialization of politics further expands the range of issues that the party is increasingly called upon to deal with, and many of those issues defy any facile conservative-progressive classification in terms of constituencies. In short, most new issues not only cut across conventional cleavages of industrial society, but also may well generate different, mutually conflicting cleavages. The coalition of constituencies for each party will shift rapidly according to issues, making it increasingly difficult for the party to perform its aggregative function in the consistent, generally predictable manner of politics in an industrial society. Changing coalitions reflecting changing cleavages caused by conflicting issues may make it very taxing for the party to maintain its internal cohesion and discipline.

Then, too, there is the problem of valuational and attitudinal change which generates increasing pressure toward greater participatory equality and erosion of conventional authority referents such as age, institutional credentials. This pressure, as we will see in chapters 6 and 7, gives rise to new types of participants, activists, and leaders who attempt to operate outside the parameters of conventional politics of industrial society. How would the party absorb and integrate them? Or would they, if unintegrated by the party, create a new type of party or political organization promoting those interests or issues that the party is incapable of promoting? In these and other dimensions, we will find considerable volatility in Japan today.

Thus, structurally and valuationally, parties in Japan are confronted with a challenge to adapt themselves to the changing environment. In the two chapters that follow, we shall examine some salient problems of the parties that emerged during Japan's industrial period, their institutional or cultural constraints and viability, and how they are reacting to the challenge of emergent postindustrialism.

4

The Ruling Party
and Its Government

Since the end of World War II, Japan has been governed
continuously by what the Japanese call "conservatives," with a
brief and unexciting interlude of a Socialist-led coalition government in 1947 and 1948. "Conservatives" had been grouped, till
1955, into a varying number of parties of the right such as the
Liberal party, the Progressive party, the Cooperative party. In
total, there had existed at one time or another before 1955
seventeen "conservative" parties, each with a rather brief life
span or with a frequent change in name or membership, merging
with or splitting from others, and party switches by their members
were frequent.[1] In 1955, the then existing conservative parties—

1. For these postwar parties and their fusions and splits before 1955,
see, for example, Tsuneo Watanabe, *Habatsu—Hoshuto no Kaibo* (Tokyo:
Kobundo, 1958), pp. 48–49; Robert E. Ward, *Japan's Political System*
(Englewood Cliffs, N.J.: Prentice-Hall, 1967), p. 63; and Robert A.
Scalapino and Junnosuke Masumi, *Parties and Politics in Contemporary
Japan* (Berkeley and Los Angeles: University of California Press, 1962),
chap. 2 and Appendix.

the Liberals and the Democrats—merged to form the Liberal Democratic party (LDP), which has since ruled the nation without interruption.

No meaningful discussion of the LDP is possible, however, without constant reference to the government bureaucracy and corporate business and industrial leadership. The LDP is not a party with political autonomy and a clear institutional identity of its own. Instead, it is the political (i.e., parliamentary and electoral) branch of an institutional triumvirate that has governed the nation since the party's formation in 1955. The other two members of the triumvirate are the bureaucracy and the corporate leadership echelon. The three members of the triumvirate have been mutually integral and reinforcing, and the past economic success of the country was the fruit of their unity and collaboration. Our discussion of the ruling party and its government in the present chapter, therefore, is unavoidably a discussion, in large measure, of the LDP as the political side of the ruling triumvirate.

RELATIONS AMONG THE PARTY, THE BUREAUCRACY, AND BIG BUSINESS

The ties among the three institutional members of the ruling triumvirate can be genealogically traced back to the late nineteenth and early twentieth centuries at the time of massive historic efforts for the modernization and development of the country. The modernizing political elite of Meiji Japan first established a government bureaucracy by mobilizing the more educated sectors of the former martial (*samurai*) class for the purpose of effective governance of the erstwhile feudal society and of strengthening its own rule over the nation. The initial stage in modernizing Japan, therefore, was the political unification of the country through bureaucratic consolidation. The role of the bureaucracy became decisive in the subsequent development of the nation's political and economic systems. In fact, both the forerunner of the present LDP and modern business and industry were creatures of the government bureaucracy.

During the period of rapid economic development and modernization late in the nineteenth and early in the twentieth century, the government bureaucracy presided over by the modernizing elite formulated, financed, and implemented various industrial and commercial plans, operated and managed them, and after turning them over to private sectors upon ascertaining their viability, guided their expansion, directed their conduct, and thus fostered the growth of the modern industrial economic sector of the nation. The giant economic cartels of prewar Japan known throughout the world by the name *zaibatsu* (such as Mitsui, Sumitomo, Mitsubishi, Yasuda) were all beneficiaries of subsidy, technical assistance, managerial guidance, and political direction of the government bureaucracy. After World War II, this peculiar relationship between the government bureaucracy and the modern corporate world experienced reconsolidation and further entrenchment. The horrendous task of economic recovery from the ashes of defeat in the war and its subsequent rapid development and growth and prosperity dictated careful allocations of resources to, coordination of, and setting of priorities for, various sectors of national economy from the center, i.e., by the government bureaucracy. The task included reorganization (including, after the end of the American occupation, a reamalgamation of the former cartels that had been dismembered after the war), planning, and guidance of the nation's economic structure, its activities, and growth. The role of the bureaucracy was as crucial, therefore, after World War II, in the nation's economic affairs and conduct of modern industrial economy as it had been more than a generation earlier. And this relationship between the bureaucracy and the corporate world continued.

The ruling LDP, too, is in an important sense a bureaucratic creation, as was its prewar predecessors. The first major party to be formed after the establishment of a parliament in the late nineteenth century was a government party led by the author of the Meiji Constitution (Hirobumi Ito) under which the parliament came into being and first prime minister under it. The imperatives of parliamentarism, the requirements of government stability, and the needs of rapid development of the nation as a modern state conspired to create a situation in which government officials and bureaucrats came to dominate the party (and subsequent conservative parties) in prewar Japan. "Conservative" parties were, in an important sense, instruments of government. And more, for an increasingly close tie developed between them and the corporate world as represented by those giant cartels.

With the emergence of parties of the left, hence of leftist or anticapitalist challenge in the political arena, the corporate world saw the need to safeguard its interest by actively, that is, financially, supporting the parties of the right. A close tie between the party of the government (or conservative parties) and the corporate world was established and continued throughout the prewar period. This completed the formation of a powerful triangular relationship among government, party, and business.

After World War II, relations between the first conservative parties and the corporate world were somewhat tenuous and ill defined because of the dissolution of the prewar cartels by the Occupation administration, the number and confusion of those parties, and the general economic dislocation and political volatility that characterized initial postwar years. By the early 1950s, however, especially with the termination of American military occupation, reorganization of the nation's economic structure and activities under the direction and guidance of the government bureaucracy had gotten under way and, simultaneously, the existing conservative groupings in the Diet (parliament) had coalesced into two major conservative parties, the Liberal and the Democratic. The rivalry between the two, however, was fierce.

Early in 1955, the warring factions of Socialists—the Right Socialists and the Left Socialists—patched up their differences and reunited to form one single Japan Socialist party (JSP). This was viewed with alarm by the resurgent corporate world as well as the government bureaucracy, especially since the resignation of the then conservative premier, because of his declining personal popularity both within the conservative camp and without, gave rise to a scramble for power between the two conservative parties. The continuing division of the conservatives into two parties gave the Socialists the power to decide which of the leaders of the two conservative parties or their own party was to head the government, and this was quite unpalatable to the corporate interest as well as to the bureaucracy. Businessmen and bureaucrats alike were particularly concerned about the need for stability in government and society at the very time when the nation was entering an era of growth and development, the collective goal to which they were committed as the paramount task of the nation. Under powerful pressures from both the corporate world and the government bureaucracy, therefore, a series of negotiations took place between the two conservative parties; as the consequence, in November 1955, the Liberals and the Democrats joined together to form a single, united conservative party. The LDP was born, powerfully backed by the bureaucracy and the corporate world. The ruling triumvirate was formed.

THE TOKYO UNIVERSITY–CIVIL SERVICE SYNDROME

In chapter 2 we talked briefly about elitism by institutional credentials, and about the prestige of Tokyo University as the topmost educational institution and the civil service as the most coveted career. This needs to be reiterated here in connection with our discussion of the LDP and the ruling triumvirate of which it is part. The best and the brightest of Tokyo graduates (and a much smaller number of graduates of other former Imperial universities) became higher civil servants in the national bureaucracy.[2] This Tokyo University–civil service syndrome has important ramifications not only for the bureaucracy but also for the LDP and leadership of big business and industry. But, first, let us examine the cause of this unique phenomenon in Japan.

As the nation began its rapid modernization and development in the late nineteenth century, Tokyo University (then called Tokyo Imperial University) was established (and thereafter other Imperial universities) by the modernizing government as a training center for government officials and leaders in order to hasten the transformation of the country into a powerful modern state. Graduates of the university were to man various decision-making organs of government and to direct the modernizing activities of the nation. They were, in short, to form the nation's ruling elite, and were so viewed by society at large and by themselves. Hence the prestige of the Tokyo diploma and the bureaucratic career. All this, incidentally, was consistent with the tradition of East Asia. In Imperial China, for example, the government officials (Mandarins or bureaucrats), who all attained their status through rigorous civil service examinations, were the most respected, indeed revered, group of people, for they combined in themselves educational excellence (tested by civil service examinations) and selfless service to the emperor and the people. A bureaucratic career was the highest calling.

2. As of this writing, all top twenty career officials of the powerful Ministry of Finance, for example, are Tokyo University graduates. Elsewhere in the higher echelons of the bureaucracy, nearly 80% of the officials are Tokyo graduates, and combined with graduates of other former Imperial universities, they constitute 92.4% of the higher civil servants. See Daizo Kusayanagi, "Kanryo Okoku Ron—Okura Sho," *Bungei Shunju*, June 1974, pp. 162–78; "Naze Tokyo Deigaku Ka?" *Sande Mainichi*, 7 April 1974, p. 19; and Akira Kubota, *Higher Civil Servants in Postwar Japan* (Princeton, N.J.: Princeton University Press, 1969), p. 69.

In Japan, the new Tokyo University–civil service elite contained the same ingredients that had earlier been found in China, i.e., educational excellence and selfless service to the emperor and the nation. This new ruling elite was (viewed as) the model of rectitude, probity, incorruptibility, impartiality, and devotion, a model that "commoners" (or, in Japanese parlance, "civilians") would be well advised to emulate. And, to an impressive extent, these "officials" throughout the prewar period managed to establish a record of living up to the dictates of the carefully cultivated myth.

At the same time, the pace and the magnitude of the nation's modernization and development and the inadequacy of the private sector to meet some of their requirements made it imperative that the government perform a vastly extensive and overwhelming role in directing and managing the national task, especially the economic development. In the process of fostering and directing the growth of a modern economic sector—business and industry—bureaucrats were sent into its leadership echelon so as to maximize the effectiveness and supervision of various modern enterprises and their advance. The movement of officials into the leadership stratum of the economy was desirable not only for the government but also for the recipient enterprises because, apart from the prestige of their education and career credentials, those former government officials brought with them the valuable asset of old-school and career ties and personal connections with their former colleagues in the government that could be effectively exploited for the benefits of the enterprises concerned. As noted earlier in the chapter, the role of the government bureaucracy in coordinating and directing the economic recovery, growth, and prosperity after World War II became extensive again, and the movement of government officials into the leadership stratum of business and industry became especially pronounced because of the Occupation administration's purge of many corporate leaders and dissolution of the giant cartels that the prewar government had fostered.

The impact of the Tokyo University–civil service syndrome on the ruling LDP has been equally significant. With the purge by the Occupation administration of many prewar and wartime politicians, especially "conservative" politicians, as one of the first political steps toward democratization of the nation, there was a wide leadership vacuum in the conservative camp to be filled. This alone would attract a large number of higher civil servants eager to take part in the postwar parliamentary system in order to help shape the future of the nation (or, as the case might be, in order to seek fame, excitement, and/or fortune). This trend was further enhanced by the mistrust with which American Occupation officials viewed politicians in general and a sense of professional affinity with which they treated government bureaucrats. The result was the rise of many senior bureaucrats as foremost leaders in party and government. In fact, during the first nine years after the war, the country was led by three conservative prime ministers who were former higher civil servants, except for the short-lived Socialist-led coalition government in late 1947 and early 1948. These prime ministers, especially Shigeru Yoshida (premier 1946–47, 1948–54), brought into the party and the cabinet a continuous string of elite bureaucrats to help them run the party and the government. Since the formation of the LDP in 1955, it has largely been those top civil servants brought in by the party's predecessors and the subsequent newcomers from the bureaucracy that have controlled the party.

Both in the corporate world and in the LDP, the dominance of the Tokyo University–civil service syndrome continues. Consider the following as symptoms of such dominance.

Each year, up to two hundred retired senior bureaucrats, mostly from what the Japanese call "the economic ministries" and the National Tax Agency, move into key sectors of the corporate world as top executives, board members, and advisers. According to a recent study former administrative vice ministers of just *one* such ministry (International Trade and Industry), for example, hold the following top corporate positions (circa 1974):[3]

President, New Japan Steel
President, Toshiba Electric
President, Fuyo Petroleum Development Corporation
President, Japan Petrochemical Company
Vice President, Fuji Iron and Steel
Vice President, Arabian Oil
Executive Director, Tokyo Electric Power
Executive Director, Kansai Electric Power
Executive Director, New Japan Steel
Executive Director, Toyota Motors

3. Chalmers Johnson, "The Reemployment of Retired Government Bureaucrats in Japanese Big Business," *Asian Survey* 14 (November 1974): 957.

Executive Director, Nippon Kokan
Executive Director, Sumitomo Metals
Director, Overseas Petroleum Development Corporation
Director, Kansai Oil Corporation

These corporations are among the largest in the modern economic sector, and these fourteen former higher civil servants represent *only one* small category (administrative vice minister) of the higher civil service jobs of *only one* of twenty-odd ministries and other cabinet-rank agencies.

Within the ruling LDP, the number of former career government officials as a proportion of its parliamentary membership has increased in recent years. In 1961, it was 26 percent in the more important lower house of the Diet. By 1973, it had risen to 32 percent.[4] (In the upper house, the proportion is even higher: 37 percent). The power of former high-level bureaucrats within the parliamentary LDP, however, is vastly greater than their numerical strength would suggest. Consider, for example, that during the entire postwar period, the premiership has been held by former high-level bureaucrats for nearly 80 percent of the time. Former bureaucrats have invariably occupied far more cabinet posts (especially more important and prestigious ones such as Finance, Foreign, International Trade and Industry, Economic Planning) far more often than their numerical strength would justify. Within the party organization itself, they have more often held the three top posts of Secretary General, director of the Executive Board, and director of the Policy Affairs Board than their more numerous nonbureaucrat colleagues.[5] Membership compositions of key party committees also reflect the dominance of the party by former government officials. In the crucial Policy Affairs Board, 17 of the 25 executive committee members in 1974, for example, were former high-level career government officials.[6]

The Tokyo University–civil service educational-career sequence indeed constitutes the axial personnel principle for the ruling triumvirate of the party, the bureaucracy, and the cor-

---

4. Scalapino and Masumi, *Parties and Politics in Contemporary Japan*, p. 171; and Takayoshi Miyakawa, ed., *Seiji Handobukku* (Tokyo: Seiji Koho Senta, 1973), pp. 3–90.

5. Kokumin no Seiji Kenkyu Kai, ed., *Kutabare Jiyuto* (Tokyo: Eru Shuppan Sha, 1970), pp. 42–43.

6. *Seiji Handobukku*, pp. 3–138 and 172–73.

porate leadership. In all fairness, it must be said that this principle in the past served the nation well in its ability to promote economic recovery, growth, and prosperity, to maintain a widespread political consensus in the arena of central policy making as well as stability in society at large. Whether and to what extent it could still serve the interests of society, however, would be determined largely by its relationship with the set of new problems and issues that have arisen as the result of the country's emergence as a postindustrial society. The rest of the present chapter unfolds against the background of this critical question.

THE PARTY AND THE CORPORATE LEADERSHIP

We noted earlier that, in industrial politics, each major alignment between party and constituency is based largely on social and economic cleavages characteristic of industrial society. For the Liberal Democratic party, the most potent "industrial era" constituency has been business and industry the leadership stratum of which is customarily referred to as *zaikai*. Literally, the term *zaikai* means "financial circle," but its more descriptive meaning would be that top echelon of the corporate world consisting of leaders of big business. According to Yanaga, the corporate leadership consists of the top executives of four big-business organizations, i.e., the Federation of Economic Organizations (*Keidanren*), the Japan Federation of Employers' Associations (*Nikkeiren*), the Japan Committee for Economic Development (*Keizai Doyu Kai*), and the Japan Chamber of Commerce and Industry, plus top officials of the Japan Industrial Club.[7] The relationship between the LDP and the corporate world is not exactly one between a party and its effective constituency. It is more like one between two partners with a division of labor whose line of demarcation is not always clear. Bluntly stated, the division of labor between them is something like this: the party organizes and manages the operation of formal institutions of public policy making such as the cabinet and parliament and the corporate leadership provides the party with necessary financial sustenance to help it maintain its parliamentary majority (and electoral majority or plurality), hence its control of formal organs of government on the one

7. Chitoshi Yanaga. *Big Business in Japanese Politics* (New Haven: Yale University Press, 1968), p. 32.

hand; on the other, it engages in very effective and substantive participation in policy making offstage on the basis of which the party as the ruling party conducts its public business in those formal institutions of policy making. In the area of effective policy making the party and the corporate leadership converge.

Let us consider a bit further this convergence of party and corporate leadership in the realm of effective policy making. This realm, of course, is participated in by the bureaucracy, whose role is indeed powerful and extensive. We shall, however, defer our discussion of the role of bureaucracy and its relations to the LDP until later.

That the corporate world or its leadership attempts to influence policy making is no news to the reader, for the phenomenon is evident in any industrial society. The engine and motive force of industrial society is business and industry because the objective of such a society is constantly to expand the size of the pie of benefits of industrialism. Apart from the basic political conflict over the distribution of those benefits of industrialism, business and industry must be pampered, constantly encouraged, and, if need be, provided with various forms of authoritative assistance so that it may with the maximum efficiency and economy continue to expand the economic pie and keep workers employed. Whatever may be said for or against business and industry, it is the most favored institution in industrial society whose occasional illness or malfunction sends shivers through the entire society and whose needs and demands receive the most deliberate and concerned attention of the authoritative policy-making bodies. The case of Japan, however, is unique in the degree of explicitness, pervasiveness, impact, and penetration of the corporate leadership's efforts at both formal and informal levels of policy making.

Perhaps the most interesting facet of the relationship between the LDP and the corporate leadership in the realm of effective policy making is the high degree of routinization of multiple channels of direct interaction between the two. Virtually by custom, leaders of the party (including the premier and senior cabinet members) and members of the corporate leadership hold regular meetings to discuss a wide range of policy issues both actual and potential.[8] And it is from these meetings

8. On these meetings at various levels of the party-corporate leadership relations, see Yomiuri Shimbun Seiji Bu, ed., *Sori Daijin* (Tokyo: Yomiuri Shimbun Sha, 1972), pp. 144–46.

(some held monthly, others biweekly, still others weekly, in addition to emergency sessions when occasions warrant) that much of general policy direction for the party emerges, well before formal processes of policy research and formulation begin to operate. The exact extent to which the corporate leadership wields its influence over policy making, of course, is impossible to ascertain. All participants in those meetings are quite understandably discreet about what is discussed and rather remarkably chary of confidences with newsmen or, for that matter, any outsiders. There is no doubt, however, that these meetings, among other means of interaction between the party and the corporate world, provide a powerful mechanism for the corporate leadership's substantive input into the ruling party's policy making. The corporate posture regarding its effort to influence such policy making is aggressive and unabashed, as manifest in a remark made by one of its top executives: "We do not present a petition to the party . . . we make demands on it."[9] Stories abound of instances in which a phone call from corporate leadership caused last-minute changes in the party's legislative proposals or executive directives. Yanaga observed: "Organized business does not engage in lobbying activities,"[10] and that is simply because there is no need to. It does appear that Guillain was not extravagantly exaggerating when he said, "The *zaikai*, or their leaders, are the government behind the government," and complained that LDP leaders "are virtually the delegates of the managerial class, their representatives in power."[11] (When we later discuss the role of bureaucrats, we will have to modify Guillain's observation a bit.)

Another aspect of the LDP–corporate leadership relationship that would at least indirectly suggest the extent of the role of the corporate leadership in effective policy making of the party is that most corporate leaders and party leaders and influentials share a common educational and career background (Tokyo University–civil service). They are former classmates or at least come from the same university; the common school ties, however removed in class or years, are a powerful property of close, exclusive interpersonal relations in Japan. And they are also

9. Quoted in *Asahi Shimbun*, 28 July 1970, p. 4.

10. *Big Business in Japanese Politics*, p. 71.

11. Robert Guillain, *The Japanese Challenge*, trans. Patrick O'Brian (Philadelphia and New York: Lippincott, 1970), pp. 56, 58–59.

TABLE 4.1. OFFICIALLY DISCLOSED LDP POLITICAL FUNDS

(In billion yen)							
Year	1968	1969	1970	1971	1972	1973	1974
Amount	4.3	5.2	7.8	8.8	9.5	18.6	18.9

Source: *Asahi Shimbun*, 28 September 1974, 25 December 1974, 22 June 1975.

former higher civil servants in various ministerial bureaucracies where they were colleagues or had superior-subordinate relations. Common career ties are as powerful a property of interpersonal relations as common school ties. They are, therefore, both members of the same club, so to speak. There is a natural community of interest, a commonalty of cultural predisposition, values, and attitudes, all fostered during their university years and bureaucratic careers in the height of the nation's struggle for the growth and development of industrial society, in the period obsessed with the expanding pie of modern industrialism.

Then, too, there is another, in more senses than one, disturbing aspect to their mutual relations in the realm of effective policy making that tends to corroborate the contention that the corporate influence upon LDP policy making is indeed considerable, and here we refer to heavy corporate financial contributions to the party.

Corporate Financing of the LDP

Corporate financing of the ruling party in the postwar period began to be salient in 1956 with the formation of the Economic Reconstruction Council (*Nihon Keizai Saiken Kondan Kai*), the sole purpose of which was to unify the theretofore disparate channels of political contributions by business and industry to the LDP for more effective use of corporate financial prowess in politics. Since then, corporate financial contributions to the ruling party rose from, for example, 740 million yen in 1959[12] to 18.9 billion yen for 1974.[13] Table 4.1 shows LDP political funds during a recent seven-year period, over 90 percent of which were contributed by corporate leadership. These figures were reported

12. Scalapino and Masumi, *Parties and Politics*, p. 88. Also see Yanaga, *Big Business*, pp. 78–87.

13. *Asahi Shimbun*, 22 June 1975, p. 1.

by the party's Finance Committee to the government according to statutes, and that means they were not all that the party got by way of political contributions. Even so, they were still rather large amounts. Take the figure for 1974: 18.9 billion yen was approximately $65 million. Of this, 97 percent came via the National Association (*Kokumin Kyokai*), the LDP's fund-raising arm, which was, like its predecessor, the Economic Reconstruction Council, a creature of the corporate leadership, consisting of close to 10,000 corporate members.[14] What was of significance about these figures was that they constituted the tip of an iceberg the precise bulk of which it was extremely difficult to fathom. And this for the following reasons.

Within the realm of legality, there were, outside the direct contribution to the party through the National Association, two additional channels through which corporate leadership transferred funds into the LDP: to individual factions and to individual MPs. For the first *six* months of 1974, for example, the five major LDP factions (regarding factions and factional politics within the LDP, see pp. 97–101) reported to have received a combined total of 2.8 billion yen (approximately $10 million).[15] Contributions to factions were channeled through various "research" organs created by and/or for those individual factions. Amounts of corporate contributions to factions vary according to donors' assessment of relative strengths of those factions. Hence, the larger a faction, assuming other things to be equal, the better its chance of playing a prominent, even a decisive role in the party, the larger the amounts of contributions to its coffer.

The third form of corporate political contribution was one made directly to individual members of the party. Not every LDP MP rated such favors, of course. The general rule of thumb was that one had to be at least a "middle-stratum" member within the party, with a good chance of political longevity and influence.

14. "Goto Yonraku no Shushi Kessan," *Sekai*, August 1974, p. 223. In February 1975, the National Association was reorganized and renamed the National Political Association—*Kokumin Seiji Kyokai*—headed by a former chairman of the Japan Broadcasting Corporation, in an effort, according to LDP and corporate leaders, to modernize and democratize political contributions to the party. Its head, who had upon assuming the post advocated proportionately equal contributions to noncommunist opposition parties, resigned a few months later, and in the view of most observers, the change in the fund-raising organization was more apparent than real.

15. *Asahi Shimbun*, 25 December 1974, p. 3.

Various sectors of the corporate world established "clubs" for such an MP and contributed funds to those clubs as monthly membership dues, assessed on the basis of the corporate members' capital assets and the recipient's standing and prospects in the party.

In any event, the total amount transferred from corporate leadership to the LDP through these three routes reached far beyond the $65 million reported by the party's Finance Committee for the year 1974. But, even here, we are still talking about the amounts reported to the Ministry of Autonomy (*Jichi Sho*). How about those funds that were never reported? Over the years, there had emerged a general consensus among knowledgeable observers as well as between them and corporate leaders that the actual amounts of corporate money channeled into the various levels of the ruling party were up to ten times the figures officially reported as received through the National Association.[16] Inasmuch as corporate leaders themselves admitted this, there was no reason to doubt its general accuracy. For 1974, then, it would be reasonable to assume that the actual amounts of money moving from the corporate world to the LDP were somewhere in the neighborhood of $650 million. A very tidy sum, indeed.

In the summer of 1975, the Diet, under mounting pressure of public dismay about the blatant financial ties between corporate leadership and the ruling party, passed a lukewarmly revised Political Funds Control Law, limiting the amounts of contribution individuals and corporate bodies were allowed to make to parties, factions, individual MPs, and other political organizations, and establishing more stringent requirements for public disclosure of incomes and expenditures by parties.[17] It would, however, be naive to conclude from the passage of this law that corporate contributions to the LDP would be effectively curtailed and decline. As political operatives and the business community in any industrial society know, illegal flows of political funds cannot be effectively curtailed, let alone eliminated. Some illegal contributions would be discovered and even prosecuted, but for every instance, there would, it seems from past experience, be ten cases going undiscovered. Besides, investigation and prosecution of illegal contributions would be entirely in the hand of the LDP government. We could not be

16. *Asahi Shimbun*, 28 September 1974, p. 3.

17. *Asahi Janaru*, 13 July 1975, pp. 98–99; and *Japan Times Weekly*, 12 July 1975, p. 2.

accused of any inordinate bias if we said that the vigor and vigilance with which the government would perform its duty in this regard would be somewhat less than exemplary.

But, the reader may ask, why such outlandishly lavish corporate contributions to the ruling party? Simply put, the party, it was and still is felt, could not survive without them, and the corporate leadership wants it to stay in power. Corporate leadership fears the rise in power of opposition parties, especially the Socialist. Quite unlike, say, in Britain, the major opposition party (the JSP) in Japan has never been regarded as the loyal opposition by many significant sectors of society, especially the corporate world. That is to say, the supporters of the LDP in general and businessmen and industrialists in particular view the opposition party as inherently dangerous to the stability of society and the well-being of the corporate interest. Corporate leadership would, therefore, go to any length to prevent the opposition party from capturing power; conversely, it would do everything in its power to maintain the conservative LDP in power. The LDP wants to stay in power; the corporate interest wants it to stay in power, for any alternative to the LDP would be inimical to the corporate interest. Hence the quid pro quo: the corporate world provides the LDP with funds to ensure its permanent hegemony in parliament and government; the LDP reciprocates by its policy making. Each gets what it wants from the other, or so it seems.

And the money is needed more perhaps by the LDP as a whole and its individual members than by other parties, in part because of the nature of the core electoral support they receive in an increasingly postindustrial society.

LDP MEMBERSHIP AND THE NATURE OF CORE SUPPORT

In the past the LDP always received the widest electoral support of any parties. Even though the rate of voter support kept declining ever so slightly, the party managed to receive more votes than all opposition parties combined. In the 1972 general election, however, for the first time since 1955, its voter support dipped below what other parties received. The trend in the past had pointed in this direction; nevertheless, when the inevitable came, there was great shock and alarm within the LDP and within corporate leadership. In the 1950s and 1960s, voters, preoccupied as they were with material pursuit, kept returning the LDP to power with comfortable margins because they viewed the LDP as most able of the parties to promote growth and prosperity. It was the politics of industrialism; there was little strain, if any, between the expectations of voters and the value and orientation of the LDP (and, we might add, corporate leadership and the government bureaucracy). With the rise of postindustrial problems and issues, however, increasing stress and strain gradually emerged between a rising popular concern with them on the one hand and the continuing industrial orientation of the party as the political branch of the ruling triumvirate. Both in public-opinion polls and electoral votes (local as well as national elections), the rate of LDP popular support began to drop with continuing pace, to the rising alarm on the part of the party and corporate leadership. Their reaction came in the form of what has since come to be termed "money power" politics, i.e., efforts to shore up the party's declining electoral strength with infusions of ever increasing amounts of money at various levels of LDP politics, especially at the level of vote gathering.

Like every other party in Japan, the LDP is not a mass party. It was organized at the national level by notables (civil or bureaucratic) for electoral and parliamentary purposes. The party in 1973 claimed a registered membership of over 900,000,[18] but even its own MPs believed the actual figure to be no more than 280,000.[19] Even if this latter figure were accurate for statistical purposes, it definitely would not reflect the real size of "party" membership, for the following reasons.

At the national level, the LDP is the parliamentary LDP. At the local level, the party is a congeries of personal support clubs (*koenkai*) for individual MPs with, more often than not, mutual rivalry. There is little organizational infrastructure of the "party" as such at this level because the LDP is not a mass party and was organized at the national level. Each LDP MP, instead of depending upon and working through what little "party" apparatus there may be at the local level, creates and maintains his own local support club. Most local "party" members, therefore, are *his* supporters, not the party's.[20] They join his support club for a

18. *Seiji Hando Bukku*, p. 171.

19. *Sande Mainichi*, 23 December 1974, p. 19.

20. For the origin, organization, and functions of the local support club (*koenkai*) of individual MPs, see, for example, Nathaniel B. Thayer, *How the Conservatives Rule Japan* (Princeton, N.J.: Princeton University Press, 1969), pp. 87–110.

variety of motivations most of which are traditional in character, e.g., personal obligation, personal connections arising out of common school ties, business associations, social acquaintance, friendship with the MP concerned or with others who are already club members, especially more influential members of the club. What characterizes the behavior of members of this support club is not a sense of party unity, party loyalty, a common ideological commitment, or even a common range of policy preferences, but rather personal loyalty and obligation to the MP or, again more often than not, to one another. Many, if not all, club members become dues-paying members of the party (recommended by two party members and paying an annual membership due of 1,000 yen—about $3.40), because the MP would like to report to the national party headquarters an increase in party membership in his district. But they are party members only statistically, for the club membership has little, if anything, to do with the party as such. It is not a party organization; it is a personal club. "Party branches exist, but usually in name only. Look behind the party signboard and you usually find some one's *koenkai*."[21]

Maintenance of this personal support club is a necessary but expensive requirement for the individual LDP MP for his political survival. Actual management in the club and recruitment of its members are done by local influentials and politicos, in many cases local assemblymen who are the MPs' clients and underlings. How successfully the club is managed and how many people are recruited into the club depend entirely upon the degree of dedication and vigor of those underlings. And the fuel for such dedication and vigor is money spent in a variety of ways and for a variety of purposes. The MP must help his underlings or local bosses when they run for assembly seats, that is, finance much of their campaigns; provide them with sufficient operating funds for his own support club as well as their own affairs (for they have their own underlings), slush funds for special political errands and dealings; and also defray the costs of various community activities, organizations, and events carried out or held to keep club members happy and beholden, hence to make the MP and his underlings and local bosses look good, concerned, and effective in the eyes of club members and their friends and families. Influential members of the club often visit the MP in Tokyo to seek favor or assistance from him on matters that concern them; they may bring other members as well. In all

21. A local politico as quoted in ibid., pp. 97–98.

such cases, the MP is expected to entertain them well, befitting their respective standings in the club or in the district.[22]

During the election campaign, the MP's (or a fresh LDP candidate's) need of funds rises far above the level normally required to keep his local underlings and other supporters content and beholden to him. "Money power politics" becames blatant. In the 1969 general election, it was widely agreed that it cost, on the average, 100 million yen (approximately $280,000) for the candidate to carry out a successful campaign.[23] In the 1972 general elections, the average cost per successful LDP campaign allegedly rose to 200 million yen.[24] In the House of Councilors election of 1974, per seat campaign costs for LDP victory were said to be 500 million yen ($1.7 million).[25] These sums are staggering, and they could not possibly be raised by most individual MPs. They need outside sources of funds, and they were corporate contributions to different levels of the party.

With the growing valuational and attitudinal change taking place among people and subsequent decline in conventional political and interpersonal referents and behavioral inhibitions, the traditional properties of personal and social relations that have been the organizing principles of MPs' personal support clubs are likely to suffer further erosion. The continuing decline in LDP electoral support at least in part reflects this tendency. The urge would become correspondingly more powerful for the LDP and corporate leadership to compensate for such decline with greater expenditures of money, more unabashed resort to "money power politics" (*kinken seiji*) if they are to persist in the industrial politics as usual. The Revised Political Funds Control Law would be not nearly as effective, at least in its application, as it might seem in preventing the ruling party and its corporate supporters from doing what they feel they must in order to protect their strength and interests. The party wants to remain in power, and the corporate interests want it to make policies that are in their interest.

22. One senior LDP MP told the author in 1972 that every time he made a two-day visit to his district, it would cost him 5 million yen.

23. See, for example Hans Baerwald, "Itto-Nanaraku: Japan's 1969 Elections," *Asian Survey* 10 (March 1970).

24. Takashi Tachibana, "Tanaka Kakuei Kenkyu—Sono Kinmyaku to Jinmyaku," *Bungei Shunju*, November 1974, p. 94.

25. *Asahi Shimbun*, 4 July 1974, p. 2.

The influence of corporate leadership on the LDP in terms of policy making cannot but be considerable judging from the several dimensions of their mutual relationship discussed. We should not infer from the above observations, however, that corporate leadership, representing the modern sector of national economy, is distinct in its commitment, preference, and orientation. As mentioned earlier in the chapter, the corporate leadership is one integral part of the triumvirate that has ruled the nation throughout most of the postwar period. Its commitment and orientation are, therefore, closely enmeshed with policy preferences of the third member of the ruling triumvirate, the bureaucracy, and its influence on the LDP in policy making is more often than not convergent and tangent with that of the bureaucracy.

THE PARTY AND THE BUREAUCRACY

Former high-level government bureaucrats in the LDP are as valuable to the party as their former bureaucratic colleagues in corporate leadership are to big business and industry: they are members of the highest educational-career elite with a vast network of personal, old-school, and career connections in the government bureaucracy and corporate leadership. In short, they have enormous power and influence, which the party can utilize to its benefit and to the benefit of its members. They dominate the party. This bureaucratic domination of the party's high-level personnel is as powerful as the corporate domination of the party's finance. Consider the following.

Of the nine postwar "conservative" LDP prime ministers (as of 1975) five were former senior bureaucrats, and they occupied the premiership for 80 percent of the postwar period of "conservative" LDP rule. Even though they are a numerical minority within the party (less than one-third of its parliamentary membership), former bureaucrats occupied two-fifths to three-fifths of cabinet posts in the past, and the more important portfolios ("economic ministries," Foreign) tended to go to former higher civil servants. Senior party posts, too, more often than not, are occupied by them.

The personal, old-school and career ties between members of the leadership stratum of the party and the government bureaucracy in itself would suggest a very considerable impact of the bureaucracy on the party's character and policy making. There seems to be a powerful continuity and penetration of the culture, attitudes, preferences and values of the bureaucracy into the party, and many observers and scholars fear that they dominate the politics of the LDP.[26] There is, however, another aspect to the role of the bureaucracy in Japanese politics that suggests a far more crucial kind of influence upon LDP policy making. I am talking about the phenomenon, not limited to Japan, of the rising direct impact of the bureaucracy on political decision making.

Both the volume and technical complexity of policy matters have increased rapidly in recent decades. The range of issues and problems impinging upon the political system, i.e., being politicized, has expanded manifold, precipitating an increasing number of offices and bureaus and programs within the existing ministries and agencies and the establishment of new cabinet-rank agencies, e.g., the Science and Technology Agency, the Economic Planning Agency, the National Land Agency, the Environment Agency, to cite a few examples. At the same time, the contents and mutual relations of the issues and problems, both old and new, have become extremely complex for management and resolution, increasingly calling for what Boguslaw calls "large-scale computer-based command and control systems"[27] that are ministerial and agency bureaucracies. Bureaucrats are, as a result, becoming highly expert, sophisticated "technocrats." Members of the ruling LDP are expected to handle and manage those problems and issues in a manner that would be beneficial and responsive to public needs and collective well-being. Apart from the former higher civil servants among them, however, they are largely amateurs, more concerned about pork-barrel matters and about their own respective political fortunes and intraparty factional politics than about devoting their time and energy to rational management and resolution of issues and problems. In their general predisposition and qualifications, therefore, they are becoming more and more dependent for policy making upon those bureaucratic experts and their "technocratic counsel." Indeed, they are barely able to scan legislative proposals and other relevant documents that cascade into their offices. One very conscientious and hard-working LDP MP admitted that he could

26. See, for example, Fukuji Taguchi, *Nihon Seini no Doko to Tembo* (Tokyo: Miraisha, 1964) and Rei Shiratori, "Seiji no Kakushin no Motomete," *Jiyu*, November 1970.

27. Robert Boguslaw, *The New Utopians: A Study of System Design and Social Change* (Englewood Cliffs, N.J.: Prentice-Hall, 1965), p. v.

familiarize himself with less than 10 percent of those materials emanating from various ministries and agencies.[28] And cabinet ministers are little more knowledgeable. In parliamentary interpellation, each minister is accompanied by bureaucratic subordinates of the section chief or bureau director level whose role it virtually is to do the answering and explaining for him. And the cabinet meeting has been reduced, according to one highly informed source, to being a rubber-stamping ritual ministered to bills, proposals, and other documents prepared by the Conference of Administrative Vice-Ministers.[29]

It seems obvious that this growing phenomenon presents serious problems for LDP policy making. In the first place, party autonomy, which was suspect from the beginning, is further eroded, as the party's dependence on the bureaucracy's counsel and guidance increases. The party is in danger of becoming simply a political appendage of the government bureaucracy. This problem is greatly compounded by the party's internal factional politics. Factionalism within the ruling party revolves not so much around policy as around personnel.[30] And this for good internal political reasons. (Each faction is more or less heterogeneous in ideological leanings and policy preferences.) One of the major unwritten rules of factional politics is that serious ideological and policy conflict be eschewed, for such conflict would lead to the destruction of existing factions by polarizing each faction and necessarily expanding the universe of debate beyond the confine of the parliamentary LDP. Such conflict inevitably (as has happened to the opposition JSP—see pp. 127–30) would increase the types and number of participants in the intraparty conflict. Personnel dispute (i.e., who from which faction is to get which cabinet, party, or parliamentary post) automatically confines the universe of debate to the finite number of those posts and also clearly delimits the number of participants (the qualified MPs) in the universe, with no outsiders, no troublemaking intruders. A serious ideological or policy dispute, however, would change the entire nature of the ball game. Unlike personnel, ideology or policy of necessity spills over into the outer world of larger and heterogeneous constituencies. Since it

28. *Asahi Shimbun*, 24 July 1970, p. 4.

29. *Sori Daijin*, p. 46.

30. For a cogent discussion of LDP factional politics, see, for example, Hans Baerwald, *Japan's Parliament: An Introduction* (London and New York: Cambridge University Press, 1974), pp. 47–65.

is in the nature of serious ideological and policy conflict for each advocate to seek to convert and win as many bystanders as possible without regard to their positions in society, outsiders (to the parliamentary LDP) would be drawn into the universe of party conflict. Not only would this pit one group (now defined in terms of ideological leaning and policy preference and not in terms of patron-client relations) of MPs against another with an escalating intensity of hostility and passion, it would surely destroy factions as they have existed. In an important sense, one of the causes of the LDP's success in maintaining its supremacy in Japanese politics is that it has attempted judiciously to avoid serious internal policy disputes that would lead to the erosion of control of the party by its MPs.

The implication of this cardinal "don't" of factional politics is serious for the autonomy of the party, especially in view of the rising influence of technocratic counsel of the bureaucracy on the party. In short, the LDP, as one of the most concerned and reform-minded of its members has pointed out, is really "a party without policies."[31] The ruling party, then, seems to make policies on the basis of a strange kind of political eunuchry. Its policy making, especially as the volume and technical complexity of issues and problems expand, is based on a more or less uncritical acceptance of the preference and recommendation of the bureaucracy directly expressed to the party and indirectly transmitted and reinforced through corporate leadership, which is dominated by former senior bureaucrats.

The impact of the dominance of bureaucracy in policy making on society at large seems to be more subtle but nonetheless significant. Citizens are being effectively divorced from the arena of policy making because their elected representatives are themselves becoming less effective participants in policy making and becoming, instead, legitimizers of policies that are in effect made behind a screen of bureaucratic secrecy by technocrats whose accountability the public is unable to ascertain. Democracy in Japan is said to be based on the integrity of parliamentarism and party politics. If that integrity is seriously undermined by bureaucratic self-interest, technical complexity, and subsequent political obfuscation, then democracy is in critical danger of losing its meaning and viability. The public retains power over the bureaucracy only as long as the bureaucracy is responsive to

---

31. Tokuma Utsunomiya, as quoted in Kenzo Uchida, *Sengo Nihon no Hoshu Seiji* (Tokyo: Iwanami, 1972), p. 90.

its needs or its elected representatives and the cabinet can maintain their autonomy and power over it.

COMBINED IMPACT OF THE BUREAUCRACY AND CORPORATE WORLD ON THE LDP

The LDP, thus far, has been a ruling party without policies of its own. This suggests a number of considerations regarding the party's policy making. Given the role and influence of former bureaucrats in corporate leadership, there seems to be a very close sense of community between the bureaucracy and corporate world. A dimension of this community of interest may be viewed in patterns of interaction between the two institutions. At the formal level, there are numerous permanent as well as ad hoc advisory councils (*shingikai*) and panels for various ministries and agencies in which leaders of the corporate world play prominent roles. For example, there is a permanent consultative body called the Economic Advisory Council (*Keizai Shingikai*) concerned with problems of long-range economic planning and consisting of twenty-nine members. Its chairman (as of this writing) is the executive secretary of the Japan Committee for Economic Development which is one of the four pillars of the corporate leadership structure, and eighteen of its twenty-nine members are corporate leaders. This body regularly gives policy advice to such government organs as Ministries of Finance, of International Trade and Industry, and the Economic Planning Agency. Other important advisory councils, such as the Council on Industrial Structure (*Sangyo Kozo Shingikai*), the Council on Financial Policies (*Zaisei Seido Shingikai*), the Council on Foreign Investment (*Gaishi Shingikai*), are all chaired by corporate leaders, and their memberships are dominated by corporate representatives. Other members of these bodies are higher civil servants from relevant ministries and agencies, MPs, and "civic" representatives such as academics and journalists who are carefully chosen by the ministry officials to ensure their sympathy and cooperation with corporate and government representatives. These councils provide a channel of formal policy interaction between the bureaucracy and the corporate interests. There are, of course, other regular channels, both formal and informal, of interaction between various sectors and levels of bureaucracy and various areas of the corporate world that fall in their administrative or policy jurisdiction.

In an important sense, it may be said that the LDP, throughout years of economic growth and prosperity and technological advances, translated the common interest and goal of these two powerful institutions into political and parliamentary terms and implemented them as the ruling party. In this general pattern of corporation and coordination of the ruling triumvirate, economic advance was the primary objective and technology the major tool. In this process the real power, Macrae once noted, came "into the hands of a dynamic business-cum-civil service machine."[32] In the meantime, the LDP ceased to be (or never really was?) the ruling party but instead became the agent, the political enunciator, of the other two members of the triumvirate, and Macrae's "business-cum-civil service machine" became what Galbraith called the "technostructure" whose increasing autonomy in society was "a functional necessity" of advanced industrialism.[33] We can perhaps best describe the relationship within the triumvirate in terms of policy making by a diagram, figure 4.1.

The influence of the bureaucracy and corporate leadership on the LDP as we have discussed it thus far seems to pose some serious problems for the emerging postindustrial society in Japan, especially because the ruling party seems without policies of its own. The primary problem here, of course, is that of adaptation to the changing environment. The distributive politics of industrial society, at which the ruling triumvirate has demonstrated a remarkable degree of accommodative and mediative skill in the past, is now conjoined by the preventive and redressive politics precipitated by the politicization of costs of modern industrialism. These two types of politics seem frequently to call for mutually exclusive kinds of management and resolution, and political difficulty resulting from the divergence in character between them is further compounded by the rise of intensity in status politics and expressive politics as well as the trend toward trivialization of politics. Could the LDP as the ruling party (or as the political side of the thus-far ruling triumvirate) modify some of its important aspects so that it may be able to adapt itself to the new set of circumstances that is emerging? What forces might help its adaptation? What constraints are against it? Would there be possibilities of some fundamental restructuring of the ruling triumvirate? We shall discuss some of these forces

32. Norman Macrae, "Pacific Century, 1975–2075?," *Economist*, 4–10 January 1975, p. 21.

33. John K. Galbraith, *The New Industrial State* (Boston: Houghton Mifflin, 1967), p. 393.

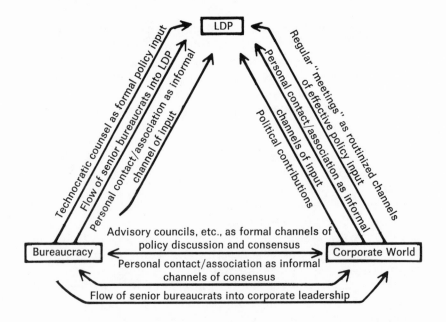

FIGURE 4.1. THE RULING TRIUMVIRATE

in chapters 6 and 7. The remainder of the present chapter looks at the LDP prime minister and his cabinet, their role in governance of the country, and then reflects on certain stirrings within the LDP and the unique role the bureaucracy might play in this period of important transition as it did in earlier transitional periods.

THE PRIME MINISTER AND HIS CABINET

A combination of constitutional prescriptions and the semipermanent supremacy of the ruling LDP confers upon the prime minister an enormous range of power over the entire governmental system of Japan. Indeed, the power at his disposal is far greater than the power allotted to his counterpart under the authoritarian prewar Constitution.

The prewar prime minister was merely the *primus inter pares* among the members of the cabinet, which was designed as the collegial advisory body to the emperor. In case of a serious disagreement with any of his colleagues, the prime minister was, by custom, to resign, together with his cabinet, as an indication of his failure. Under the democratic postwar Constitution, the prime minister is considerably more than the *primus inter pares*: he is *sine pares*, in a cabinet that is itself the sole source of executive power. He has the power to appoint and dismiss members of his cabinet "as he chooses." He is vested with power to appoint judges of the Supreme Court and inferior courts, and to designate a chief judge of the Supreme Court who will be formally appointed by the emperor. He can dissolve the House of Representatives, and the fact of the perennial supremacy of his Liberal Democratic party in addition gives him the effective power also to designate the Speakers of both chambers of the Diet, to be routinely ratified by the majority (i.e., his party) in these chambers; to select chairmen of parliamentary committees; and to determine the agenda for parliamentary debate and vote. In short, the Japanese chief executive effectively presides over all three branches of government. His office is the locus of all governmental power. On paper, therefore, it appears as though he enjoys an almost Caesarean potency.

The reality of the prime minister's power, formidable as it may appear, however, is far more complex and circumscribed by a welter of constraints (some of which we have already alluded to) that have nothing to do with the Constitution or statutes. These constraints seem at times quite capable of reducing his otherwise awesome power to near-impotence. They are inherent in the nature of the party, in the process through which he attains his office, and in the relationship between his party and his office on the one hand and the bureaucracy and corporate leadership on the other. These aspects, which powerfully define the operational predicament of the prime minister, have prompted a widespread impression perhaps best summarized by Guillain when he observed that, while the prime minister is "one of the prime movers" in government, he is "not the most important one."[34]

The Prime Minister and His Party

The prime minister is elected, not by popular vote, but by the 743 members of the Diet. In effect, he is chosen by the more powerful House of Representatives (491 members) since, in case of a disagreement between the two houses, the decision of the lower house prevails. Moreover, inasmuch as the ruling LDP enjoys a comfortable majority in the lower house (while pre-

34. *The Japanese Challenge*, p. 55.

cariously guarding a slim 7-seat majority in the upper house), the choice of the prime minister is solely in the hands of its partisan MPs (plus one delegate from each of the 47 prefectures) gathered at the biennial party convention. It is significantly inaccurate, however, to conclude that the LDP MPs (and those 47 prefectural delegates) in fact democratically elect the premier (who is also party president) on the basis of leadership quality and capability. Why? Two considerations: a seniority system (see pp. 25–26) and factionalism.

Seniority System. The seniority element of sociocultural tradition of the country is still potent in party personnel and is clearly manifested in the roster of postwar prime ministers. The age of the Japanese chief executive at the time of his assumption of office is, on the average, sixty-five. (Average age of cabinet officers in the past four years was sixty-three, rest of the party MPs fifty-seven, circa 1974.) Within the LDP, nobody can normally hope to become a cabinet member unless he has served seven or eight consecutive terms in the House of Representatives (or, in the case of those rare members of the upper house included in the cabinet, a minimum of two six-year terms). One LDP MP, who was first elected to the lower house in his mid-thirties, at the time publicly expressed his ambition to his constituents: to become a cabinet minister in his fifties and premier in his sixties. Vocally ambitious though he was, he apparently did not envisage a probability of being appointed to a cabinet post during his first two decades in the Diet. (Recently, in his late fifties, he served briefly as a cabinet minister. It is highly unlikely that he will ever achieve the premiership.) For upward mobility and promotion within the LDP in terms of government, party, and parliamentary posts, one has to wait his turn. MPs who are senior to him in service (assuming, of course, other things to be equal, such as educational and career backgrounds) must be taken care of before he is. It is bad form, as we observed in chapter 2, to be personally ambitious and aggressive and to compete for promotion even with one's peers.

By general rules of thumb, the seniority system within the ruling party operates in the following fashion: a third-termer (in the lower house) can normally expect a parliamentary vice ministership in one of the some twenty ministries and cabinet-rank agencies; a six-termer the chairmanship of a parliamentary committee; and an eight-termer a cabinet post or one of the top party posts such as Secretary General and director of the Executive Board or the Policy Affairs Board.[35] To be party president and prime minister, one must be a very senior man, indeed. The seniority system, as the major criterion for selection, is ascriptive. As such, it disregards considerations that are objectively far more pertinent to promotion and selection, such as ability, achievement, vision, commitment. It is therefore not very compatible with the necessity of strong, committed, imaginative leadership. And this problem is greatly compounded by the phenomenon of deep and pervasive factionalism within the ruling party.

Factionalism. Factionalism as such is observable in the political parties of other countries, of course. What is unique about LDP factionalism is a depth and pervasiveness that produce some important consequences for the selection and power of the prime minister.

Factionalism within the LDP arose for a number of specific reasons, including the multimember electoral district system and political funds.[36] We shall, however, look at two of those factors that seem either peculiar to the LDP or to Japanese society. One is a certain element of sociocultural tradition. Traditional interpersonal relations in Japanese society are based on a vertical tie between a senior and a junior (a leader and follower, superior and subordinate, patron and client, *oyabun* and *Kobun*, as students of Japanese politics and society would variously have it). They are reciprocal relations, whereby the superior looks after the well-being of the subordinate in return for the latter's loyalty and support. The really important dimension of traditional social relationships is not the horizontal tie or a sense of solidarity among equals but rather this vertical tie between the superior and the inferior.[37] Society, therefore, is vertically stratified, giving rise to its oft-repeated characterization as "an open society made up of closed components."[38] Within the ruling LDP,

35. *Sori Daijin*, p. 24.

36. For a list and discussion of these causes, see, for example, Watanabe, *Habatsu*, p. 4; and Baerwald, *Japan's Parliament*, pp. 47–59.

37. The title of one of the recent books on Japan is quite descriptive in this regard: Nobutaka Ike, *Japanese Politics: Patron-Client Democracy* (New York: Knopf, 1973).

38. Scalapino and Masumi, *Parties and Politics in Contemporary Japan*, p. 141.

therefore, MPs cluster around various *oyabun* or influential senior members to form those "closed components," i.e., factions.

The other factor for factionalism has to do with the origin of the party. The LDP, as we recall, was formed in 1955 by a merger of the then existing two conservative parties (Liberals and Democrats) each of which, in turn, had been formed by a series of shifting coalitions and alignments of various conservative groupings that emerged during the first postwar decade. Initially, therefore, there were natural tendencies among LDP MPs to gravitate toward their respective former partisans and leaders: former Democrats getting together and former Liberals doing likewise. More often than not, within each of those two constituent groups of the party, members who had shared trials and tribulations of earlier mergers and splits of more numerous conservative forces gravitated toward one another, thus forming a series of distinct groupings within the new party. This, combined with the first factor for factionalism, resulted within one year of the LDP formation in the emergence of eight separate factions, each led by an influential notable or senior politician. Five of these eight faction leaders would become party presidents and premiers in subsequent years.

Factions rise and decline because faction leaders (*oyabun*, patron, and so on) rise and, by the sheer process of biological necessity or by unexpected political misfortune, recede from the scene. A faction leader may also "retire," as is normally the case with a former prime minister. When the leader of a faction retires or dies, his followers may disperse into other factions (in search of a new patron), or his faction may be taken over by one of his senior lieutenants, or split into smaller factions to be led by rival lieutenants. In any event, during the two decades since the birth of the LDP, factional formations have changed considerably. Today there are five major factions plus a few minor ones in the party. By a major faction is meant here one that is large enough (by common agreement and past experience, at least close to forty members) that its leader can be considered a serious possibility for the party presidency/premiership.

As indicated earlier, the relationship between the faction leader and his followers is based on quid pro quo. *Quid* that the leader assumes on his part is a variety of vital assistance to his followers: he sees that his more senior followers receive cabinet appointments, parliamentary committee posts, and party committee chairmanships according to seniority both within the party and within his faction; he provides each of his followers with campaign funds[39] and other expenses that he requires not only during the election campaign but also between elections (see pp. 84–87); and he helps his followers in their dealings with government agencies in behalf of their constituencies. In return, he receives *quo* from his followers in the form of their personal allegiance to him and support for his quest for power in the party and ultimately for the party presidency/premiership. Each faction is a personal grouping; in ideology and policy preference, it is more or less heterogeneous.

Factional Politics.   Faction, or, rather, faction leaders, and not individual MPs are the units of competition for the party presidency/premiership in the LDP. Theoretically, of course, any parliamentary member of the party can run for the post, but that simply is theory. The pattern of competition among factions for party and government leadership, therefore, is of a particular kind and character. It is fierce, intriguing, more subtle than apparent, frequently conspiratorial, and usually fascinating. Of course, insofar as the incumbent premier (president of the party) decides to run for another term (the presidential term is three years), he obviously has a considerable edge over his rivals for reasons that are peculiar neither to the LDP nor to Japanese politics. This is not to say that the incumbent, when he runs, automatically receives party convention votes for another term. In fact, he has to engage in all sorts of maneuvers (e.g., shuffling cabinet posts, promises of payoffs, and the like) prior to announcing his intention to seek another term in order to ensure his reelection. Prices for reelection can be very dear.

Let us take the situation in which a new party president/ premier-designate is to be elected. The leader of each major faction wishes to run, and long before the party convention, he starts running. The major strategy is to form a winning coalition of competing factions for his election or, if he does not think he can win the race, to belong to one. Of course, politics being a gamble with high stakes, there usually is no assurance that the coalition he has formed or belongs to is in fact the winning coalition until the convention actually votes. The formation of

39. One study indicated that only 20% of LDP MPs' or new candidates' campaign expenses were covered by the subsidies from the party itself, meaning that faction leaders had to provide them with much financial assistance. See Haruhiro Fukui, *Party in Power: The Japanese Liberal Democrats and Policy-making* (Berkeley and Los Angeles: University of California Press, 1970), p. 130.

such a coalition of factions is the sine qua non for the capture of the party presidency, since the aspirant needs an absolute majority of the convention votes, most of which are controlled by factions. Behind-the-scenes negotiations take place among faction leaders as well as among their followers, and much to the constant disgust of the public, large sums of money change hands, amounting to millions of dollars.[40]

By the time the convention opens, a general contour of the battle royal emerges, though it is never officially or publicly admitted by the contestants or the party, the whole affair presumably being a model of open democracy and fair competition. The leader of one major faction is promised support from, say, another faction, or even two factions. Another faction leader manages to obtain a promise of support from still another major faction, and so on. Sometimes there are more than two major contenders; there may be a dark horse. Minor factions may or may not commit themselves to one candidate or another. Speculations are rife in the newspapers and other media, and committed supporters of each candidate scurry frantically in search of delegate votes in an effort to ensure his victory. Circulation of large amounts of money erodes factional discipline, and MPs with less than exemplary fortitude against temptation accept bribes from any number of candidates (or their emissaries) without, of course, divulging that they are accepting similar gifts from the others. In fact, they often raise the ante as the ballot approaches.[41]

On the first ballot at the convention, the opposing factional alignments may immediately manifest themselves; or each faction, including minor ones, may vote for its leader. In the latter case, inasmuch as no candidate receives a majority of the votes, the behind-the-scenes agreement within each factional coalition, if adhered to with sufficient discipline, will be implemented on the second (or third) ballot. These patterns, of course, vary from one convention to another, but the general outline is fairly accurate and common. Usually on the second or the third ballot the winner emerges, the one who has successfully put together

40. The last time (as of this writing) the party convention elected a new president (1972), it was reported by the mass media (and never denied by the party) that anywhere from $20 million to $40 million circulated. For further details, see pp. 105–6.

41. For an interesting description of money, weakness, betrayal, and the like, at the convention, see, for example, "Jiminto Sosaisen," *Mainichi Shimbun*, 27 June 1972, p. 2.

a winning coalition of factions. He delivers an acceptance speech, appealing for party unity now that the contest is over, and outlining the party's and government's policy direction under his leadership with varying degrees of generality and obfuscation. The convention concludes with a shouting of three *banzai* in unison. The party president, hence the premier-designate, has been chosen. In a day or two, he is duly elected by the LDP majority in the Diet as prime minister.

How powerful or effective is the prime minister thus elected? Frankly, we can hardly escape the impression: not very. But, let us look a bit further, both backward and forward, to see if the impression is fair.

The very process by which the premier has successfully won his office places a range of stringent constraints upon his conduct. From a normative viewpoint, it is not entirely unreasonable to say that the process of his selection does not confer on him any kind of meaningful popular mandate, as a popular and popularly elected chief executive may be said to have been given a mandate. Indeed, it appears to be more accurate to say that the Japanese prime minister has no popular mandate whatsoever, and this not because he is elected by the Diet (which is popularly elected) but because his election really has nothing to do with the wish and preference of individual representatives who might otherwise vote in a manner that could variously approximate the preference of their respective constituencies. Theoretically, the prime minister's constituency is the public at large, for he is the head of government. In the reality of political equation, it is not the public or the nation, but rather those other faction leaders within his party who have, with varying degrees of enthusiasm or reluctance, agreed to support his election to the office. We should note here that the nature of constituency defines the politician's conduct of office. Let us see the working of this loose dictum in one of the most important tasks of the prime minister: organization of his cabinet.

The Cabinet. The prime minister owes his election to having put together a winning coalition of factions within his party. His office, then, is built on a stack of political IOUs. After all, every faction leader wanted to be premier himself, and none of them, including those who in the end agreed to support the new premier, wanted to see him elected in the first place. He was elected because his allies, for a variety of not necessarily consistent reasons and mutually compatible motives, wanted to see his major opponents elected even less. In his successful attempt to put together his winning factional coalition, the premier had to negotiate with other faction leaders and their lieutenants and make promises that were attractive enough to entice their support for his election. Those promises usually have to do with personnel, rather than policy, e.g., who from which faction is to get which cabinet, subcabinet, parliamentary, or party post. The leader of each coalition faction expects a senior cabinet post, such as Finance, International Trade and Industry, or Deputy Premiership, or the most coveted party post of Secretary General.[42]

The reason for each allied faction leader's demanding an important cabinet or party post for himself and other posts for his followers is perhaps understandable. The same phenomenon is observed in other countries, e.g., in the United States when the newly elected President attempts to form his cabinet and reorganize his party's National Committee. There is, however, another reason for this that is unique to the context of factional politics within Japan's ruling party. Every LDP MP sooner or later expects a government, party, or parliamentary post, as we briefly discussed in connection with the seniority system. Now, one of the indispensable requirements for the leader of a faction is that he manage to obtain those posts for his followers at regular intervals according to their respective seniorities and, if circumstances permit, other qualities, ascriptive or otherwise. His followers expect him to do so because that is one of the important aspects of the relationship of quid pro quo between the leader and the followers. If he fails to meet this expectation, he will lose his followers to other factions whose leaders are more capable in discharging their duties as patrons. After all, being a cabinet minister is the pinnacle of success for most MPs. In addition, the cabinet (or, for that matter, subcabinet and other) post confers upon its holder a rather considerable increment of public prestige, which is readily translated into enhanced standing with constituents. So, for personal as well as electoral reasons, every MP, on the basis of the seniority system, covets the post. The pressure upon each faction leader, emanating as it does from this normal pattern of expectation on the part of his followers, therefore, is quite heavy, and this pressure is transferred by the faction leader onto the prime minister. Much in the same sense that the faction leader will lose the loyalty of his followers if he

42. For the ranking of cabinet posts, see Kokumin no Seiji Kenkyukai, ed., *Kutabare Jiminto* (Tokyo: Eru Shuppan Sha, 1970), pp. 149–50.

fails to meet their expectations, the prime minister will readily be abandoned by leaders of his coalition factions if he fails to meet their expectations.

From the outset, therefore, the prime minister seems to be severely handicapped. He does not enjoy the luxury of being able to choose men of genuine competence, political affinity, and promise of leadership for his cabinet. If, on occasion, he chooses a man of outstanding quality, that is more often than not accidental, not by design. Each faction leader of the winning coalition (now collectively referred to as the mainstream of the party, the losing coalition being the anti-mainstream) literally or in some other way presents the premier with a list of those among his followers who, by custom and seniority within the party as well as within his faction, he thinks have waited long enough for cabinet and other posts, and their names are listed in order of rank and preference. The premier is normally expected not to go outside this list in picking his ministers and vice ministers. Should he violate this unwritten rule of the game, his factional allies are quite capable of retaliation.

The cabinet the prime minister forms and heads, then, is in effect a coalition cabinet, "a composite of the representatives of key factional groups."[43] In theory, he is *sine pares*; in the reality of political equation, he is frequently little more than the *primus inter pares*, inasmuch as his factional allies sit in his cabinet with potential sanctions to be used against him. The constitutional prescription that the premier appoints and dismisses members of his cabinet "as he chooses" is a legal fiction several degrees removed from political reality. The range of his "choosing" is severely circumscribed, though not entirely absent. True, ministers are appointed and replaced with great frequency, but that has nothing to do with the premier's "choosing." All but the most senior cabinet posts are musical chairs, occupied by one set of deserving (or undeserving) men of appropriate seniority (recommended by faction leaders) and then occupied by another set of such men (rarely a woman), perpetuating the phenomenon called the "one-year ministers" syndrome. This is because of the necessity for each faction leader to reward his loyal followers in order to keep them satisfied with him.

Politics, especially factional politics within the LDP, being unpredictable like the woman's mind (pardon the reference)

43. Peter P. Cheng, "The Japanese Cabinets 1885–1973: An Elite Analysis," *Asian Survey* 14 (December 1974): 1056.

depicted in a famous Beaumarchais libretto, the prime minister cannot be assured of the fidelity of his initial coalition. He must, therefore, see to it that the danger of defection from his camp be minimized and that the existing opposition (the anti-mainstream factions) be weakened or won over to his side if at all possible. This imperative is another cause for frequent cabinet changes or reshuffling of cabinet posts which, to the uninitiated, might give the impression that the Japanese chief executive is very hard to please or that he is powerful. The fact is that the prime minister is compelled sometimes desperately to manipulate allocations of cabinet and other posts to strengthen his current position and to try to ensure reasonable prospects of survival in the long run. These posts are given, observed Leiserson, "not simply as rewards for supporting a Prime Minister in the past but also as encouragement to support him in the future. Indeed, posts may be given to factions simply to keep them from stirring up trouble, to silence them, or to weaken them internally." And "the Prime Minister uses the posts in two ways: as payments on debts he incurred in the election, and as capital investment."[44] He is a very busy man, harried by internal factionalism of the party he is presumably the head of, more often than not second-guessing himself, and attempting to maintain in his favor the precarious equilibrium of forces within the party and the cabinet. At times, it almost seems that the paramount preoccupation of the prime minister is survival in office rather than governance of the nation.

Under this kind of climate, it is extremely difficult for the prime minister to stir a serious political debate within his party or within his cabinet. Added to this problem is that rule of factional politics we mentioned earlier (eschewal of serious ideological and policy dispute). Therefore, there is an understandable disinclination on his part to take bold initiative in reorienting basic policies of party and government. Any radical departure from business as usual is likely to generate intraparty policy dispute, thus running the serious risk of violating that cardinal injunction of factional politics and of quickening his own demise as premier and party president. In fact, his party is so shy of serious political debate that it does not even like to be sucked into an intense dispute with opposition in the Diet or

44. Michael Leiserson, "Factions and Coalitions in One-Party Japan: An Interpretation Based on the Theory of Games," *American Political Science Review* 62 (September 1968): 779.

outside it. Of course, the party is accustomed to the standard criticism and ritualistic parliamentary harassment to which opposition (the JSP, the JCP, the CGP, and the DSP) habitually subjects it. And the level of such criticism and harassment is quite predictable; the LDP expects it as a matter of course. It is like being bitten by a mosquito; it is annoying, but really not worth getting uptight about. But then, beyond this normally expectable level, the LDP is very loathe to incur a really serious argument even with the opposition. So, even in terms of relations with opposition parties, there is a kind of "don't" for the LDP. There were in fact a few memorable instances of prime ministers having to resign the office because they seriously annoyed their party by causing a critical intraparty policy dispute or by generating an intense struggle with the opposition.

Corporate Leadership and the Selection of the Prime Minister

Infusion of corporate funds into the ruling party naturally affects various aspects of its operation, and the election of the party president/premier-designate is in a sense the most important party affair. As we touched on earlier, large sums of money change hands before and during the party convention. At the time of the 1972 party convention, for example, it was variously speculated that anywhere between 5 billion to 10 billion yen changed hands among 478 delegates (i.e., approximately $20 million to $40 million at the then prevailing exchange rate, or roughly $40,000 to $80,000 per delegate).[45] Clearly, in a situation where such large sums of money circulate, the more money a faction has at its disposal, the better its leader's chance of getting elected,[46] of winning the competitive bidding for delegate votes.

The fact that money plays such a crucial role in the party signifies that those who supply the money play a crucial role in the party. Corporate leadership, for reasons that are not at all difficult to fathom, is very much interested in the selection of prime minister. It wants as premier a person who is both supportive of its interest and knowledgeable about its problems. It is no accident that three of the LDP prime ministers, who among them occupied the office for fifteen of the first twenty

45. "Jiminto Sosaisen," *Sande Mainichi*, 9 July 1972, pp. 142–46.

46. Kin'ichi Fukuda, "Kinken Seiji to sono Kusanone," *Asahi Shimbun*, 5 December 1974, p. 3.

years of the party history, were former high-level officials in three of the so-called economic ministries with close working relations with business and industry. Yanaga's observation "candidacy for the premiership is unthinkable without [corporate leadership's] tacit approval"[47] may well be a bit exaggerated if taken literally, but there seems to be little doubt that, through money, corporate leadership exerts an important influence upon the selection of prime minister. Else, there would not circulate such horrendous amounts of money during the party convention.

The Bureaucracy and the Cabinet

At least in theory, the cabinet, as the body of the premier's closest lieutenants who are popularly elected representatives, exerts power and command over the various ministerial bureaucracies. In practice, the picture looks quite a bit different from the constitutional prescription. In the first place, as we alluded to earlier, an average cabinet minister is little more than the nominal head of his ministry, even when he is endowed with appropriate educational and career credentials. In the second place, again as we hinted earlier, both the volume and technical complexity of issues and problems his ministry must cope with have expanded enormously to the point where the minister, even if he is a former bureaucrat, finds himself increasingly dependent upon counsel of his bureaucratic subordinates. Those bureaucrats are said also to be resistant to an occasional maverick of a minister who attempts to impose his ministerial will, reformist, unorthodox, or otherwise. In the ensuing struggle, the minister appears to be the more likely loser. One former cabinet member lamented: "You cannot do anything once bureau chiefs and administrative vice minister unite against you."[48] Also, there is truth to the argument that bureaucrats are capable of punishing a maverick minister or, for that matter, any LDP MP who would incur their ire. Elected representatives are vulnerable to the bureaucratic pressure because they must act as middlemen between their constituents and government agencies and see that their respective constituencies receive their shares of government funds, permits, licenses, and other benefits that are dispensed at bureaucratic discretion. One seasoned observer noted: "Cabinet

47. *Big Business in Japanese Politics*, p. 32.

48. Quoted in *Asahi Shimbun*, 15 July 1970, p. 4.

ministers . . . more often than not are the bureaucracy's instruments for the control of the party rather than the party's instruments for the control of the bureaucracy."[49]

Our foregoing discussion of the prime minister and his cabinet generates a pattern of interaction and influence between him and his cabinet on the one hand and the party, the bureaucracy, and corporate leadership on the other. Such a pattern may be summarized in figure 4.2, which is built on figure 4.1 on p. 94.

This diagram clearly indicates an enormous range of institutional constraints under which the premier as leader of party and government must operate. Especially during a period of transition, as Japan is today, how and to what extent of effectiveness society can adapt itself to the changing environment depends critically upon the courage and capability of its leader or leaders.[50]

In this sense, the Japanese government seems incapable of generating effective political leadership. This is further exercebated by absence of any meaningful devices that could variously countervail those forces and constraints in policy making that emanate from the bureaucracy and corporate leadership. The prime minister does not have a policy staff of his own; the cabinet secretariat is a management instrument, not a policy-formulating or recommending body. Structurally, the premier and his cabinet have the party's Policy Affairs Board with numerous councils, committees, and subcommittees under it, each focusing on a specific policy area, but the Board is where powerful policy inputs from the bureaucracy and corporate leadership converge and where former government bureaucrats dominate. One sometimes gets the impression that the cabinet is a sort of rubber-stamping board of directors of the ruling triumvirate, and the premier is its genial but powerless chairman. Perhaps one corporate leader had this in mind when he observed, "It really does not matter who becomes Prime Minister. It's all the same."[51]

49. Watanabe, *Habatsu*, pp. 69–70.

50. For the crucial role of political leadership, see Taketsugu Tsurutani, *The Politics of National Development: Political Leadership in Transitional Societies* (New York and London: Chandler, 1973).

51. Hideo Shinohara, president of Mitsubishi Chemical, as quoted in "Sato Sokkin no Tetteiteki Kaibo," *Bungei Shunju*, March 1971, p. 93.

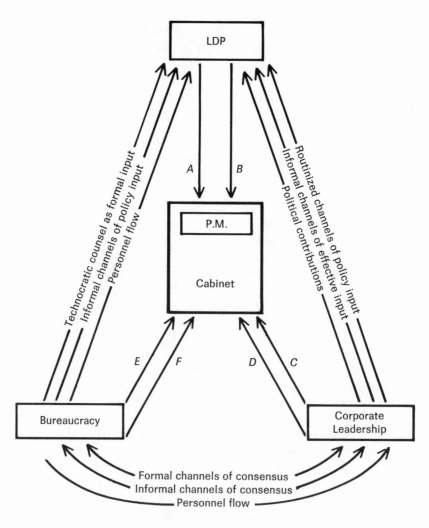

A: factional personnel
B: factional politics' avoidance of ideological and policy dispute
C: policy input via "meetings" between P.M. and other ministers and corporate leaders
D: corporate fund's role in selection of the P.M.
E: technocratic counsel
F: bureaucratic resistance

FIGURE 4.2. CONSTRAINTS ON THE PRIME MINISTER AND HIS CABINET

THE LDP IN POSTINDUSTRIAL JAPAN

The picture of the ruling party in Japan that emerges from our discussion thus far is one of a virtual puppet of the bureaucracy and corporate leadership. We should, of course, not indulge in exaggeration. The picture, however, is difficult to suppress. Are there any prospects of significant change in the party's aspects? We can only speculate at this moment. And hazard inheres in any speculation. Nonetheless, I do not believe it is entirely futile to engage in speculation on the basis of what we know about the party and about its relationship with the other two institutional members of the current ruling triumvirate.

The future of the LDP seems to depend on two considerations: internal changes and changes in its relations with the bureaucracy and corporate world. In both considerations, generational metabolism seems to be crucial. The valuational and attitudinal change in Japan to which we referred in chapter 2 is affecting the party, albeit slowly and more or less imperceptibly. Politicization of the costs of modern industrialism and subsequent emergence of preventive and redressive politics, especially at the local level, are giving rise to the new breed of younger, more "postindustrial" political activists and candidates even for the LDP, many of whom would eventually move up to the arena of parliamentary and party politics at the national level. (For these new types of politicians, see chapter 7.) These aspects of the changing environment caused by the nation's transitional travail from industrial to postindustrial society are already producing some subtle but significant impact on the ruling party. One clear symptom of such impact is the rise during the past few years of suprafactional policy study groups consisting mainly of younger MPs. These groups are entirely independent of those numerous boards, councils, committees and subcommittees within the party that are formally charged with tasks of research, deliberation, and recommendation in specific policy areas. One student of LDP factional politics contends that these study groups may be viewed as "adaptive responses to increasingly complex issues that can no longer be handled solely within the context of the faction."[52] As *Asahi Janaru* notes, these cross-factional groups of younger MPs are ideologically diverse, but they are commonly more sensitive and attuned to trends in

52. Daniel I. Okimoto, "LDP in Transition: Birth of the Miki Cabinet," *Japan Interpreter* 9 (Spring 1975): 397.

public opinion and public needs.[53] And these younger MPs' impatience with the business-as-usual orientation of their seniors within the party may be seen not only in these cross-factional study groups but also in the emergence of another type of intraparty groupings independent of the formal internal organizational structure of the party. These are "classes," so to speak, formed by MPs across factional divisions on the basis of year of first election to the Diet. These two types of groups commonly indicate the younger MPs' increasing challenge to the seniority system, their growing disenchantment with factional politics, and their rising concern with the party's lack of adequate responsiveness in policy making to critical new issues and problems that are largely postindustrial in character. The generational metabolism, at once physical and valuational, manifest in the rise of these new types of groups, is bound to continue and accelerate and to have a variety of implications for operation, organization, and orientation of the party.

The LDP's relationship with the bureaucracy and corporate world, too, would be modified significantly, if not in terms of the structure of the current triumvirate, at least in some of its fundamental aspects, especially in the realm of policy making. Generational metabolism is as relevant a fact within the bureaucracy as in the party, and it would gradually develop a corps of less industrial- and growth-oriented, more democratically disposed civil servants who are more attuned and responsive to the temper, values and attitudes of a more and more postindustrial population. But how about the corporate world? the reader may ask. Whatever change that might emerge within the corporate world, even its leadership, in terms of attitude, value, and orientation, would be minimal and extremely dilatory. This difference in pattern and pace of change between the corporate world on one hand and the party and the bureaucracy on the other arises out of differences among them in the nature of basic interest. Let us take a brief look at this difference.

The paramount interest of the corporate world—business and industry—is profit making. This basic interest subsumes all other considerations, such as expansion, technological progress, rationalization of production, amalgamation, conglomeration. The corporate world is preeminently industrial in attitude, value, and orientation, and it is precisely for this reason that the corporate interest has played such a dominant role in both

53. "Dai San ki no Nihon," *Asahi Janaru* 16, no. 50 (13 December 1974): 8.

politics and society in the period of industrialism. It is the creature of industrialism; it is sustained by and feeds on industrialism. In contrast, neither party nor bureaucracy is intrinsically committed to industrialism as such. True, parties rose in large measure in industrial society, and bureaucracies developed and expanded most rapidly during the industrial period. Parties and bureaucracies alike, however, emerged and developed in industrial society, not to promote profit making and industrial growth and expansion as intrinsic values, but to manage various forces and groups that industrialism generated and to reduce issues and problems (conflicts) to the level whereby society might be maintained on the basis of reasonably predictable and routine patterns of interaction among individuals and groups. This is particularly true with bureaucracies, for their primary concern is the stability of society and the predictability of its behavior. In the case of Japan, partly because of the tradition of sociopolitical authoritarianism, the modern bureaucracy came to assume basic political leadership as well in its innovative, mediative, and consolidative dimensions.[54] It imported, fostered, and guided industrialism, not because it saw some intrinsic value or principle in industrialism as such, but because it viewed industrialism as functional to an end that was of greater importance and independent of industrialism as such in its substance: the well-being of the nation. Japan's industrial economy was the bureaucracy's creation, engineered for an end that was preeminently political, though its subsequent development resulted in the emergence in society of the essentially same range of social, economic, and political phenomena that are cross-nationally comparable to other industrial societies. And it is easy to overlook the fact that the relationship initially developed between the government bureaucracy and industrial economy in Japan has remained basically unaltered. And it is this relationship that, in the words of Shaplen, confers upon "the experts of the bureaucracy . . . virtually free rein to control much of [the corporate world] . . . by means of periodic 'administrative guidelines,' a euphemistic phrase for a directive that is tantamount to an order."[55] In an

---

54. For these basic dimensions of political leadership, especially in modern Japan, see Taketsugu Tsurutani, "Political Leadership: Some Tentative Thoughts from Early Meiji Japan," *Journal of Political and Military Sociology* 1, no. 2 (Fall 1973).

55. Robert Shaplen, "A Reporter at Large: From MacArthur to Miki—II," *New Yorker*, 11 August 1975, p. 52.

important sense, therefore, the corporate world in Japan is powerful only as long as its fundamental interest (or the dictate of its own dynamics) coincides with the functional view the bureaucracy has of it. Throughout the industrial period, and especially during the postwar period of recovery, rapid growth, and expansion, there was a close harmony between the self-interest of the corporate world and the functional interest the government bureaucracy took in it. It may well be, however, that this harmony is beginning to decline in the face of the rising postindustrial issues and problems.

The LDP, precisely because it is a party without policies thus far, would most likely move in the direction of where power is. For this reason, in case of a serious divergence of interest and orientation between the corporate world and the bureaucracy, it would side with the bureaucracy. This observation is borne out by past experience in the pattern of interaction among the party, the bureaucracy, and the corporate interest. Most of the significant welfare and social legislation, for example, in the past was enacted despite resistance from the corporate interest because the bureaucracy, more sensitive and responsive to the need of the collectivity than business and industry and concerned in its sense of responsibility with the maintenance of social and political stability, counseled, encouraged, sometimes even pushed the party to promote it in the formal arena of politics. Indeed, many policies went, in their provisions, far beyond what the opposition parties had demanded.[56]

The primary purpose of a party is to capture power and stay in power. The LDP has in the past managed to capture and retain power because it subscribed as its operative principle to the general expectation of the populace concerning economic growth and prosperity and to the functional conjunction of interest between the bureaucracy and the corporate world. But the fortuitous harmony between the kind of popular expectation on which the party based its electoral strength on the one hand, and the functional conjunction of interest between the bureaucracy and corporate interest on the basis of which it made its major policies on the other, now seems to be declining. A new alignment of forces and expectations is emerging, and this new alignment may well be one between a new pattern of popular expectation and need and the bureaucratic adaptation to them,

---

56. See, for example, Yasushi Haga, *Gendai Seiji no Choryu* (Tokyo: Ningen no Kagaku Sha, 1975), pp. 44 and passim.

with the corporate interest increasingly in conflict with it. This, combined with generational metabolism and all that it seems to signify within the LDP, tends to suggest that the party will gradually distance itself in policy making from the corporate world.

As well, there is the inevitable electoral consideration for the party. The impact of the growing disjunction of the customary LDP politics and the shift in popular expectation as a consequence of Japan's transition to postindustrial society is already visible in the party's strength in the Diet. In the upper house (House of Councilors), the ruling party's margin of majority has already been reduced to seven seats—a virtual parity with opposition. With the continuing decline of its electoral popularity and a corresponding rise in the number of opposition seats in that chamber, a drop in the number of LDP seats below the majority seems imminent. In the more important House of Representatives, the party still maintains (as of this writing) a 77-seat margin over the combined opposition strength (284 vs. 207) despite its consistently declining voter support, but this is due mainly to inequality in electoral districting which invariably favors the ruling party (see chapter 7, pp. 215–17). Neither the party nor the public at large expect that the LDP can maintain this margin of strength in the lower house in future elections unless some significant changes are made in various aspects of the party.

Apart from the inevitable generational change in the party and the bureaucracy, we should perhaps note another very important aspect in these institutions, and that is the process of decision making. As we all know, what decision is made is frequently influenced, if not entirely determined, by how it is made. In strict confrontation majoritarian decision making (e.g., the UN General Assembly), a decision that is acceptable only to the majority results. In compromise majoritarian decision making (e.g., the U.S. Senate), the decision that emerges is at least partially acceptable to the minority. But these are not the only modes of decision making.

One mode of decision making, as has been pointed out by numerous students of Japanese politics and society, is consensual. We implied in chapters 2 and 4 in connection with the seniority system and factional politics that conflict is assiduously eschewed within any organization. In terms of decision making, the same obtains, albeit from a slightly different perspective. No Japanese organization or institution is static. In fact, one of the major

reasons for the remarkable record of the nation's rapid modernization before the war and its even more rapid recovery and
advance after the war is that its organizations and institutions
(especially the national bureaucracy) are adaptable and flexible,
or they variously were. This means that new ideas are proposed
and eventually adopted, replacing existing policies and preferences, more often than not against considerable resistance.
Decision making, however, is still consensual. How?

Consensus, in an important sense, pertains to the horizontal
relationship among equals at each relevant level of the entire
decision-making structure in an institution, e.g., bureaucracy.
Vertical dissensus is permissible; in fact, it is encouraged. At
the level where consensus must obtain among equal participants
for final policy making, one might get the following impression,
among others, unless one is familiar with the presence of vertical
dissensus. At this level alone, say the top level of decision making,
such as the cabinet meeting or the executive committee of the
party's Policy Affairs Board, or the Conference of Administrative
Vice Ministers, we can of course visualize certain tendencies
generated by the necessity of consensus. Consensual decision
making tends to favor erring on the side of the tried and true
rather than on the side of the bold and the innovative. It seems
to resist daring experimentation and creative imagination. It
tends to discourage radical departures from the prevailing norms
and goals. It also tends to delimit the range of relevant variables
to be taken into account, for introduction of certain types of
topics or considerations would necessarily both expand the range
of discussions and raise the level of intensity of debate. Thus,
consensual decision making seems to encourage conformity in
thought and behavior. All this would be true if that element of
vertical dissensus were absent.

To a surprising extent, the direction and the thrust of each
decision in Japan is upward from the lower stratum of the
decision-making structure rather than downward from the upper
stratum.[57] From the outside, it might appear that superiors wait
for subordinates' recommendations, just sitting back and sipping
tea. There is logic to this, however. The fact of the critical thrust
for decisions originating at the lower stratum of the structure of
decision making enables a maximum freedom of debate on a

57. For an insightful and detailed discussion of this mode of decision
making in Japan, see Frank Gibney, *Japan: The Fragile Superpower* (New
York: Norton, 1975), pp. 213–19.

given policy issue without imperiling the consensual mode of decision making at the higher level, where it must formally and authoritatively be made. At the lower level, disagreement with and departure from the existing norms and goals are allowed. In fact, superiors tend to view their hard-working subordinates with fond condescension and their aggressive, innovative, even unorthodox ideas and recommendations always with equanimity, frequently with approval and envy, and never with hostility. Indeed, being a maverick with one's superior is a sign of character; being a maverick with one's equals is bad form. In any event, the whole structure of decision making characterized by vertical dissensus between the superior and the subordinate and horizontal consensus at the top level of formal decision making aims at maximizing initiative and innovation at the one level where no public accountability is applicable (i.e., where there is the maximum freedom of debate), and harmony and collective responsibility, i.e., consensus, at another level where public accountability rests. Horizontal consensus and vertical dissensus are viewed as mutually complementary and promotive of organizational adaptability without undermining internal harmony and cohesion.

The basic thrust for a decision starts at the junior-rank level and moves upward; the recommendation emanating from that level is modified, reinforced, or endorsed at each successive level in consultation with and with the agreement of each lower level. Of course, the extent to which the formal decision arrived at by consensus at the top level reflects innovativeness and vigor of the junior-rank level where it originated differs from case to case. It nonetheless seems that, given the fact of generational metabolism and general shifts in valuational and attitudinal orientations within society, consensual decision making turns out to be considerably more generative of an adaptable outlook and orientation for both the bureaucracy and the party.

The LDP is indeed inhibited by many constraints that emanate from the particular manner in which it developed as the ruling party, the unique configuration of forces with which it became tied, the political ethos of industrial society according to which it became so accustomed to making policies, and special ways in which it operated internally. There is, therefore, a legitimate anxiety about the party's ability to adapt itself to the changing environment and to meet the challenge of post-industrial society. It seems equally clear, however, that internally and externally there are forces at work that would eventually help modify the party in some of its important aspects, including its policy orientation. It is entirely too early to argue that the party is doomed. How soon and how effectively those forces converge and combine at various relevant levels of the party to transform it into a meaningful postindustrial political party, however, remains to be seen.

5

Opposition Parties

There are four parliamentary opposition parties in Japan, all variously claiming to be "progressive." Ideologically they range from the more or less centrist Decocratic Socialist party to the Communist party. The difference among them in this regard, however, is not always as clear to the public as it is to the parties concerned. The public presumption has long been that the Communist party (JCP) is most leftist, with the Socialist party (JSP) slightly to the right of the Communists and the Democratic Socialist party (DSP) and the Clean Government party (CGP) falling somewhere between the JSP and the ruling LDP. Ideological differences among the opposition parties are further obscured by the factionalism within the JSP, the revisionism of the JCP, political ambiguity of the DSP, and the recent leftward shift of the CGP. These parties all deplore the LDP as conservative, but they quarrel among themselves more intensely than they cooperate to challenge the ruling "conservative" party. Their mutual quarrels in the past dissipated their energy and potential strength as opposition to the LDP, significantly helped the ruling

117

party retain its semipermanent supremacy in politics and government, effectively permitted it to continue its politics as usual in harmony with the bureaucracy and corporate leadership, and discouraged the necessary development of adaptive capacity on the part of both themselves and the ruling party in the changing environment.

All opposition parties are naturally in the habit of blaming the ruling LDP for every major problem in society but, collectively, they too must share the blame. The condition and predicament of the LDP discussed in chapter 4 are the results not only of the forces of the bureaucracy and corporate interests but also of the weaknesses and shortcomings of opposition parties. The present chapter examines and evaluates each of the opposition parties, their impact on Japanese politics, and their future prospects and roles in it.

THE JAPAN SOCIALIST PARTY

The second largest party in Japan, the JSP was long expected to grow into a genuinely viable alternative to the conservative LDP. This expectation had arisen out of certain conventional political wisdom generated by experiences in other industrial nations. Industrialization and subsequent urbanization were presumed to result in a rising popular electoral support for "progressive" or "socialist" parties. In fact, this happened in Britain, West Germany, and elsewhere in the industrialized world. Both the Socialists and conservatives thought that Japan would follow a similar kind of change in popular party support, conservatives with trepidation and Socialists with eager anticipation. Unfortunately for the Socialists and their sympathizers, this has failed to materialize. Instead, what we have seen is a fairly consistent decline of the JSP and a simultaneous advance of society in industrialization, urbanization, and all that they entail. What has happened? Is Japan so different from other industrial societies that Socialists were doomed to fail from the beginning? Several factors help explain the weakness, stagnation, and failure of the JSP, and they do not seem to suggest that the failure was preordained.

Causes of Failure

Table 5.1 shows that the JSP share of the seats in the more important House of Representatives by and large consistently

TABLE 5.1. PARTIES IN THE DIET

House of Representatives

Election Years	1958	1960	1963	1967	1969	1972
Liberal Democratic party	287	296	283	277	288	271
Japan Socialist party	166	145	144	140	90	118
Japan Communist party	1	3	5	5	14	39
Clean Government party				25	47	29
Democratic Socialist party		17	23	30	31	19
Others	18	6	12	9	16	15
Total	467	467	467	486	486	491

House of Councilors

Election Years	1959	1962	1965	1968	1971	1974
Liberal Democratic party	124	143	141	137	138	126
Japan Socialist party	81	66	73	65	62	62
Japan Communist party	2	4	4	7	11	20
Clean Government party		15	20	24	23	24
Democratic Socialist party		11	7	10	11	10
Others	43	11	5	7	7	10
Total	250	250	250	250	252	252

declined since 1960. The decline in Socialist representation in the Diet, however, does not directly reflect a more serious type of decline in popular support for the party, especially among the sectors of the electorate that are traditionally viewed as crucial to the party's survival and growth. In 1960, 44.0 percent of white-collar workers, 43.2 percent of manual workers, 35.0 percent of the well-educated, and 37.1 percent of the 20–29 age group supported the JSP. By 1972, however, party support had declined drastically, to 27.8 percent of white-collar workers, 28.5 percent of manual workers, 17.5 percent of the well-educated, and 21.9 percent of the 20–29 age group.[1] Thus the erosion in the strength of the JSP is much greater than the decline in its parliamentary membership may indicate. Several causes for this phenomenon suggest themselves, and they all have to do with the structure, organization, and internal operation of the party.

1. Joji Watanuki, "Japanese Politics in Flux," in *Prologue to the Future: The United States and Japan in the Post-industrial Age,* ed. James W. Morley (Lexington, Mass.: Heath, 1974), pp. 72–74.

Factionalism

The JSP is plagued by internal factionalism, to the extent that has prompted a highly knowledgeable observer to conclude: "In certain respects, the JSP is even more badly split than the LDP."[2] The major causes of factionalism discussed or alluded to concerning the LDP (see chapter 4) also apply to the JSP in large measure; but perhaps the most important among them for the JSP factionalism is political affiliations that preceded the formation of the JSP in 1955. There had been different socialist and socialistic affiliations before the war (which exerted influence upon various groupings and coalescences among them after the war and before 1955). The first postwar Japan Socialist party was formed by "an assortment of left-wing elements ranging from Marxist theoreticians and militant labor leaders on the left to Fabians and Christians on the right,"[3] and it split in at least four ways in late 1940s and early 1950s. In 1948 a moderate faction bolted from the party to form the Social Renovation party, and a left-wing group seceded to form the Labor-Farmer party. The Social Renovation party in 1951 changed its name to Social Democratic party and shortly thereafter merged with the Japan Progressive party (the most progressive of the then conservative parties) to form the Cooperative party. In the meantime, the Japan Socialist party itself split into two parties—Left Socialists and Right Socialists. A little later, the Cooperative party was dissolved and its former Socialist members drifted into the Right Socialist party. Finally, in 1955, the two wings of the former Japan Socialist party were reunited to form the current Japan Socialist party. A year later, members of the Labor-Farmer party joined the JSP. In short, the JSP, upon its final unification in 1955, contained as many different currents as did the LDP on its formation later that year.

Quite unlike the LDP, factionalism in the JSP has been more intense, vocal, and often public and acrimonious precisely because it involves serious ideological differences. Wounds are more frequently inflicted and open humiliation of losing factions is not rare. Moreover, the ideological dispute has expanded the range and types of participants in it to outside the parliamentary

2. Hans H. Baerwald, *Japan's Parliament: An Introduction* (New York: Cambridge University Press, 1974), p. 65.

3. George R. Packard III, *Protest in Tokyo: The Security Treaty Crisis of 1960* (Princeton, N.J.: Princeton University Press, 1966), p. 17.

JSP. A united front or a consensual surface, therefore, is far more difficult for the JSP to project than for the LDP. This is not to say that ideology is the sole cause of factional politics within the JSP. The actual situation of factionalism is a bit ambivalent, for, while ideological concerns may, as Scalapino suggested, give the impression that "the quotient of modernity in Socialist factionalism is higher than that in Liberal Democratic factionalism,"[4] they also serve as convenient pretexts of interfactional competition for party personnel and leadership.[5] By involving ideology in factional competition (which LDP factional politics carefully eschews, as we observed in chapter 4), then, the JSP greatly aggravates the ills of factionalism without any compensating benefit to the party. LDP factionalism seems carefully to minimize tension; JSP factional politics openly maximizes it.

Within the parliamentary JSP, three major factions of more or less equal sizes can, from their past behavior and orientation, be viewed, respectively, as right, left, and center, plus a group of "unaffiliateds" that equals in size any of the three major factions. There are also a handful of "radical leftists." The "right" faction, which initially became distinct in the party early in the 1960s, wants to transform the JSP from a class (i.e., proletarian) party to a national party to appeal to all classes of citizens. The faction originally called this plan "structural reform" with a stress on gradual, incremental reform of society through the existing democratic parliamentary process and nonviolent popular pressure with the view to achieving some sort of amalgam of British parliamentarism, the Soviet social security system, the American standard of living, and Japan's Peace Constitution. In short, the faction abandons Marxism as it has been adhered to by the party and intends to transform the party into one similar to a Western European socialist party.

The left faction has attacked the right's structural reform as "rightism, opportunism, and a betrayal of the class struggle."[6] Though anti-JCP, this faction is Marxist and committed to class

4. Robert A. Scalapino and Junnosuke Masumi, *Parties and Politics in Contemporary Japan* (Berkeley and Los Angeles: University of California Press, 1962), p. 101.

5. See Chae-lin Lee, "Factional Politics in the Japanese Socialist Party: The Chinese Cultural Revolution Case," *Asian Survey* 10 (March 1970): 243.

6. Packard, *Protest in Tokyo,* p. 311.

struggle and to the overthrow of capitalism. The major operational problem within the JSP during most of the 1960s was how to maintain an outward appearance of unity and how to minimize the danger of outright left-right confrontation within it. During this period the center faction played a key role in maintaining a personnel balance between the right and the left, especially the two topmost positions of party chairman and secretary general. When a rightist, or somebody sympathetic to the right, was chairman, therefore, a leftist was elected secretary general, and vice versa. This continued throughout the 1960s.

By the party convention of 1970, however, both the right and the left had become weary of the inconclusive series of balancing acts. Also, the near-disastrous setback the JSP had suffered in the 1969 general elections had persuaded the intraparty adversaries of the necessity of a definitive change in the party's popular image and decisiveness in its policy and ideological direction. Moreover, the right faction, after the 1969 electoral debacle, had been promoting the idea of a realignment of opposition parties together with sympathetic support and collaboration of the Democratic Socialist and Clean Government leadership, though the idea itself had originally been suggested by the then DSP chairman.

In this party convention, the left faction managed to secure a majority of convention delegate votes (for reasons that we shall discuss shortly) and established its hegemony within the party, inflicting what one paper called "a crippling blow to the attempt by the right wing."[7] For the first time, the right was excluded from any of the topmost leadership positions and obtained only 3 of 24 seats on the Central Executive Committee.

Since then, the JSP came effectively to be dominated and controlled by leftists, and the right faction became the antimaincurrent, with little influence on party decision making. Both the center faction and many unaffiliateds moved toward the left for intraparty personnel considerations, that is, for purposes of securing party posts in the Central Executive Committee and other party bureaus and committees. Factionalism, however, did not abate. Not only did the right faction survive and continue to hold a sizable proportion of the Socialist MPs in its camp but also to persist in its attempt to recapture its former influence in the party. In short, factionalism within the JSP is as persistent and intense as it has ever been.

7. *Japan Times Weekly*, 12 December 1970, p. 1.

Party Membership

The JSP, despite its claim to be the party of the working masses, is no more a mass party than the LDP. Much like the LDP, the JSP was organized from the top after the war by socialist "notables" who had been active in various socialist movements before the war. Because of this, the JSP shares the "exclusive, semiclosed" nature of most organizations in Japan.[8]

For a party representing the working masses, the JSP's membership is very small indeed. Even if the party is not exaggerating, membership is less than 50,000. *Asahi Shimbun* estimated that it is actually little more than 30,000.[9] This indicates that the party is very weak at the grass-roots level, as other parties are. The JSP membership figure has rarely reached the 60,000 mark, fluctuating most of the time between 30,000 and 50,000 though it reached 95,000 in 1947–48 when the party headed a weak coalition government. Yet the party has consistently drawn an electoral support of over 10 million votes (though increasingly smaller proportions of the total electorate) in general elections. The gap between the size of electoral votes for the party and its membership is impressive when contrasted to European socialist parties. The JSP membership as a proportion of the party's electoral support has been extremely small, in fact infinitesimal. With the exception of the 1947 election when it was 1.3 percent, the figure has fluctuated between 0.3 and 0.5 percent, while the comparable figures for European socialist parties in the early postwar years ranged from over 5 percent in Britain (excluding the Trades Union Congress membership) to around 37 percent in Austria.[10] Much of the JSP support, then, seems to have been on very weak partisan identification. This is one of the serious shortcomings of the JSP, for, as Epstein observed of European socialist parties as mass-membership parties, "How could a movement that challenged the existing economic order seriously compete politically unless it organized many of the class in whose name and interests the challenge was being advanced?"[11] In fact, the number of urban districts where

8. Robert A. Scalapino, "Japanese Socialism in Crisis," *Foreign Affairs* 38 (January 1960): 320.

9. *Asahi Shimbun*, 9 February 1973, p. 2.

10. See the table in Maurice Duverger, *Political Parties* (New York: Wiley, 1963), p. 95.

11. Leon D. Epstein, *Political Parties in Western Democracies* (New York: Praeger, 1967), p. 130.

the party had its own organizations was quite small even when the party membership was up (one-third of those districts when the membership reached 60,000 late in the 1950s),[12] and a recent report indicated that in one major prefecture, there were only 277 party members.[13]

What this signifies, then, is that Socialist MPs or candidates do not and cannot depend upon votes of the party members. While nearly 40 percent of the JSP delegation to the House of Representatives are former union officials and a large bulk of the party membership consists of members of organized labor, a Socialist MP's or candidate's appeal cannot be directed toward the party membership but must be made to the general electorate. Moreover, since whatever there is by way of party organization at the local level is neither extensive nor effective, he must cultivate his own personal support clubs (*koenkai*) much in the same manner that his LDP counterpart does. Such support clubs, as we noted in the preceding chapter, are based on personal connections and other traditional properties of interpersonal and social relations as the basic organizing principles. Ideology has little to do with them. In comparison to his well-heeled LDP counterpart, however, the JSP MP is very much at a disadvantage; although he, as an MP, can perform services for members of his support clubs and their friends, his financial ability to help his local underlings for local offices, for example, is limited. This is one reason for the JSP's failure to increase its power and influence at the local level. It is difficult for the JSP MP to aggrandize his influence at the grass-roots level and, consequently, his base tends to be less secure than his LDP counterpart's.

In addition, JSP members at the local level, in large measure, are no more party members than LDP members at that level are party members, and for different reasons. JSP members are unionists and members of a certain ideological study group; the object of their primary loyalty is not the party.

Effective Constituencies

Perhaps the most serious problem for the JSP is that the party became heavily dependent upon a few apparently exclusive segments of society for its survival. These groups are ideologically

12. Scalapino, "Japanese Socialism in Crisis," p. 320.

13. "Kinken ni Yowakatta Shakaito," *Asahi Janaru*, 27 December 1974.

dogmatic, organizationally restrictive, and preeminently industrial in political orientation. They are the ideologically militant sector of organized labor and the militant Marxist revolutionary ideologues of the Socialism Society (*Shakaishugi Kyokai*).

The General Council of Trade Unions of Japan (Sohyo). The JSP became inordinately dependent upon *Sohyo* (a Marxist labor federation consisting mostly of politically militant public employees' unions) for personnel, organizational activities, and finance. Its dependence upon *Sohyo* in these respects is as great as, even greater than, the LDP's dependence upon the corporate world for party funds. That a party of the left is aligned with organized labor is not new. It has a long and, in some senses, honorable tradition elsewhere. In Britain, for example, the Labour party grew, in the words of the late Ernest Bevin, one of its great prewar and postwar leaders, "out of the bowels of the TUC."[14] But the relationship between the JSP and *Sohyo* is quite different from that between Labour and the Trades Union Congress. Despite continuing tension between Labour and the TUC and even occasional challenge and defiance from the TUC, the Labour party in Britain seems to retain an upper hand over its effective constituency, though levels of that "upper hand" vary from time to time, depending upon the personalities and prestige of Labour leaders and also upon whether or not the party is in power. The Japan Socialist party was not created as the political arm of organized labor, let alone of *Sohyo*. (In fact, the first labor unions were organized by Socialists early in this century.) The latter came into being only in 1950 through the coalescence of some of the union movements that had become active with the end of the war but had been engaged in mutual internal squabbles.[15]

Initially, the JSP was quite autonomous. Starting in the mid-1950s, especially after the unification of conservatives into the LDP, however, the ties between the JSP and *Sohyo* became increasingly close, for understandable reasons. *Sohyo*, the largest labor federation, consisting mainly of politically militant public employees' unions (but not civil servants) such as teachers,

---

14. Quoted in Samuel H. Beer, *British Politics in the Collectivist Age* (New York: Vintage Books, 1969), p. 113.

15. For a good description of postwar labor movements in Japan in English, see Solomon B. Levine, *Industrial Relations in Postwar Japan* (Urbana, Ill.: University of Illinois Press, 1960), chaps. 1 and 3.

national railway workers, and telecommunications employees, and led by vocally leftist leaders, feared the consolidation of the conservatives in government. It was also and still is dedicated to the overthrow, however nonviolent, of capitalism. The JSP, on the other hand, lacking a political and organizational infrastructure of its own, needed an organizational base of support for its attempt to challenge the conservative dominance of government. In short, they needed each other, or so they thought. What has happened since, however, is neither the development of a strong Socialist party nor the growth of a united and politically effective *Sohyo*, but instead, a growing dependence, some call it subservience, of the JSP upon *Sohyo*, whereby the party, instead of maintaining its institutional integrity and political and organizational autonomy, has become a virtual mouthpiece of *Sohyo*. The party in fact is sometimes referred to as the labor federation's "political department." We have noted the decline of the JSP; but *Sohyo*, too, has largely stagnated. While its membership increased from a little over 4.2 million in 1965, for example, to 4.3 million in 1973, its share of total organized labor steadily declined from 38.8 percent in 1968 to 36.9 percent in 1970, then to 35.5 percent in 1972.[16] Apparently the mutual stagnation has also contributed to the strengthening of the mutual ties between the party and the labor federation, resulting in a situation in which the party is so dependent upon the federation that it has become, in the word of one observer, virtually "a one-pressure group party."[17]

There are several aspects to JSP dependence upon *Sohyo*, and they all seem seriously to undermine the party's integrity as an autonomous organ. They involve party organization, activity, personnel, and finance.

Organizationally, the party depends upon the federation and its member unions and their local branches since it lacks its own grass-roots organizations. The size of the party membership, as noted, is small; many party members are in fact *Sohyo* unionists, with the result that party branches at the prefectural and local

---

16. *Nihon Tokei Nenkan Showa 48–49 Nen* (Tokyo: Sorifu Tokei Kyoku, 1974, pp. 74–75; and *Nihon Rodo Nenkan* (Tokyo: Hosei Daigaku, Ohara Shakai Kenkyu Jo, 1974), pp. 198–200. According to the Ministry of Labor, 37.9% of male and 29.4% of female labor were organized in Japan early in 1970s. *Asahi Shimbun*, 20 June 1971, p. 8.

17. Scalapino, "Japanese Socialism in Crisis," p. 322.

levels are usually *Sohyo* branches in fact if not in name. Financially, the JSP is as dependent upon *Sohyo* as the LDP is on the corporate world. For 1974, for example, the total revenue for the JSP as officially reported was approximately 1.1 billion yen, but close to 80 percent of it seems to have come from *Sohyo*'s Political Action Committee and its three major leftist member unions.[18] As Passin once observed, "since power goes with money even in proletarian organizations, the dependence of the Japan Socialist Party on the financial support of the unions makes it more responsive to political pressures from the leftist unions than *vice versa.*"[19]

The fact of JSP dependence on *Sohyo* for organization, personnel, and finance, hence the party's political dependence upon the federation, resulted in an increasing dominance in the parliamentary JSP of many MPs who are former unionists and in an equally increasing influence of militant leftism of *Sohyo* in it. Earlier we noted the factions of the right, the left, and the center, plus a body of the unaffiliated within the parliamentary JSP. It is interesting to note that the dominant left faction, as of this writing, contains the highest proportion of unionists in its membership (62 percent in contrast to less than 14 percent of the right faction, 35 percent of the center faction, and 26 percent among the unaffiliated).[20] In educational background, on the other hand, the left faction has the fewest relative number of university graduates (one-third of its members), with the anti-maincurrent right faction and the unaffiliated showing the highest (67 percent each), followed by the center faction (56 percent). The victory of the left faction in the 1970 party convention meant in effect a victory of the political pressures of *Sohyo* and its leftist unions.

The Socialism Association (Shakaishugi Kyokai). JSP factionalism involves ideology, unlike its LDP counterpart. Ideology, as we suggested in the preceding chapter, expands the factional conflict beyond the universe of factions and their members within

18. *Ashai Shimbun*, 25 December 1974, pp. 1–2, and 22 June 1975, p. 1.

19. Herbert Passin, "The Course of Protest in Japan," *American Political Science Review* 56 (June 1962): 398.

20. Abstracted from Takayoshi Miyakawa, ed., *Seiji Handobukku* (Tokyo: Seiji Koho Senta, 1973).

the parliamentary JSP. It by necessity widens the range of conflict and debate outside the factions concerned, precipitates the participation in conflict of outsiders, and compounds the acrimony and intensity of debate. In so doing, it deprives the party of its own control and direction. This is precisely what happened to the JSP.

We have already seen the impact of *Sohyo* in this factional conflict within the JSP. In numerical terms, the left faction is a minority within the parliamentary JSP. It achieved power in the party in 1970 precisely because of the participation of outside forces on its side. *Sohyo* was one such powerful force. Another outside (for the Parliamentary JSP) group to play an increasingly potent role in JSP factionalism is the Socialism Association, a radical theoretical and ideological organization. It was organized in 1951 by Marxist academics as the theoretical underpinning or support group for the party, but with the emergence early in the 1960s of an intraparty dispute over what came to be known as the "structural reform" (see p. 121), it became even more militantly revolutionary Marxist, defining itself as Marxist-Leninist and aggressively advocating "the establishment of a revolutionary socialist regime" and "the dictatorship of the proletariat."[21] It now regards the Japan Communist party as no longer revolutionary. Ideological factional politics within the JSP inevitably (in part because the leftist faction needed allies and supporters and also because of the nature of activist membership) brought the Socialism Association into the arena of intraparty factional struggle, and by the end of 1975, the Association had become the most influential single force within the party (within *Sohyo* there is intense rivalry among its member unions), and at the same time penetrated local party membership and *Sohyo* branches, therby expanding its influence beyond the realm of ideological disputation into organizational activities and personnel of the party.

Of the close to 50,000 JSP members in the nation, approximately one-third were, in 1975, said to be members of the Socialism Association, and combined with its supporters among other members, 20,000 were said to be under the effective control of the Association.[22] On the other hand, only 3 JSP MPs (114 in the lower house and 62 in the upper) are definitely aligned with the Association. Whence comes its influence over the party?

21. "Shakaishugi Kyokai no Taido," *Chuokoron*, April 1973, pp. 40–41.

22. *Tokyo Shimbun*, 16 January 1976, p. 2.

Domination by Radical Activists

The JSP is dominated, not by its MPs, as is the LDP and as socialist parties in Western countries are, but by leftist activists from the Socialism Association and *Sohyo* who predominate in the party's local organizations. This becomes most apparent in the party's national convention. The convention, of course, is the highest formal organ of the party and draws up the party platform, elects the party's Central Executive Committee (CEC) and party chairman who heads it. Unlike their LDP counterparts, however, the Socialist MPs do not have votes in the convention unless they have been elected delegates by party members in their respective prefectures. (Before rule changes in 1958, MPs did have votes by virtue of their parliamentary positions.) Since prefectural party branches are dominated by leftist activists from the Socialism Association and *Sohyo* unions, whom they keep at an arm's length and by whom they are in turn frequently distrusted as not sufficiently dedicated to class struggle, most Socialist MPs do not risk a humiliating rebuff by them in seeking election as delegates to the national convention. (Convention delegates are elected at a ratio of 1 for every 100 party members.) For example, apart from 16 MPs who were also members of the then incumbent Central Executive Committee, only 51 MPs (of 176) were included among the delegates in the 1974 party convention.[23] They constituted only slightly over 10 percent of the convention delegates. (In contrast, the MPs constitute 90 percent of the delegates in the LDP convention.)

The JSP convention, therefore, is dominated by leftist activists, i.e., *Sohyo* unionists and ideologues from the Socialism Association, and it is they who set the tone of the convention proceedings and largely determine the content and results of the convention. Most MPs, having no votes, must content themselves with being voiceless bystanders to the entire proceedings. In the 1974 convention, 180 of the 500 delegates were members of the Socialism Association, and many of the remainder were either *Sohyo* unionists or sympathetic toward the Association.[24] The JSP convention was heavily stacked against the moderates within the parliamentary JSP, who include, not only the right faction, but also a majority of the center faction and the unaffiliateds.

23. Toshiaki Kaminogo, "Shakaito Soso Koshin Kyoku," *Bungei Shunju,* September 1975, p. 122.

24. *Tokyo Shimbun,* 16 January 1976, p. 2.

This development in the JSP conventions in recent years catapulted the left faction into the foremost role in party affairs. Convention votes put members of this faction (perhaps fewer than one-quarter of the entire JSP parliamentary delegation) and its partners in a *mariage de convenance* on the Central Executive Committee to control the parliamentary JSP, plus two of the three MPs openly affiliated with the Socialism Association. All this resulted in a strange character of the structure of the party. Schematically, the distribution of power/personnel at three salient levels of the party may be seen as follows:

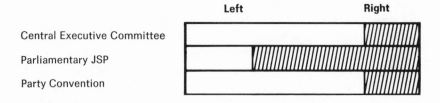

From this representation, it is clear that there is very little in common between the parliamentary JSP on the one hand and the party's Central Executive Committee and the party convention on the other. The CEC is the creature of the party convention, not of the parliamentary JSP. The parliamentary JSP, for reasons discussed earlier in this chapter, is not the creature of the party membership though many leftist MPs receive logistical support from local membership in election campaigns. By virtue of party rules, the parliamentary JSP is effectively barred from, or at least critically curtailed in its participation in, the party convention. But, then, it is the CEC that speaks in the name of the party in general and the parliamentary JSP in particular. It is the leftist pronunciamentos that the public hears. Insofar as the parliamentary JSP is concerned, the minority rules and calls the tune. Insofar as the public is concerned, what issues from the JSP (through its CEC) is incorrigibly leftist, dogmatically Marxist.

Ideological Posture of the JSP

The JSP's dependence upon, even domination by, *Sohyo* and the Socialism Association has had a potent influence on the party's behavior in the open political arena. Put simply, the party has given the impression of being simplistic, doctrinaire, backward-looking, obsessed with theoretical disputation, and consequently, lacking in relevant pragmatic concern and meaningful political thrust.[25] In a very important parliamentary sense, this is an unfortunate impression for the party to generate. As we noted, a majority of the Socialist MPs are moderate, and they operate in the practical political arena of parliamentarism. They negotiate with the ruling party on legislation, make alternative proposals, and induce the LDP to modify many of its bills. As a result, the JSP usually supports over 70 percent of LDP legislative proposals.[26] (This fact, of course, annoys and frustrates leftist activists who run local party branches and dominate the party convention.) No party in an open political system, however, can hope to make much electoral headway unless it not only focuses, but also gives a clear public demonstration of focusing, on issues that are of more immediate concern to the voters, and this is especially true as the general political predisposition of the masses regarding ideological differences undergoes change (as it is undergoing in Japan and elsewhere in the industrial world). The leftist domination of the party convention and the CEC forces the party or at least its leadership to give a constant public appearance of revolutionary confrontation with the "capitalist" LDP. In a sense, therefore, there are, we might say, two JSPs, even at the parliamentary level: one operating discreetly behind the scenes to help shape legislations in pragmatic manners, the other a "public" JSP acting in a manner more or less consistent with the preference and orientation of its effective constituencies, i.e., *Sohyo* unions and the Socialism Association. It is this "public" JSP that the public sees, and it is in this sense that we can agree with Baerwald's observation that the party's "excessive dependence" upon these constituencies "has tended to rigidify the policy stance adopted by the Socialists and has made it difficult for them to appeal to other interest groups."[27] The dogmatism of *Sohyo* and the Socialism Association pervades the public JSP, and this is paralyzing to the party. Socialists, in this public context, have given an indelible impression of harping on "a pattern of

25. See surveys reported in Nihon-jin Kenkyu Kai, ed., *Nihon-jin Kenkyu* (Tokyo: Shiseido, 1975), 2:67.

26. *Asahi Shimbun*, 20 June 1971, p. 2.

27. Hans H. Baerwald, "Factional Politics in Japan," *Current History* 46 (April 1964): 227.

grievances drawn mainly from traditional ideological sources and spelling out the future either in utopian or apocalyptic terms,"[28] of entirely disregarding the leveling effects of economic growth and prosperity in their insistence on the overthrow of capitalism, and of constantly spouting abstract generalities in the face of the specific and concrete policies of the LDP government. The doctrinaire jargon and ideological platitudes with which the JSP continues to embellish its pronouncements might have been attractive before the war, but they became either annoyingly or tragicomically incongruous with the changed and changing realities of postwar Japan. Policy debates within the public JSP are conducted in esoteric ideological vocabulary and theoretical terms and not in language that is clearly comprehensible to the people. They seem to be "rituals" rather than substantive discussions. But, then, all this seeming inveteracy of the party—its affliction with abstract disputation and haughty ideological posturing—is the inevitable reflection of the essentially elitist arrogance of its increasingly powerful support groups, i.e., *Sohyo* and the Socialism Association, vis-à-vis the masses they purport to represent and serve. As manifest in much of their writing, those doctrinaire ideologues and leftists feel that the electoral weakness of the JSP is owing to the lack of "enlightenment" and the grievously low level of class consciousness and revolutionary awareness of the working masses, that it is the JSP (i.e., those radical ideologues and leftists that dominate the party convention and select the Central Executive Committee) that knows what is in their true interest, and that the party is anointed by history to enlighten and guide the semi-ignorant masses toward a just society.[29]

The widespread impression that the JSP "indiscriminately opposes everything proposed by the government party and pro-

---

28. Scalapino and Masumi, *Parties and Politics in Contemporary Japan*, p. 46.

29. For incisive criticism of the JSP by its MPs in this regard, see Saburo Eda, "70 nen dai no Kakushin Undo," *Gekken Shakaito* 164 (October 1970); Saburo Eda, "Kakushin Seiken wa Toreruka," *Jiyu* 14 (February 1972); and Masamichi Kijima, "Jibun Jushin ni tote mitakoto," *Sekai*, March 1970. For samples of elitist arrogance and condescension by those leftist ideologues and activists (what Eda calls "reactionary conceit"), see Itsuro Sakisaka, "A Correct Platform and a Proper Organization," *Journal of Social and Political Ideas in Japan* 3 (April 1965); Itsuro Sakisaka, "Kodoryoku aru Seito e," and Noboru Sato, "Kakushin teki no Daigaesaku o," *Asahi Shimbun*, 15 April 1970.

poses nothing by way of concrete and constructive alternatives"[30] is the consequence precisely of the hidebound, anachronistic, confrontation-ideology posture the party has been compelled to take by its excessively close, politically counterproductive ties with radical *Sohyo* unions and the ideologues of the Socialism Association. One survey found that nearly two out of every three voters, even when they disregarded policy differences and considered only instrumental competence, viewed the JSP as unreliable, while a clear majority (54 percent) regarded the LDP as dependable.[31] This general public view of the JSP has been further reinforced by the party's local branches' inability or unwillingness to concern themselves with grass-roots problems of ordinary people. These branches are mostly controlled by *Sohyo* unionists and members of the Socialism Association. With their disdain for the alleged backwardness of the masses and their preoccupation with ideological debate as well as internal mutual rivalry, they tend to have little meaningful contact with or concern for grass-roots problems. The party at this level, one editorial writer commented, "would not condescend to concern itself with the problems of ordinary people. Its basic attitude is that it would listen to you if you took the trouble of petitioning to it. The party shows no readiness positively to solicit people's views and grievances and to present to the government party concrete demands based on public needs."[32] And he suggested that the JSP was "an invisible party" because people in need of help from political parties as channels of communicating their wants and grievances could not see it. You could hear its loud polemics and haughty pronouncements, but it never is where you need it.

Internal factionalism, heavy dependence upon *Sohyo* and the Socialism Association for organizational, personnel, electoral, and financial sustenance, and their resultant ramifications all tend to be mutually reinforcing for the JSP. Such a mutually reinforcing tendency of the internal problems of the party is further compounded by the knowledge that power is beyond reach. This sense of security that it has no practical prospect of

---

30. *Sekai*, May 1970, p. 159.

31. Rei Shiratori, *Nihon ni okeru Hoshu to Kakushin* (Tokyo: Nihon Keizai Shimbun Sha, 1973), p. 83.

32. Tokuro Irie, "Nichijo Katsudo towa nani ka," *Chuokoron*, March 1970, p. 157.

assuming the responsibility that comes with power, for example, encourages the debilitating factionalism within the JSP. (Contrariwise, the knowledge that power is secure permits factional infighting within the LDP.) This knowledge also prevents the JSP from making pragmatic and determined efforts to develop more relevant organizational infrastructure at the local level and from reorienting its public posture to accord with the rising postindustrial concerns of the public. Penchant for dogmatic ideological debate may well be viewed as a function of the party's sense of powerlessness.

The JSP as a Party of Industrial Politics and Society

It is important to note that those effective constituencies of the JSP—*Sohyo* and the Socialism Association—are the type of groups that, together with others, characterize industrial society, its politics, and its values. *Sohyo*, as a federation of labor unions, is one of the major actors in the politics of industrial society, and apart from the material interest it seeks to satisfy and increase, it is deeply embedded in the kind of ideological struggle that is one of the features of industrial society before it begins to be dissipated by the rising *embourgeoisement* of the working masses. In the case of Japan, this labor federation itself is still bound to the attitude and mentality of the ideological struggle even though such a struggle has already ceased to be largely relevant, not only objectively (i.e., in terms of the level of material well-being of the masses) but also subjectively (i.e., the perception of the working masses who view themselves as middle class). There is therefore a wide gap between the attitude and mentality of the labor federation and those of the people in whose interest it claims to be speaking. Likewise with the Socialism Association. Its commitment, language, and values are all taken directly out of the jargon, clichés, and platitudes of the ideological struggle of an earlier stage of industrialism, out of what Willy Brandt, the West German socialist leader, once characterized as "those books and brochures."

Thus the JSP is as deeply bound to industrial politics as is the ruling LDP. In the transition of the nation from industrial to postindustrial society, labor, in an important sense, does not seem to be any more a progressive force than business and industry because its interests, mores, attitudes, and values are as born of and embedded in the politics of industrial society as are those of the corporate world. In this developmental sense, nor does the Socialism Association. Dependence upon these forces constitutes an enormously burdensome political baggage for the JSP, in this era of transition into postindustrial society. In the case of the LDP, while its ties with the corporate world inhibit its adaptation to the changing environment, it does have a potentially countervailing force in its alliance with the government bureaucracy, which views industrialism not as an intrinsic but only as functional value and instrument of society. None of the forces upon which the JSP has depended for sustenance and whose interests it has in effect represented, however, seems to be able to forsake the attitude, preference, and value characteristic of industrialism and industrial politics. Neither within the party nor among its major effective constituencies does it seem there is any institutional countervailing force against the persistence of industrial politics. The only force that would help free the JSP from its constraining ties with the industrial politics, then, would have to come from some act of will on the part of members of the party itself.

What would the future of the JSP be? Earlier, in our discussion of the membership and the party convention of the JSP, we spoke of the domination of the party convention, its formal leadership apparatus and its local organizations by leftist activists and ideologues of *Sohyo* and especially of the Socialism Association. The left faction within the parliamentary JSP, the very faction that had, by its doctrinaire class-struggle advocacy, caused the incursion of *Sohyo* leftists and the radical ideologues of the Socialism Association into party organizations and eventually the domination of the party convention by them, recently began to manifest signs of uneasiness about the alarming rise of the power and influence of these radical extraparliamentary activists, especially of Association members.[33] This faction is now said to be seeking a kind of modus operandi with the right faction (and the center as well as the many anti-left unaffiliateds) that would prevent a complete takeover of the party convention and party organization, especially the party personnel, by these radicals. The bitterness that was generated among these factions within the parliamentary JSP by the fierceness and acrimony of their past factional struggle, however, seems to militate against any ready reconciliation, let alone smooth cooperation, among them in the face of the danger of the further growth in power of,

33. See, for example, *Tokyo Shimbun*, 13 January 1976, p. 2.

and eventual takeover of the party by, the radicals.[34] Reconciliation between the "structural reform" thesis of the right and the
Marxist class struggle thesis of the left would be no easy task.[35]
Moreover, many MPs within the left faction are reportedly
resisting any move that would antagonize those radical activists
since the latter provide much organizational support and other
logistics for their election campaigns.[36] Thus, the JSP seems to
suffer from a wide range of organizational and political constraints that render its adaptation to the changing environment
very difficult.

Perhaps the greatest weakness of the party in the emerging
postindustrial Japan lies in its lack of effective organizational
and political infrastructure at the local level. What organization
there is at this level is an extension of leftist *Sohyo* unions and
the Socialism Association, and even within it, there is as much
factional strife as there is within the party at the national level,
among member unions (or their local branches) and between
them and the Association. Their allegiance is not to the party but
first to their respective unions (or the Association), and the party
seems to come in last in this regard. Their major concern is the
strengthening of their respective groups within the local party
organization vis-à-vis one another. Attention to grass-roots
problems of postindustrial society is very low on their list of
priorities. The party's virtual "invisibility" at this level, especially
where postindustrial problems are more acute, i.e., urban and
metropolitan areas, has already resulted (see pp. 219–21) in
pronounced popular rejection of the party—and this is ironic
since it is precisely in these areas that the JSP had hoped to
increase, à la Western socialist parties, its popular support in
order to challenge the LDP domination of politics and government. Most of what we discussed as postindustrial issues and
problems in chapter 3 are locally politicized and acute and,
as such, they are quite different in character and thrust from
the conventional problems of the distributive politics of industrial
society. The JSP, with its ties with *Sohyo* and the Socialism

34. For the high level of strain in the relations within the JSP, see, for
example, "Dai San-ki no Nihon," *Asahi Janaru*, 12 December 1974, esp.
p. 9.

35. For intra-JSP attempt at a modus operandi, see, for example, *Asahi
Shimbun*, 13 July 1974, p. 1.

36. *Tokyo Shimbun*, 13 January 1976, p. 2.

Association, persists in talking and behaving in a manner that is no longer very pertinent in the eyes of the masses to their daily problems. Thus, there is a fundamental disjunction between the JSP's pattern of conduct, especially at the local level, on the one hand and popular needs and expectations in postindustrial society on the other. Perhaps more than the LDP, the JSP needs some fundamental reorientation in many of its aspects. Without such endeavors, the future of the party in postindustrial Japan would be very uncertain at best.

THE JAPAN COMMUNIST PARTY

One of the most surprising, and, to many, alarming, phenomena in the past several years in Japanese politics is a remarkable electoral growth of the Japan Communist party (JCP). Its rising popularity coincided with the rise in salience of cross-stratal and other novel issues, hence with the emergence of postindustrial society in Japan. Or was this a mere coincidence? There is reason to doubt that it is, as the following pages demonstrate.

Vicissitudes of the JCP

To a significant extent, the JCP may well be the most adaptable of the five political parties in Japan. The JCP was brutally suppressed and outlawed before and during the war, but with the coming of the American occupation administration after the nation's surrender, it was legalized. Its members emerged from prison and underground or returned from overseas to reorganize the party. In the first general election held under the new Constitution, the party received a million votes, or 3.7 percent of the popular vote, and won 4 seats in the House of Representatives; two years later, it nearly tripled its popular vote to close to 3 million and won 35 seats in the same house. Its rapid advance in two years was at least in part the result of popular disenchantment with the ineffectiveness of the Socialists when they were the senior partners of a coalition government in 1947 and 1948. This was quite apparent because, in the 1949 election, while the JCP's popular votes nearly tripled over 1947, the Socialist party's declined by 42 percent and its lower house seats decreased from 143 to 48. The JCP advance, of course, was aided by the party's assiduous efforts to rid itself of its former image of a secretive, fanatical band of subversives committed to the violent overthrow of government and by the popular temperament of the time, i.e., the rejection of all past values and beliefs.

Early in the 1950s, however, the party suffered a virtual political decimation. The victory of the Chinese Communists over Chiang Kai-shek's corrupt Nationalists after a bitter, prolonged civil war, the intensification of the cold war, and the outbreak of the Korean war caused a persistent, often blatant Soviet and Chinese pressure to be exerted upon the JCP in the direction of a violent revolutionary struggle to liberate the nation from American colonialism and domestic monopoly capitalism. While the party itself was not banned, its leaders were driven underground (or out of the country as in the case of its then Secretary General, who fled to Peking and died there shortly thereafter), and in the 1952 general election, the party's support declined by 70 percent over the previous election and no Communist candidate was elected. Nevertheless, the party's violent tactics, more or less forced upon it by Moscow and Peking, continued throughout the first half of the 1950s, until both the Russians and the Chinese changed their broad political direction with the rise of Khrushchev and his de-Stalinization and China's effort to cultivate friends among Afro-Asian nations starting from the famous Bandung Conference.[37]

The electoral debacle of 1952 and the decline in Sino-Soviet pressures on the party after 1955 generated an intense search for a new strategy and direction within the JCP. With the emergence of the Sino-Soviet ideological rift, the search quickly led to a polarization of the Japanese Communists into a pro-Peking or Maoist faction and a more or less pro-Soviet "revisionist" group. Subsequent debates and struggles within the JCP, however, made this neat pro-Chinese–pro-Russian dichotomy less and less clear. During the course of subsequent events, many party leaders originally identified with the pro-Russian faction were expelled from the party, but it cannot be said that any pro-Chinese view triumphed. What eventually emerged from a protracted intraparty policy struggle was more or less an independent "Japanese" line, aligning the party neither with Peking nor with

37. For the predicament of the JCP during this period see, for example, Hirotake Koyama, *Sengo Nihon Kyosanto Shi* (Tokyo: Mitsuki Shobo, 1958), chaps. 2–4. Perhaps the most concise description of the same in English is Paul F. Langer, *Communism in Japan: A Case of Political Naturalization* (Stanford, Calif.: Hoover Institution Press, 1972), pp. 48–57.

Moscow, promoted by those who clearly recognized the changed and changing environment of a highly advanced industrial society and the need for strategies and tactics that were consonant with the new reality.

By late 1960s, the public began to realize the significant change in the JCP posture—one of a "lovable Communist party," nonviolent, open, law-abiding, obviously committed to the existing parliamentary system, concerned about ordinary people's problems. A combination of this new image assiduously cultivated by the party, the inevitable generational metabolism and the party's virtual dormancy for nearly two decades in which the nation had been entirely preoccupied with the pursuit of economic recovery, growth, and prosperity caused a significant decline in the traditional visceral fear of and antipathy toward the Communists on the part of the Japanese masses. Among people in their twenties and thirties, positive images and negative images of the JCP became just about equal, while among those over forty, negative images still outstrip positive images.[38]

This trend in the public's view of the party is manifest in the Communists' electoral growth: after the debacle of 1952 in which the party failed to win a single lower house seat, for nearly two decades there were at the most only 5 lower house seats held by Communists; and the party never reached the 5 percent level of voter support, though the increase in the voter support was consistent, rising steadily in one election after another. In 1969 the party scored its first radical rise in its lower house seats from 5 to 14, and in the 1972 general election the party nearly tripled its lower house seats to 38 (10.8 percent of total popular votes), becoming the third largest party by surpassing the Democratic Socialists and the Clean Government party. The subsequent upper house election held in 1974 indicated that the rise in the JCP in the Diet seemed to be closely related to changes in the popular view of the party. For example, four months before the 1972 general election, 41 percent of the Japanese still held negative views of the party and only 15 percent held positive views. Four months after the election, those holding negative views of the party declined to 32 percent and those holding positive views had increased to 19 percent.[39] It was clearly no accident that the party nearly doubled its upper house seats from 11 to 20 in the 1974 election.

38. *Asahi Shimbun*, 13 May 1973, p. 4.

39. Ibid.

Today the JCP is viewed as favoring civic order and discipline and publicly opposed to violent disruption of extremist movements; consequently, its old image as a radical, conspiratorial, and violence-prone party has been erased to a very significant extent. In fact, many people view the JSP as more extreme than the JCP precisely because of its alignment with the Socialism Association (which regards the JCP as no longer revolutionary). The JCP also attempted to enhance its new public image of reason and moderation by a series of policy statements. It pledged itself to the total defense of the present Constitution, and a minimum nationalization of economy (only energy industries). While still insisting on the abrogation of the Japan–U.S. Security Pact, the party also committed itself to the maintenance of friendship with America and Japan's Self Defense Forces.[40] In order to reiterate the party's pledge to the total defense of the Constitution, its chairman in 1974 enumerated "three freedoms" to be specifically guaranteed under a Communist government in Japan: "freedom of life, civil and political freedom, and national freedom." The first two need no explanation here, but the third, national freedom here means "the freedom to choose any social system, and the freedom to take a completely independent line in foreign affairs,"[41] with which few could quarrel. Other parties all continue to express their doubt that the JCP is really committed to what it says, in part out of genuine suspicion, in part because they fear the rising popularity of the Communists at their expense. It does seem clear, however, that a considerable, and most likely increasing, proportion of the electorate is inclined to give the party the benefit of the doubt.

Sources of JCP Popularity

A changing image is not the only reason for the rising popularity of the JCP. There indeed seems to be a close conjunction between the rising political fortune of the JCP and the emergence of postindustrial society in the country with all that it implies. The Communists are perhaps most attuned among all political parties to issues and problems of postindustrial society with which the population at large is increasingly concerned. As an opposition party, they have been doing what the Socialists have demonstrated a remarkable lack of willingness to do:

40. *Asahi Shimbun,* 16 September and 10 October 1973, p. 2.

41. *Japan Times Weekly,* 8 June 1974, p. 1.

grass-roots activities. Communists act as efficient and incorruptible channels for transmitting the concerns and grievances of ordinary citizens to relevant public authorities and extracting action from those authorities. A recent observer of the JCP notes: "The party has focused more and more on reforming the distortions in capitalist society. The mundane but politically potent issues of pollution, taxation, rising prices and the traffic congestion now receive more treatment from the Communists than the hated Mutual Security Treaty with the U.S., thus enabling them to capitalize on voter dissatisfaction with the government party's handling of these problems."[42] We must perhaps add here that voter dissatisfaction extends to other opposition parties, especially the JSP, in this regard, for reasons discussed in the section on the Socialists.

Another observer reports that the Communists have become electorally successful "in large measure because they have concentrated on key social and economic issues rather than on ideological dialectics,"[43] which, indeed, is in sharp contrast to the inveterate tendency and conduct of the JSP. Specifically, while a typical LDP membership is likely to be nominal, having registered as a member only out of social obligation emanating from his participation in the personal support club of an LDP MP representing his district, and while a typical JSP member is a *Sohyo* or Socialism Association activist concerned primarily with ideological debate and/or factional competition within the local party branch, the JCP members are engaged in what the Japanese call "daily activities" (*nichijo katsudo*) in their localities. Where the party holds seats in assemblies, the JCP legislators act effectively as ombudsmen for citizens, and everywhere, party members visit neighborhoods affected by pollution and other problems, solicit concerns and grievances from neighbors, discuss matters with them, gather other relevant information, report their findings to local party leaders who, in turn, put pressure on relevant authorities to deal with those matters, or negotiate with them to resolve the problem. Their pattern of activity, geared as it is toward the needs and concerns of ordinary people at the grass-roots level, has been producing salutary effects for the party. Citizens who are initially apprehensive or skeptical of Commu-

42. Karl Dixon, "The Growth of a 'Popular' Japanese Communist Party," *Pacific Affairs* 45 (Fall 1972): 394.

43. Robert Shaplen, "Letter from Tokyo," *New Yorker,* 20 May 1974, p. 116.

nists and their motives soon learn that it is those Communists, not members of the LDP or the JSP, who are most concerned and hard-working in soliciting their grievances and problems and remarkably expeditious and efficient in delivering what they promise by pressuring or negotiating with authorities for the redress of those grievances.[44] "Persistent grass-roots activity set the rhythm for the JCP advance," observes Totten. "The party went to the people to explain its policies, criticizing the LDP for its neglect of the people's welfare in pursuing economic growth."[45] The JCP, in short, began to focus its attention and energy in the very category of issues and problems on which other parties, especially the ruling LDP and the JSP, are most vulnerable and which are in fact accelerating their further decline. These are the issues and problems of postindustrial society.[46]

Communists do not attempt to sell their ideology. In fact, ideological rhetoric is largely absent from their public statements. Instead, they have found their new métier in cultivating the people's trust and support by performing the role of concerned, problem-oriented, community-centered intermediary between the powerless and frustrated citizens on the one hand and the all too often inertia-ridden, unresponsive public authorities and other industrial-growth-oriented institutions on the other. JCP activities, therefore, are eminently compatible with the rising concern of citizens with the worsening problems of advanced industrial society. Popular support for the party has increased, as a direct and directly observable result, not only in national elections, but also (and this is more persuasive as evidence of the effect of the party's grassroots activities) in local elections: between 1970 and 1974, the party's share of prefectural assembly seats rose by 150 percent, of municipal legislative seats by 74 percent, and at the town and village level by 54 percent.[47]

44. In this connection, it is of interest that a recent survey found that housewives, traditionally conservative, hence LDP-leaning, became, after white-collar professionals, the least anti-Communist among the electorate in the country. This seems to be very suggestive of the effects of JCP grass-roots activities in their behalf. See "Hankyo to Kyosanto," *Sande Mainichi*, 16 November 1975, p. 146.

45. George O. Totten, "The People's Parliamentary Path of the Japanese Communist Party—Part I," *Pacific Affairs* 46 (Summer 1973): 194.

46. Also see Shiratori, *Nihon ni okeru Hoshu to Kakushin*, pp. 61–65.

47. *Asahi Shimbun*, 23 February 1975, p. 2.

Parliamentary JCP

The JCP membership in the House of Representatives is noticeably younger than its JSP or LDP counterpart. Its average age (circa 1973) of 51.0 contrasts rather sharply with the LDP's 57.2 and the JSP's 55.1. More significant, perhaps, is that the JCP membership shows a very different pattern of age-group distribution, as shown in table 5.2, in comparison to the two larger parties. The table indicates that the preponderant age group for the LDP is 51 years old and above, with the largest concentration of MPs in the 61–70 group. The JSP shows a not very dissimilar pattern. For the JCP, however, the majority of its lower house members are in the two youngest age groups. Another interesting aspect of the JCP MPs is their educational background. Table 5.3 is a comparison of the LDP, the JSP, and the JCP in this regard. The JCP MPs are indeed well-educated; in fact they are the second best-educated parliamentary group, far surpassing the JSP and the CGP (40 percent university graduates and 7 percent Tokyo graduates) and well ahead of the DSP (64 percent with university diplomas and 10 percent from Tokyo University). It is no coincidence that both the party chairman and the secretary general of the JCP at this writing are Tokyo graduates.

In occupation or career background, the JCP reflects not only its high level of education but also its basically postindustrial character. Fewer than 14 percent come from a labor background (in contrast to nearly 40 percent for the JSP). Over one-half of the Communist MPs come from professions such as law, education, and medicine. In fact, lawyers constitute the largest single occupational group within the parliamentary JCP (32 percent), followed by educators (17 percent). There are even one former high-level bureaucrat, one business executive, and one author. The remainder come from local politics (assemblymen) and party organizations. Both in educational and career backgrounds, the JCP is a highly trained, intellectual, sophisticated party.

Relevant, also, is the nature of districts that the Communist

TABLE 5.2. THREE POLITICAL PARTIES, BY AGE GROUP

	25–40	41–50	51–60	61–70	71 and above	Total
LDP	8.2%	19.1%	28.5%	33.7%	10.5%	100.0%
JSP	3.4	23.9	46.2	22.2	4.3	100.0
JCP	7.7	46.2	28.2	12.8	5.1	100.0

TABLE 5.3. THREE POLITICAL PARTIES, BY EDUCATIONAL BACKGROUND

University Graduates (Tokyo graduates)		
LDP	83%	(32%)
JSP	54	(8)
JCP	72	(24)

MPs represent. All but 5 of the 39 Communists in the House of Representatives represent highly urban increasingly postindustrial districts. Fifteen of them were top vote-getters in their respective multimember districts in the latest (1972) general elections. One urban district (Kyoto's first district) elected two Communists. Perhaps of some ancillary interest: the average age of the urban Communist MPs at the time of their latest election was 46.

Thus, the nature of the demographic basis of their popularity, the level of their education, the pattern of their career background, and their relative age all combine to suggest, if not demonstrate in themselves, that the Communist MPs are in large measure in the mold of postindustrial society.

Party Membership and Penetration

The JCP is indeed a young and vigorous party. Its current membership is in excess of 320,000, of which one-third is said to be female. While we do not have a breakdown by age of this membership, its youthfulness might be inferred from the age composition of the party congress. At the November 1973 JCP Congress, 39 percent of some 2,000 delegates were in their twenties and thirties and 44 percent in their forties.[48] The 320,000-plus members constitute the party's organizational and activity infrastructure extended throughout the country. Not only does the JCP membership numerically far surpass the JSP membership and in all probability exceed the LDP's, but as we noted, it is characterized by dedication and diligence in its activities at the grass-roots level. The JCP membership seems qualitatively different from its LDP or JSP counterpart.

Apart from the general "daily activities" in which JCP

48. Takuro Suzuki, "Kyosanto Dai 12 kai Taikai o Kaibo suru," *Jiyu*, January 1974, pp. 81–90. On the other aspects of the party membership, see Fukuji Taguchi, "Nihon Kyosanto no Yakushin to Kongo no Kadai," *Sekai*, February 1973.

members are engaged in their respective localities, which all suggest their highly admirable sensitivity toward a number of problems that plague ordinary people, we may briefly mention a few salient examples of the party's organizational efforts of cross-regional magnitude, in order to highlight the extent to which the party's endeavor has come to be congruent with citizens' problems and needs.

One of the worsening grass-roots problems in highly urban Japan is the inadequacy of health service and medical care. The number of doctors in Japan, while large even among industrial nations, is such that, especially with the national health insurance that tends to encourage citizens to seek medical counsel and treatment more often than they would without it, medical service provided by the practicing doctors is frequently behind what is demanded or needed.[49] In terms of demand and supply, therefore, the doctors have an enormous advantage over patients and they are, at least from time to time, under stress and strain of work, wont to take advantage of this situation, not in terms of charging extra fees necessarily, though this does happen, but rather in terms of handling patients, preventive medicine, and office hours. Also, with rising urban congestion, public sanitation and health services are lagging behind. As a result, there has been an increasing popular discontent. The JCP has stepped into this service vacuum to take the initiative in organizing what has since come to be called the All-Japan Democratic Medical Facilities League (*Zen Nihon Minshu Iryokikan Rengokai*). This organization now consists of clinics, volunteer doctors, nurses, medical students, and case workers that are available twenty-four hours a day. They are available not only for medical treatment and medical consultation, but also for health consultation, consultation about diet, and related problems. They also help citizens concerning welfare qualifications and applications, domestic problems, legal problems; and when problems involved require governmental action, they are researched and presented to local authorities, directly or through JCP assemblymen and lawyers.

49. According to a Ministry of Health and Welfare survey, there were, in 1973, 128 doctors for every 100,000 inhabitants. The Ministry contended that this number should be increased at least to 150. *Showa 48 nen ban Kosei Hakusho* (Tokyo: Kosei Sho, 1973), p. 162. The minimum legal standard specified by the Ministry of Health and Welfare calls for one public health clinic per 100,000 inhabitants, but the actual condition in, for example, Tokyo was only one such clinic per 180,000 by the end of the 1960s. Goro Hani, *Toshi no Ronri* (Tokyo: Keiso Shobo, 1969), p. 378.

As of 1973, the League had developed a network of 318 hospitals and clinics throughout the nation, most of them located in urban areas, with support personnel and corps of volunteers. They are financed by contributions from the party, from individual citizens and former patients, and from funds raised through a variety of fund-raising campaigns.[50]

Another interesting example of JCP membership activities focusing on extensive grass-roots problems is the Democratic Commerce and Industry Association (*Minshu Shoko Kai*). This, too, was organized through the initiative and leadership of the JCP and its members in various localities for small businessmen and merchants to deal with the complex tax problems that customarily plague them, including what they consider the officiousness of and harassment by the National Tax Agency. The Association has been an enormous assistance to these small businessmen and merchants and factory owners who have little experience on legal and tax matters and/or could not afford to hire expensive tax lawyers. The Association's activity, however, has expanded beyond tax matters to include credit and financing, management consultation, and related services to these people who would otherwise have to depend on their own limited wits. As noted in chapter 2, a great bulk of the total of Japan's business and industrial firms consists of small and marginal enterprises that operate at the mercy of the domineering triumvirate of the ruling LDP, the bureaucracy, and big business and industry. There are varying degrees of disjunction and tension between the top layer of the Japanese economic structure occupied by giant modern corporations on the one hand and the remainder of the pyramid on the other, though such disjunction and tension have traditionally been cushioned and mitigated by peculiar social and interpersonal relationships that obtain in society. They are, however, likely to become increasingly manifest as Japan attempts to cope with the problems of postindustrial society. In any event, as of January 1973, the Association was reported to have a membership of 216,000 and aimed at enrolling by 1975 10 percent of the estimated 4 million small businessmen, merchants, and factory owners.

One clear indication of the vigor and diligence of JCP members is a phenomenal increase in the circulation of the party's paper, *Akahata* (The Red Flag), as seen in table 5.4 compared

50. These examples of party activities in this section are drawn from *Nihon Kyosanto*, pp. 95–138.

TABLE 5.4. THREE POLITICAL PARTIES: PARTY PAPER CIRCULATION, 1974

LDP	600,000 (weekly)
JSP	180,000 (semiweekly)
JCP	2,500,000 (550,000 daily and 1,950,000 Sunday)[a]

[a] The latest figure reported is over 3 million for *Akahata*: 660,000 daily and 2.4 million on Sunday. See Yomiuri Shimbun Sha, Yoron Chosa Shitsu, eds., *Senkyo o Tettei Bunseki suru* (Tokyo: Yomiuri Shimbun Sha, 1975), p. 53.

with its LDP and JSP counterparts. Indeed, *Akahata* has the largest circulation of any Communist newspaper outside of the Communist nations, far exceeding that of *l'Humanité* of the French Communist party (fewer than 400,000) and *l'Unità* of the Italian Communist party (500,000 copies).[51] It may be of some significance that 40 percent of *Akahata* readers are said to be women.[52] The increase in circulation of the Communist newspaper, which continues, is an important sign of the rising penetration of JCP members at the grass-roots level. It appears, therefore, that Totten was entirely correct when he observed, "The Communists have discovered that they can grow from the bottom up, outside the ranks of organized urban labor, with a posture of peacefulness, friendship, and service."[53]

Party Finance

The vigor of the JCP is apparent also in party finance. Table 5.5 shows the finances of the five parties for the calendar year 1972, as reported officially by these parties. The financial prowess of the JCP does not seem to have declined at all since then. Consider table 5.6, party revenues for 1974 on p. 148.

As is clear from these tables, the financial condition of the JCP seems very solid. While the authenticity of the LDP revenue is clearly suspect (for reasons discussed in chapter 4), few seem

51. There are over 300,000 card-carrying Communists in France. In Italy, though the party boasts a membership of 1.5 million, apparently only one out of three of them subscribes to the party paper. See *Nihon Kyosanto* (Tokyo: Asahi Shimbun Sha, 1973), p. 290; and *World Strength of the Communist Party Organization* (Washington: Bureau of Intelligence and Research, Department of State, July 1973), pp. 24–28.

52. Dixon, "The Growth of a 'Popular' Japanese Communist Party," p. 397.

53. George O. Totten, "The People's Parliamentary Path of the Japanese Communist Party—Part II," *Pacific Affairs* 49 (Fall 1973): 384.

TABLE 5.5   FINANCES OF FIVE POLITICAL PARTIES, 1972

	Revenue (in million yen)	Expenditure	Political Contribution as % of Revenue
LDP	9,480	9,480	87.8
JCP	5,170	4,910	2.9
CGP	3,720	3,430	5.4
DSP	940	940	79.1
JSP	770	770	31.2

Source: From Yoshikata Aso, "Jiminto wa Jiyu o Mamotte iruka," *Jiyu*, January 1974, p. 105.

to doubt the credibility of the JCP finances. In 1972 and 1974, according to these tables, JCP revenue is well above half that of the LDP. The per MP revenue was by far the highest for the JCP in both those years, surpassing the LDP's by more than two to one. (In 1974, for example, the per MP revenue for these parties were: 171 million yen for the JCP, 94 million yen for the CGP, 48 million yen for the LDP, 30 million yen for the DSP, and a minuscule 6 million yen for the JSP. Of course, the LDP most likely had the highest per MP revenue when we consider the widely accepted assumption that the actual revenue for the party was up to ten times the figure officially reported by the party. See pp. 81–83.) This in itself suggests the organizational potency of the JCP. More significant, however, is the fact that the JCP, apart from the CGP, is the only party that is financially on its own; other parties are all beholden to outside sources for political funds. In fact, the JCP at least in 1972 showed the highest degree of financial independence among all the parties. The LDP is heavily dependent on funds provided by the corporate world and other special interests. The JSP would be totally bankrupt without

TABLE 5.6.   REVENUES OF FIVE POLITICAL PARTIES, 1974

	Revenue (in million yen)
LDP	18,880
JCP	10,070
CGP	4,960
JSP	1,130
DSP	860

Source: *Asahi Shimbun*, 22 June 1975, p. 1.

Sohyo financial assistance, and the DSP, as we shall see, relies heavily upon the Japan Confederation of Labor (*Domei*), the major rival to *Sohyo* within organized labor. Contributions as proportion of the total JCP revenue in 1972, for example, were 2.9 percent, and in 1974, indications were that they were even smaller, 2.5 percent, part of which is said to have come from its chairman's own household.[54] Virtually all JCP revenue comes from incomes generated by its paper, *Akahata* (over 70 percent), other publications and advertisements in them (approximately 20 percent), and membership dues.[55] Membership dues are assessed at 1 percent of personal income, but exceptions are provided.

The fact that the JCP is not financially beholden to any special interest is of considerable significance. Precisely for this reason the party is able to engage in effective "daily activities" at the grass-roots level: it need not fear stepping on any special interest's toes. It does not have to fear angering any institutional group or entrenched interest, since the party is not supported by any of these groups, including labor. The LDP would incur the wrath of business and industry if it engaged in aggressive grass-roots activities to cope with many postindustrial problems because such activities are inimical to the interest of the corporate world. The JSP would alienate the Socialism Association and much of *Sohyo* leadership if it undertook (assuming, that is, it could) problem-oriented activities that call for instrumental orientation, because those leftist groups are primarily concerned about ideological authenticity and revolutionary purity rather than about the practical solution of mundane problems. The JCP, on the other hand, can, because of its freedom from ties and obligation to organized interests of industrial society, deal more effectively with various grass-roots problems of postindustrial society from the perspective of citizen needs and grievances.

Adaptive Capacity of the JCP

The Japan Communist party, the party of popular anathema in the past, seems destined to grow into a power seriously to be reckoned with. Its major strength lies in its freedom from the constraints of the politics of industrial society, its freedom from the kind of ties and resultant obligations to entrenched interests

54. See *Asahi Shimbun*, 28 September 1974, p. 3.

55. *Nihon Kyosanto*, pp. 75–76.

that would seriously inhibit its adaptation to the changing environment as Japan undergoes the transition from industrial to postindustrial society. The party, in an important sense, is untainted and unfettered by the conventions, preferences, commitments, and values that are characteristics of parties and politics in industrial society. It owes no allegiance to any group of any sector of society, including labor (except in a theoretical Marxist sense). Labor, in fact, has never really supported the JCP, though the party in the past attempted assiduously to cultivate its support. The fact that labor has never supported the party has turned out to be a blessing in disguise, for the party has unwittingly avoided being trapped into the maze of special-interest politics of industrial society. The party continues to attempt to generate labor support, and it has been reported that some member unions of the JSP-bound *Sohyo*, notably the Japan Teachers Union, disillusioned by the decline of the JSP, are at various levels moving away from the *Sohyo* rule of exclusive JSP electoral support. It is doubtful, however, that the JCP, in view of its sound and entirely independent party finance, its organizational autonomy and integrity, and its rising cross-stratal popular support through successful engagement in grass-roots activities, would succumb to the role of a malleable client of any special interest as have the JSP and the LDP. Indeed, the JCP's total independence from the essentially parochial, industrial-era interests of organized labor is manifest in its candor in stressing that workers (especially in reference to militant public-sector employees such as municipal and prefectural employees and public school teachers who constitute the two largest unions within *Sohyo*) should, while entitled to legitimate rights and privileges, be mindful that they are servants of local residents and therefore should not indiscriminately oppose measures (by incumbent governments) to streamline personnel and retrench personnel finances of government and other public institutions. This is indeed the kind of advocacy or admonition that is taboo in organized labor and among "progressive" parties.[56]

The JCP seems better suited than either the LDP or the JSP to adapt to the demands and requirements of postindustrial society because of the character of its membership. It has won increasing popular support at the grass-roots levels precisely because it has engaged in effective activities that address themselves to the more relevant issues and salient problems at this

56. See *Asahi Shimbun*, 23 March 1975, pp. 1–2.

level, namely issues and problems that are more characteristic of postindustrial society, and in the interest of ordinary citizens who have no effective channels of access to the powers that be. In so doing, the party has eschewed ideological platitudes and political rhetoric and instead concentrated on efforts tangibly to help resolve ordinary citizens' immediate problems with local authorities, business firms, tax offices, medical problems, pollution, and congestion. It must be noted, both by us and by the JCP itself, that popular support for the party has increased, not because it is Communist (i.e., a party of ideological politics of industrial society), revisionist or otherwise, but because it serves certain political functions that other parties do not, and serves people in ways where other parties have been derelict, in manners that are visibly instrumental in dealing with the rising problems of postindustrial society. The electoral growth of the JCP, therefore, is strictly on functional merit. It is thus that the emergence of postindustrial society and the rise in popularity of the JCP are no mere coincidence.

THE CLEAN GOVERNMENT PARTY

The Clean Government party (CGP), called *Komeito* in Japanese, is unique within the context of Japanese politics and the party system in more senses than one. It did not emerge as an autonomous political grouping of notables at the national level, as other parties did (including the JCP). Instead, it rose as the political arm of a mass socioreligious movement that was peculiar to a particular period in the evolution of Japanese society. The movement out of whose womb, so to speak, sprang the CGP needs some description here. It is called the Value Creation Society (*Soka Gakkai*).[57]

The Value Creation Society

The Society was created as a movement to revive what its leaders regarded as the quintessence of Japanese tradition and culture based on the teaching of Nichiren Shonin, founder of an activist Buddhist sect in the tumultuous thirteenth century. Its origin goes back to the prewar period, but it came to appeal

57. For a good description and analysis in English of *Soka Gakkai* as a mass movement, see James W. White, *The Sokagakkai and Mass Society* (Stanford, Calif.: Stanford University Press, 1970).

widely only after the war, especially in the 1950s. The rapid rise in its popularity was the function of convergence of two major factors: the Society's teaching and the predicament of postwar Japanese society.

The fundamental popular thrust of the Value Creation Society was nationalistic, antibureaucratic, anticapitalist, anticommunist, and moralistic. It deplored the blatant materialism of industrial capitalism, the soulless atheism of modern ideologies, especially communism, the barren impersonality of modern bureaucratic society, the mindless decadence of Western culture, and the lack of spiritualism and sense of community in contemporary life. It attempted, therefore, to revive the national pride in Japan's moral, religious, and cultural tradition, the close sense of community that presumably had characterized the nation's long history, and, hence, the unique national identity of the Japanese people. These aspects of the Society's thrust were eminently attractive to a large segment of the Japanese populace at a time when there was a vast and disturbing moral and cultural vacuum as the result of the defeat in the war and all that ensued in consequence: the denigration of everything Japanese; the popular rejection of the past tradition of the country as antiliberal, reactionary, and backward; national self-flagellation in collective guilt over militarism and the war; and the subsequent mass penchant for indiscriminate emulation of everything Western, especially American. There emerged, therefore, a high degree of disquieting moral anomie pervading many sectors of society, a crisis, we might say, of identity. This vacuum, or identitive ambivalence, soon gave rise to a number of so-called *parvenu* religious sects (*shinko shukyo*), and the Value Creation Society became by far the most aggressive and appealing among them. Like all other *parvenu* religious sects or movements, it had its greatest appeal to those sectors of society whose identitive ambivalence was compounded by their socioeconomic marginality, hence insecurity.

Economically, the segments of the Japanese population to which the Society had the greatest appeal were those that were left out of the rising growth and prosperity: largely the lower and lower-middle classes. Socially, too, they were not in the mainstream of modern society. Members of these social segments were relatively isolated, not belonging to large and powerful interest groups and associations. They were mostly without higher education. Occupationally they were small merchants, tradesmen, operators of marginally viable small enterprises, and their workers. Politically and culturally, they were conservative, narrowly moralistic and intolerant, simplistic, largely antidemocratic, and hostile to new ideas. They were, in the word of one observer, "lower middle class puritans."[58] In one sense, Value Creation Society membership had a disturbing resemblance to those groups in other industrial societies as well as in prewar Japan that have most ardently supported ultrapatriotic, antirational, and illiberal political movements that were at once anti-corporate-capitalist and anticommunist. And, not incidentally, it was characterized by a high degree of organizational cohesiveness, internal unity and discipline, and a fervent sense of mission and élan.

By the early 1970s, the Society boasted a nationwide membership of over 15 million (or 7.5 million households)[59] and a spate of affiliate organizations, including a university, high schools, a symphony orchestra, youth organizations, artistic associations, publishing firms, a daily newspaper, a theater troupe, and various "research" institutes. It was aggressive in its effort to recruit converts, and its frequent strongarm tactics in this endeavor engendered sporadic public criticism and outrage.

The Rise of the CGP

The CGP's origin dates back to the local elections of 1955, when the Value Creation Society first fielded candidates from among its members for legislative assemblies. At that time, the Society had a membership of 300,000 households, and 52 of the 54 of its candidates were elected.[60] Thereafter, Society members became increasingly successful in running for local assemblies. At the national level, the Society entered the formal political arena in the 1956 House of Councilors election in which 3 of its 6 candidates were elected. Total Society votes for its candidates were close to one million (3.5 percent of the total popular votes cast), representing a little over 2 votes per member household (Society membership at that time was approximately 400,000 households). Encouraged by continuing success in local and upper house elections, the Society organized the Clean Politics

58. Norman Macrae, "Pacific Century: 1975–2075?," *Economist*, 4–10 January 1975, p. 18.

59. Yukio Hori, *Komeito Ron: Sono Kodo to Taishitsu* (Tokyo: Aoki Shoten, 1973), p. 147.

60. For a good description of the CGP in Japanese, see also Shigeyoshi Murakami, *Komeito* (Tokyo: Shin Nihon Shuppan Sha, 1970).

League (*Komei Seiji Renmei*) in 1962 as its full-fledged political department and in 1964 reorganized it into the Clean Government party as a formal political party. In 1967 the CGP entered the races for the all-important House of Representatives for the first time and elected 25 candidates by garnering a total of nearly 2.5 million votes (5.4 percent). In the meantime, the CGP had done very well in local elections, and the party reached its peak strength at the national level when it attained 24 seats in the House of Councilors in 1968 and 47 in the House of Representatives in 1969.

The CGP, in the meantime, was distinctly subordinate to the parent Value Creation Society, according to the principle of "unity of politics and religious teaching" (*seikyo itchi*). Its parliamentary members, therefore, were representatives of, hence accountable to, the Society for all practical purposes, and were politically not autonomous. At the same time, however, their party could confidently rely upon the electoral support of the dedicated Society members, their families, relatives, and friends, not only for votes but also for election campaigns. This gave the CGP both its electoral vitality and limitations. Society members were motivated by the religious zeal and activist devotion that permeated the entire organization, and they could be counted on to spare no efforts to promote campaigns of CGP candidates. On the other hand, its relationship with the Society made the CGP a party of distinct limitations. For example, as we mentioned, the Society's aggressiveness was viewed with wariness by the populace, and its tactics in attempting to acquire converts to its cause had been severely criticized and incurred antipathy and fear among citizens outside the Society. Moreover, as one of the "*parvenu* religious movements" playing upon fear, insecurity, and ignorance, the Society was widely viewed with something resembling contempt and derision by nonmembers. This, combined with the absence of any clear-cut policy direction, would prove to be a serious handicap for the future prospects of the party. In short, for the CGP to become a genuine modern party, there was need for it to rid itself of its ties with the Society.

Separation from the Value Creation Society

Impetus for the separation of the CGP and the Value Creation Society was generated quite unexpectedly in 1969. Earlier in that year, a definitive treatise on the Society by a well-known scholar was published. The book was objective but was for good reasons critical of the predilections and tactics of the Society and explored their antidemocratic implications and dangers. The Society and the CGP then stirred a public outrage and controversy by resorting to crude attempts to prevent the book's distribution by intimidation. This raised a very legitimate question about the CGP's suitability as a party in a democratic society. The controversy raged within the Diet and elsewhere for several months, and the CGP found itself on the defensive. It escaped formal parliamentary censure only with the aid of the ruling LDP, which needed CGP electoral support for conservative candidates in certain local elections. In any event, under mounting public and parliamentary pressures against it and the Society, the CGP, in its eighth party convention in 1970, adopted a resolution to separate politics from religion, and drew up a new party constitution, thus formally severing its ties with the Society. The CGP, at least on paper, now emerged as a secular political party capable of appealing to wider constituencies.

While there was little doubt that the separation of the party from the mass religious movement had been approved by the Society's leadership for tactical reasons, the effect of the separation tended to bear out the suspicion that the party had in fact been an appendage of the Society and that it would not be a really viable, vital force without the dedicated works of Society membership. In the first general election after the party's declaration of independence, so to speak, the CGP suffered a rather drastic setback: it lost 19 of the 47 seats it had held in the lower house of the Diet, becoming the second smallest party in the national political arena. This was a clear reflection of the change in the size of party membership. Before the separation, party membership had stood at 280,000. After the separation, it declined to 120,000 (of whom 110,000 were still Society members).[61] There was a widespread speculation that the days of the party's growth had ended.

Leftward Shifts of the CGP

The radical electoral setback it suffered in the 1972 general election caused the CGP to reexamine its position and policy direction. Until then, the party had been the political mouthpiece of the Value Creation Society and, as such, it had been less than distinct in concrete policy orientation and programmatic com-

---

61. Hori, *Komeito Ron*, p. 164; and *Asahi Shimbun*, 5 January 1973, p. 2.

mitment. Apart from its vaguely militant nationalism, the CGP had expressed only ambiguous generalities such as moderation, social welfare, humanistic social policy, and so forth. General public impression had been that the party was at best only slightly to the left of the ruling LDP and a secret political partner of the same. Some observers saw much in common between the CGP and the right wing within the LDP. After the 1972 electoral debacle, however, the CGP began to move gradually to the left on the Japanese political spectrum, a move that was precipitated by several important considerations.

The 1972 experience clearly suggested that the CGP, unless it took a fresh direction, could not hope to compensate for the loss of vigorous electoral assistance of the Value Creation Society and its members it had earlier taken for granted, let alone to expand its base of popular support. Since a return to the Society was rejected (though many CGP MPs viewed it as imperative), the party had to turn to other methods for vitalizing its strength and electoral appeal. Then, too, the increasing popular disaffection with the ruling LDP and the rising popularity of the JCP indicated that the only direction the CGP could move to redefine its position and to generate popular appeal would be leftward. In addition, the rise in salience of issues and problems of advanced industrial society and the visibly increasing popular concern with them made it quite clear that, in order for the CGP to increase its electoral appeal and to expand its base of support, it must cultivate support of those sectors of society that were more seriously affected by those issues and problems, so as to project a new image as a secular "national" party.

It was thus that the CGP began to move noticeably to the left of its former vague "middle of the road" stance, advocating, for example, an immediate cancellation of the Japan–U.S. Security Treaty, thus joining, at least on this issue, the JSP and the JCP, its arch rivals and ideological enemies. In an attempt to cultivate an image of an open national party, the CGP also enunciated what it calls "humanistic socialism" that is supposed to be distinct from the "scientific socialism" of the JSP and the JCP and the DSP's "democratic socialism." The distinction among these "socialisms," however, has never been clear to the electorate, except that the CGP is still basically anti-Marxist. The party also enumerated certain of its broad policy commitments among which are (1) the defense of the Constitution and parliamentary democracy; (2) peaceful, independent, neutralist foreign policy; (3) the care and protection of the socially disadvantaged and handicapped, and promotion of social justice; and (4) a national economy committed to the priority of public interest.[62] These, however, still remain broad and general statements, and nobody but the CGP has any idea as to how they would be specified in terms of concrete contents and programs of implementation.

While its pronouncements and public rhetoric became politically clearer and its public stance distinctly more anti-LDP and opposed to socioeconomic and political status quo, therefore, the CGP's precise location on the conventional political spectrum is by no means clear. From the perspective of the politics of industrial society, the party is still rather difficult to characterize beyond its origin and evolution. This problem is not quite as serious as it might appear at a first glance, for two reasons: the politics of industrial society is in decline, or, to be less sanguine, it is being powerfully challenged by the rise of the politics of postindustrial society; and the CGP's strength or prospects seem to lie not in its place in the politics of industrial society (which in more senses than one is monopolized by the ruling LDP and the opposition JSP) but rather in its successful cultivation of popular support through its attention to the very problems that have given rise to the politics of postindustrial society. We now turn to the CGP's efforts in this new dimension of society.

The CGP and Its Grass-roots Activities

Earlier, we discussed its grass-roots activities as one of the primary causes of the rising popularity of the JCP. The JCP, however, is not the only political party to be concerned with daily issues and problems of ordinary citizens. The CGP has been concerned with these problems almost as long as the JCP. The Value Creation Society had, in its effort to expand its appeal and to seek converts, instituted a network of "citizens' livelihood discussion centers"[63] even before the organization of the CGP and the party subsequently expanded it by providing legal and other assistance to "those people discarded by politics." Since its separation from the parent Value Creation Society, the party greatly expanded its range of activities in this regard, clearly recognizing them as a practical necessity for its own survival and growth. CGP legislators, both at the national and local levels,

62. *Asahi Shimbun,* 25 October 1973, p. 2.

63. White, *Sokagakki and Mass Society,* p. 159.

are required actively to solicit grievances of citizens and aggressively to see to it that they are resolved to the satisfaction of those citizens. It was reported that over a million grievance cases were successfully processed by CGP legislators in 1973 alone.[64] In the same year, the party provided a battery of over one hundred lawyers to give professional assistance to citizens who had problems with government agencies and business establishments. In a wide range of aspects, therefore, grass-roots activities by the CGP are fundamentally similar to those of the JCP. And, not surprisingly, since 1972, the CGP's electoral popularity has been on the rise, significantly paralleling the JCP's, especially at the local level. In the 1973 and 1975 local elections, the CGP representation increased in all four major demographic areas: metropolitan, urban, semiurban, and rural, and the party's successes were clearly owing to its increasing concentration of its energy on issues relating to grass-roots social and economic problems plaguing ordinary citizens.[65] In fact, the CGP and the JCP were the only parties to experience increases in their strengths in those local elections.

There are, however, some important differences between the CGP and the JCP, differences that could cause a significant variation in electoral fortune between the two parties. These differences are in the character of membership and the general base of support.

Bases of Support and Membership. Past surveys show some distinct features about CGP supporters that are not altogether reassuring to the party. The largest proportion (32 percent) of CGP supporters is found among those with a grade-school education or less, and only 8 percent of its supporters are university graduates. In terms of occupational distribution, a survey at the peak of CGP strength (1969) indicated that over 60 percent of the party's supporters were "self-employed," i.e., small farmers, fishermen, shopkeepers, operators of marginal factories, and so on. The second largest occupational group among CGP voters (over 20 percent) was blue-collar, e.g., factory hands, waiters and waitresses, artisans, construction workers, and the like.[66] One common characteristic of these categories of CGP supporters

64. *Asahi Shimbun,* 15 April 1974, p. 2.

65. *Asahi Shimbun,* 19 July 1973, p. 4, and 29 April 1975, p. 2.

66. Hori, *Komeito Ron,* pp. 189–93.

was their socioeconomic marginality. They were among those Japanese who had benefited least from the rising prosperity and affluence because of the particular economic structure of the country described in chapter 2. This can further be seen in the fact that the largest support for the CGP came from the lowest income bracket. In short, a typical CGP supporter was a blue-collar worker or small shopkeeper with a low level of education and a low level of income.[67] He was essentially identical with a typical zealot of the Value Creation Society.

In contrast, the largest proportional support for the JCP comes from university graduates, white-collar workers, professionals, and those holding executive positions.[68] In more senses than one, CGP supporters are industrial in many of their features, while JCP supporters are increasingly postindustrial. This tends to suggest that the prospects of the CGP may not be quite as good as those of the JCP. The number of blue-collar workers, as a proportion of the entire labor force, is in decline in Japan as in other advanced industrial societies. So are the number of small shopkeepers, tradesmen, and marginal factory owners with the continuing trend toward absorption of these small enterprises by chains of supermarkets and toward business mergers, although, to a considerable extent, the dual economic system of Japan is likely to persist with greater tenacity than in other countries. More and more Japanese are better educated and more high school graduates go on to colleges and universities, as in other advanced industrial states. The number and importance of professionals are on the rise. CGP supporters as a proportion of the electorate would be bound to decrease unless the party significantly expands its bases of support, although temporary economic difficulties, such as those that the country has been experiencing since the oil shock of 1973, do tend to increase the number of voters in the area of economic marginality, thus causing a rise in popular support for the CGP.

The CGP would seem likely to suffer further if many of its voters were supporting it because of the psychic ambivalence that caused their attraction to the Value Creation Society. The identitive ambivalence or moral vacuum we referred to earlier still persists, of course, but its potency is definitely in decline for a variety of reasons. One reason is the inevitable generational

67. *Japan Opinion Poll January 1975* (Delray Beach: Fla.: Ross Snyder & Son, January 1975), n.d.

68. Ibid.; and *Nihon-jin Kenkyu*, 2:4–14.

metabolism of the Japanese population. Older generations that have most acutely felt the impact of the moral vacuum of the postwar period are receding into history; younger generations, especially those who were raised after the war, are naturally more impervious to or unconcerned with such a vacuum, for they have been acculturated and socialized in the postwar, "modern," "democratic" Japan. Second, the Japanese, as a nation, have been gradually developing a new sense of national identity, aided, no doubt, by their newly found pride in being a world power, however militarily weak, and by the increasing attention paid them by the world at large. The Japanese know, and rightly, that they are a nation to be reckoned with, that many nations in the world envy them, even are attempting to emulate their resourcefulness, energy, and successes, and that they can perform valuable services for the development of other nations and for the cause of world peace. The recent wave of publications focusing on the meaning of being Japanese suggests, not so much a neurotic search for identity as some commentators would have us believe, as an attempt to define what the Japanese already feel and know. There is a considerable degree of self-confidence in this attempt at self-definition that was never observed during the postwar period. Now, if our argument here is anywhere near correct, then the CGP's future would be quite circumscribed unless the party succeeds in cultivating a cross-stratal popular appeal. The party, in order to remain viable and to grow, must address itself vigorously to problems of advanced industrial society, and not to the apparently diminishing sectors afflicted with socioeconomic marginality, low levels of education, and identitive ambivalence.

The CGP, as of 1974, had a membership of approximately 120,000. This was more than twice the size of the JSP membership. There are, however, some problems with this membership. Of the 120,000, 110,000 were said to be members of the Value Creation Society. The party membership, then, is dominated by Society zealots, and in this sense the CGP has the same type of problem as the JSP: domination of membership by those whose primary allegiance is *not* to the party as such, and whose dominance can be ensured so long as they maintain their numerical majority in the membership. In short, there is a built-in bias in the CGP membership, as in the JSP membership, against cross-stratal recruitment of new members. Despite its grass-roots activities, therefore, the CGP, at least in its membership composition, gives the appearance of a "one-pressure group" party. The JCP membership, on the other hand, gives an increasingly "cross-stratal" impression. According to the party's report in 1970, well over 40 percent of its members were white-collar and professional,[69] and the proportion of those white-collar and professional people with high levels of education and pragmatic problem-orientation seems to be increasing.[70] There seems to be a greater degree of congruence between membership and grass-roots activities for the JCP than for the CGP.

The CGP in the past often cited the rise in the circulation of its paper (*Komei Shimbun*, Clean Government News) as evidence of its rising popular appeal. Indeed, a total circulation of 2.2 million (800,000 daily and 1.4 million Sunday) appears very impressive, when the party membership stands at 120,000. And it does give the party considerable financial autonomy, inasmuch as, according to the report of the party's tenth convention, 82 percent of its revenue came from incomes of the party paper and other publications (the remaining 18 percent was said to be generated by membership dues,[71] though this somewhat contradicts the report by the Ministry of Autonomy that 8 percent of the CGP revenue, at least in 1974, came from outside the party).[72] But the fact of the domination of party membership by members of the Value Creation Society (92 percent) and the party's past ties with the Society combine to generate a suspicion that the readership of the party's paper is largely Society members, much in the same sense that the readership of the JSP paper must be largely *Sohyo* and Socialist Association activists. The size of the CGP paper's circulation, then, may not mean what that of the JCP paper's seems to.

Then, too, there is some problem with the party's own leadership at various levels of the party's organization. The current top leadership is manned by persons who began their political careers as influential officers of the Value Creation Society, and it was only after the formal severance of the tie between the party and the Society that they resigned from Society posts. The teachings, cultural predispositions, and mental

69. *Nihon Kyosanto*, p. 36.

70. *Nihon Kyosanto no Subete* (Tokyo: Sankei Shimbun Shuppan Sha, 1973), pp. 130–31.

71. Hori, *Komeito Ron*, p. 167.

72. *Asahi Shimbun*, 25 December 1974, p. 1.

orientation of the Society, we might argue, are deeply ingrained in these CGP leaders and could affect their attempt to adapt the party to the requirements of the new politics. The same problem obviously attends at lower levels of leadership within the party's prefectural and local branches which are, as we observed, still dominated by members of the Value Creation Society. As well, there may be the problem of differential adaptation among various strata of party leadership and organization. For example, top leadership of the party may well prove flexible, accommodative, hence adaptable; but it could encounter resistance from power holders at lower levels, or vice versa.

The Future of the CGP

The future of the CGP seems to depend on whether and how expeditiously the party can free itself from the constraints of its past ties with the Value Creation Society—constraints in terms of membership, recruitment of leadership, public image, and base of support. To the extent that the party can accomplish this fundamental task, its future may be promising, inasmuch as it is not beholden to any special interests of industrial society. Its baggage, so to speak, is relatively light, in comparison to the heavy load that the LDP and the JSP carry. Indeed, the very fact that the party began after the 1972 electoral setback to undertake a noticeable, albeit perhaps reluctant and not entirely distinct change in its basic policy stance and public posture in the direction that seemed more congruent with the rising problems of postindustrial society is significant. The party, it can be said, is attempting to search an area in the political arena in which it may be able to assure its viability and growth, to seek to carve out an early homestead in the new postindustrial politics, a homestead for a more problem-oriented, citizen-centered service politics. Many obstacles remain for the CGP, but the really critical ones are internal; if the party manages to overcome them, it would be able to attract the support of the widening constituency of citizens who have become increasingly disaffected by the politics as usual of the LDP and the JSP.

All things considered, the prospects of the CGP, while by no means certain, seem considerably brighter than those of, say, the JSP. The party is indeed greatly inhibited by the nature of its origin and its early growth, but it is much less constrained by its roots in industrial politics than either the LDP or the JSP, though its future rests still on a number of contingencies most of which are internal. The next few elections should be able more definitely to indicate the extent of the party's future prospects.

THE DEMOCRATIC SOCIALIST PARTY

The Democratic Socialist party (DSP) is a grouping formed by the moderates who seceded from the JSP in 1960 at the time of the heated controversy over the revised Japan–U.S. Mutual Security Treaty.[73] It was and is a party of conservative Socialists who are opposed to the radical leftist orientation of the JSP and to the JSP's insistence on an immediate abrogation of the security treaty with the United States. In domestic policy, the DSP eschews the class emphasis of the JSP on the ground that it stymies the growth of socialist appeal, and instead stresses the need for efforts to appeal to a broad, cross-stratal constituency.[74] In more senses than one, the DSP in its fundamental orientation, strategic inclination, and tactical preference shared much in common with European social democratic parties. The party's electoral fortune, however, has been dismal since its formation in 1960. Its general election share of votes has hovered well below 10 percent: 8.7 percent in 1960, 7.4 percent in 1963 and 1967, 7.7 percent in 1969, and 7.0 percent in 1972. The party has sunk from the role of the third largest party in the first half of the 1960s to the smallest one in the 1970s, from 40 seats in the controlling lower house before the 1960 election to 19 after the 1972 election, overtaken by both the JCP and the CGP. Its viability, therefore, is in serious doubt today.

Causes of the Decline

Despite its similarities to social democratic parties of Western Europe, there is critical lack of parallels between the DSP and its counterparts in other highly industrial societies. The DSP, like the JSP, had no hand in mass enfranchisement and

73. The best English-language treatment of this controversy, as well as of the moderates' secession from the JSP, is Packard, *Protest in Tokyo.*

74. For the fundamental disagreement of the DSP and the JSP on domestic issues, see, for example, Allan B. Cole, George O. Totten, and Cecil Uyehara, *Socialist Parties in Postwar Japan* (New Haven and London: Yale University Press, 1966), esp. p. 95.

democratization of political processes in Japan, for those tasks were accomplished by fiat of the American occupation administration. No sector of Japanese society, not even labor, therefore, is indebted to the party. Second, the DSP has no more mass base for organization and electoral strength than the JSP does. It simply does not have the kind of organizational and institutional base of support its European counterparts do; for, like most of other parties in Japan, the DSP was organized as a party of notables at the national level and not generated from below as the parliamentary arm of mass organizations.

Then there are political and programmatic reasons for the decline of the DSP. The party started its career in 1960 as a middle-of-the-road party, with the hope of being a viable alternative to both the conservative, business-bound LDP and the doctrinaire leftist JSP. In its first party declaration, the DSP committed itself to fighting tyranny of both the right and the left, and to defending parliamentary democracy, and gave the public to understand that, as opposition to the LDP, it would not engage in opposition for opposition's sake or refuse parliamentary debate of any issue, as the JSP had done (for example, during the parliamentary deliberation of the revised Japan–U.S. security pact in 1960) and continued to do. The DSP also attempted to generate public support by stressing "welfare" and social services in terms that were more pragmatic than those advocated by the JSP but more progressive than those of the LDP. Perhaps these advocacies of the DSP had some positive appeal to the electorate for some time; the party, after suffering a loss of seats in the 1960 elections, did increase its lower house seats in the 1963 election from 17 to 23; in 1967 it gained 30 seats and increased to 31 in 1969.

In the meantime, the DSP's policy direction came to be coopted by other parties: the LDP had begun to move increasingly in the direction of welfare and social services, expanding the scope of national health insurance, welfare subsidies, and other programs (see p. 112); other opposition parties, including the JCP, variously modified their traditional stands regarding revolution and parliamentarism. Today, all parties, from the LDP to the JCP, profess allegiance to parliamentary democracy and commitment to orderly conduct of legislative deliberation. The DSP, then, became less and less distinct as a party. Its chairman was poignantly and entirely correct when he observed, in the wake of his party's dismal performance in the 1972 general election, "all other parties have adopted the DSP line. Our party, subsequently, has lost the uniqueness of its appeal."[75] Today the DSP stands, at least in the eyes of the public, closest to the ruling LDP politically, prompting some observers to suggest that it is now "the second LDP,"[76] especially with the leftward shift in stance of the CGP. This lack of, or perhaps more accurately, decline in, unique identity and thrust of the party clearly deprived the DSP of political dynamism, popular appeal, and a necessary sense of political drama. In recent years, opinion surveys have consistently shown that the party is short on positive image, hence voter appeal. More people think the party is closer to the LDP than those who regard it as closer to the JSP; over 40 percent of its supporters at the time of the 1972 general election (latest as of this writing) were over fifty years of age, and there were relatively few young people and women among them.[77]

Since the LDP has coopted much of policy direction that the DSP had advocated for domestic problems, the DSP has found itself supporting LDP legislation more than 80 percent of the time. While this is perfectly legitimate and even suggests the DSP's integrity, it nevertheless renders the party increasingly indistinguishable from the ruling party. What the DSP considers to be its pragmatism and honesty thus works against it: "People just don't understand that each issue has to be examined on its own merit," lamented the party's secretary general. "They want to see everything in terms of black and white. If we oppose the Fourth Defense Build-Up Plan, they say we are not different from the JSP. If we argue that the country needs self-defense forces, they think we are identical with the LDP!"[78]

Then, too, there is this problem of organizational weakness for the DSP. On this problem, the DSP is a bit like the JSP. As the JSP depends upon *Sohyo* (the General Council of Trade Unions) for organizational, personnel, and financial support, so does the DSP rely heavily upon the Japan Confederation of Labor (*Domei* for short), and this has created as much problem for the electoral fortune of the DSP as the JSP's tie with *Sohyo* has for the JSP.

Domei is a federation of private-sector unions, and while much smaller than *Sohyo*, it experienced a faster rate of growth.

75. *Asahi Shimbun*, 16 December 1972, p. 2.

76. *Asahi Janaru*, 20 April 1973, p. 108.

77. *Asahi Shimbun*, 23 September 1972, p. 4.

78. Ibid., 16 December 1972, p. 2.

Its membership increased from fewer than a million in 1960 to 2.3 million in 1973 (as opposed to 4.3 million for *Sohyo* in the same year).[79] *Domei*, unlike *Sohyo*, is politically moderate, some of its member unions even conservative, reflecting the fact that its member unions are enterprise unions in the private sector. A union in this sector is likely to be politically moderate because, in the nature of employer-employee relations in Japan, workers identify their well-being with that of the management or their company at large. If their company flourishes, they will benefit, and their benefit is ascertainable. They are therefore interested in promoting the overall interest of the enterprise of which they are employees, and not in the kind of "political struggle" that *Sohyo* unionists actively engage in. Unionists in the public sector, because their salary and wage increases are not the function of any rise in their productivity, resort to "political struggles" to extract political concession for salary and wage increases from their employers, the public corporations subsidized by tax money. Enterprise unionists in the private sector can expect to see their wages and other benefits increase only if their productivity rises and/or their firm is healthy and prosperous. This is the major reason for *Domei's* political moderation and its support for the DSP, which in turn results in the party's electorally counterproductive similarity to the LDP.

The DSP claims a membership of 50,000, but most members are in fact *Domei* unionists. They run the party branches, field candidates, and select delegates to the party convention. In an important sense, it is not the DSP that runs the party-labor alliance, but the other way around—a phenomenon not altogether unlike the one seen between the JSP and *Sohyo*. This creates a serious problem of adaptation for the DSP. *Domei* unions see an important degree of identity of interest between themselves and their employers, which are large industrial establishments, the very groups that constitute the corporate world that has a close link with the LDP. These unions, therefore, are constitutionally as resistant to problems of postindustrial society as big business and industry. In other words, they are as embedded in industrial society as are their employers. In turn, they bind the DSP to industrial orientation, as does the corporate world the LDP. The DSP, as a result, has been unable to engage in the kind of extra-parliamentary, grass-roots activities that have catapulted the

79. *Nihon Tokei Nenkan Showa 48–49 Nen* (Tokyo: Sorifu Tokei Kyoku, 1974), pp. 74–75.

JCP as a force to be reckoned with and seem to be vitalizing the CGP. The DSP confines its political activities within the parliament, and despite its protestations to the contrary, has shown little eagerness to engage in vigorous, problem-oriented, citizen-centered activities.[80] In effect, because of its ties to the forces of industrial society, the party has proved unable to carve out an area of operation in the new political arena.

The relatively unexciting, industrial-bound character of the DSP may be further seen in its selection of candidates to the Diet. The DSP more often than not recruits (or, perhaps more accurately, *Domei* prevails upon it to recruit) senior officials of *Domei* unions simply because they are well known to rank-and-file union members and also because large enterprise unions, such as those of New Japan Steel, Nissan Motors, and Toshiba, have large memberships that can be counted on to provide vigorous assistance to the candidates' campaigns and generate electoral votes for them from their relatives, friends, acquaintances, and associates. In the absence of autonomous organizational infrastructure of its own at the local level, this is the only way the DSP (much like the JSP) could carry out any political campaigns, that is, through dependence upon *Domei* for organizational and campaign efforts. What is of some interest here, moreover, is that the party, again with *Domei* urging or acquiescence, recruits candidates from management of large enterprises whose unions belong to *Domei* because they would be supported by *Domei*. Thus, for the 1972 general election, 5 of the 19 DSP candidates who were successfully elected to the lower house of the Diet were either senior members of large enterprise unions or officers of those enterprises' management. And, of the 12 DSP members of the House of Councilors prior to the 1974 election, 7 were former officials of company unions of such corporate giants as Tokyo Electric, Toyo Rayon, and Nissan Motors.[81] Because of the close sense of community that binds management and union in private corporations, when a *Domei* official runs on the DSP ticket, his company management gives him financial and other assistance; likewise, when an executive of the company runs, its union reciprocates.

The DSP's dependence upon *Domei*, and also upon corporations whose unions belong to the labor federation, is apparent

80. Shinzo Shimizu, *Nihon no Shakai Minshu Shugi* (Tokyo: Iwanami, 1972), pp. 54–57.

81. *Asahi Shimbun*, 16 December 1972, p. 2.

also in party finance. As noted (pp. 147–49), DSP finance is better than JSP, and its per MP revenue was four times larger than that of the JSP and virtually equal to that of the CGP. While much of its revenue comes from *Domei*, about one-third of the DSP's total income is said to be channeled from corporate interests through the Democratic Socialist Association (*Minsha Kyokai*), an independent fund-raising organ for the party uncomfortably akin to the National Association for the LDP. This association's membership includes dozens of large corporations including banks, utility companies, and steel manufacturers.[82] Apart from the reasons cited earlier, these large corporations make political contributions to the DSP because they would rather see DSP candidates elected than JSP or JCP candidates.

The DSP, then, is dependent not only upon *Domei* unions but also on corporate giants for its finance, operation, and electoral campaign.[83] In a sense, we could even say that the party is doubly handicapped because it combines the disadvantages of the LDP's dependence upon corporate interests and the JSP's reliance on organized labor. The political baggage of industrial society the DSP carries seems to be very heavy indeed.

Effects of the Decline

The steadily declining fortune of the DSP has produced some demoralizing impacts upon party members, especially at the national level. For example, in the wake of the electoral setback the party suffered in the 1972 general election, the third highest official of the party—vice secretary general—who was concurrently director of the party's publications and was one of a number of DSP lower house incumbents to be defeated in the election, not only resigned from his party posts but also withdrew from the party, declaring, "Never again would I run on the DSP ticket!" While his frustration was understandable (he has since become a successful political commentator), his resignation and withdrawal from the party predictably proved demoralizing to party

82. *Asahi Shimbun*, 16 December 1962, p. 2; and *Asahi Janaru*, 4 April 1973, p. 108.

83. As an eloquent testimony to the role of corporate enterprises in the DSP: when one DSP member of the House of Councilors died a few years ago, the party was unable to field a new candidate in the deceased councilor's district because Mitsubishi Heavy Industries, from which the deceased had come, would not approve of any of the candidates the party had proposed. See *Asahi Janaru*, 20 April 1973.

leadership and membership alike. The secretary general was reported to have confided that he would not mind resigning his post, either.[84]

Another phenomenon accompanying the party's decline is the absence of fresh blood in its parliamentary membership. The DSP is by far the most aged party in the Diet. The average age of the DSP MPs in the controlling House of Representatives at the time of the 1972 election was 59.6 years in contrast to 57.2 for the gerontocratic LDP and 55.1 for the JSP. By comparison, the JCP and the CGP impart an impression of youth and vigor, with the average age of 51 (a majority below 50) for the Communists and 46 for the CGP. Eighty percent of the DSP Representatives are 51 years and older, and there are no DSP MPs below age forty. DSP MPs, as a group, therefore, obviously give the public a rather conservative, cautious, uninspiring, dull-gray impression. Perhaps it is no wonder that the party has little appeal to younger generations and women.

The DSP leadership is naturally aware of many problems and the need for revitalizing the party and expanding its base of support. But, again much like the LDP or the JSP, its desire tends to outrun its ability. For example, the 1973 convention of the DSP produced a party reconstruction plan consisting, among others, of (1) a fundamental reexamination of the current party membership and an expansion of popular bases for party support; (2) reeducation of party members, (3) strengthening and expansion of "daily activities" (*nichijo katsudo*) at the grass-roots level, and reform of party finance.[85] Unfortunately, however, these general propositions have not been translated into specific and effective programs of action. The DSP is unable to reform itself either in terms of its organization or in terms of its involvement in grass-roots problems precisely because it is a party essentially of industrial society. It is tied to special interests characteristic of the politics of industrial society, beholden for its sustenance to forces that are resistant to change in the country's transition from industrial to postindustrial society. In its organization, alliance, and institutional base of support, the DSP is a party of an era that has seen its heyday, not a party of society that is emerging. It is ironic that the physics of politics by which it is bound compels the DSP to rely more heavily upon forces of the past as its prospects in the emerging society continue to decline.

84. Ibid., p. 107.

85. *Asahi Shimbun*, 2 April 1973, p. 2.

The 1974 upper house election (the latest national-level election as of this writing) witnessed a further decline of the DSP. The DSP, indeed, was the only opposition party to lose a seat in that election. And it has continued to show a downward trend or at best stagnation of its electoral appeal in local elections since.[86] It may indeed be argued that the party is moving toward a virtual extinction as a viable political force, though its individual members may continue to receive electoral support from *Domei* unionists and through many forms of personal and social and occupational connections.

The political baggage the DSP carries is very heavy; in fact it is so heavy that the party may collapse in its journey to the politics of postindustrial Japan. It is of significance in this connection that, of the 19 DSP candidates elected to the lower house in the 1972 general elections, 10 barely made it as lowest vote-getters among elected candidates in their respective multi-member districts.[87] The future of the DSP is very uncertain indeed.

FRAGMENTED OPPOSITION

Parliamentary opposition in Japan is fragmented. This fragmentation, in terms of political balance, has more than compensated for the steady decline in popular support for the ruling LDP. With the unification of the warring factions of Socialists into the Japan Socialist party and the formation of equally fractious "conservatives" into the Liberal Democratic party in 1955, a widespread expectation rose that the nation was entering a stable era of competition between two major parties as in Britain and the United States. The era of two-party competition lasted, however, for less than five years. In 1960, a moderate faction of the JSP split to form the Democratic Socialist party, opposed to the JSP as strongly as to the LDP. By 1967, the Clean Government party had emerged in the controlling House of Representatives, both to challenge the supremacy of the ruling LDP and to seek leadership of opposition. In the meantime, the Japan Communist party, virtually forgotten after its near-

86. The DSP legislative seats declined by 14% at the village/town level, by 7% at the prefectural level, and by more than 50% at the municipal level. *Asahi Shimbun*, 23 February 1975, p. 2, and 2 May 1975, p. 4.

87. *Bessatsu Kokkai Binran: Shiryo Soshu Hen* (Tokyo: Nihon Seikei Shimbun Sha, 1975), pp. 475–89.

decimatory electoral debacle in 1952, had gradually and unobtrusively been rebuilding itself and, in 1969 general elections, suddenly caught national attention by virtually tripling its lower house representation and, three years later, repeated an identical electoral feat of almost tripling its lower house seats. The rise of the CGP and the reemergence and subsequent rise in strength of the JCP, however, were accomplished not so much at the expense of the electoral support for the LDP as at the cost of a decline in the existing opposition parties, especially the JSP, and particularly in the controlling House of Representatives. (In the less powerful House of Councilors, the growth in the strength of the JCP and the CGP has been at the expense of both the LDP and the JSP.)

Fragmentation and subsequent dissipation of the power of the opposition have had critical impact upon the quality and process of politics in Japan. This impact is becoming more apparent and critical as the nation undergoes the travail of transition from industrialism to postindustrialism.

In terms of relationship between the ruling party and opposition, it seems fair to say that the LDP continued to behave in the manner of business as usual, that is, it conducted the politics of industrial society despite rapid changes taking place in society, precisely because it felt no serious danger of effective challenge by opposition to its manner of governance. Its semipermanent supremacy was a comfortable fact effectively ensured by the opposition's fragmentation. In an important sense, the ineptitude of the opposition aided and abetted the rampant intraparty factionalism and critically hindered the ruling party from the necessary task of its reform, reappraisal of its values and methods, and of the restructuring of its policy priorities. Indeed, many LDP members, especially younger ones, believe that a concrete opposition threat to the power their party has so long monopolized is the must for its reform, reorientation, and adaptation.

Fragmentation of opposition also generated certain negative tendencies within the opposition camp, especially within the JSP. One such tendency, of course, was to intensify factionalism with the JSP with the secure knowledge that power was beyond reach, hence the party would not in the foreseeable future be called upon to shoulder the heavy responsibility that inheres in such power. The remoteness of power tends to corrupt. It effectively prevents the party from reforming itself in order to adapt to the changing environment so that it may be able to challenge the entrenched ruling party and to assume the responsibility of government. Then, too, there is this tendency on the part of the JSP and the DSP alike to seek to strengthen their ties with the institutional special-interest groups of industrial society that inhibit their task of reforming themselves and making themselves more adaptable to the emerging postindustrial environment. This tendency results from a fear of further erosion in their electoral and political strength, especially under the rising tide of the JCP and the CGP. The fear, in turn, tends to rigidify and embitter the relations among these opposition parties even further, making their mutual cooperation in challenging the ruling LDP more difficult.

The only immediate hope for any effective challenge to the ruling LDP—challenge not necessarily in terms of threatening to topple the government but rather in terms of inducing the LDP seriously and concretely to reassess its policy direction— seems to lie in a further growth in strength of the JCP and, mutatis mutandis, the CGP. As discussed, the JCP seems to be attitudinally, valuationally, organizationally, and programmatically most attuned among the five parties to the problems and requirements of the emerging postindustrial society. Formerly the party of greatest ideological intensity and political bellicosity, the JCP today gives all the impression of genuine problem-orientation and instrumental outlook. If it can maintain this impression, and the only effective way to maintain it is vigorously to practice it at the grass-roots level, the party may well attract further popular electoral support, and the pace at which it has increased its electoral strength since 1969 may foretell the extent of its future growth. The CGP, as noted, does have some serious internal problems that could negatively affect its prospects. These problems, are, on balance, less burdensome than those of the JSP. If the CGP manages to overcome them, then its growth in electoral support may well follow the pattern of the JCP's.

Any significant quantitative rise in the parliamentary and electoral strength of the JCP and, perhaps, also of the CGP would cause serious efforts on the part of the ruling LDP to reorient itself in a manner that would be more consistent with the magnitude of issues and problems of an increasingly postindustrial society. But there is more. The persistent fear of communism—justified or merely residual—on the part of the LDP and its effective constituency (e.g., the corporate world, the bureaucracy) most likely would provide an additional impetus for the party to make those necessary efforts, perhaps much sooner and with a greater unity than it otherwise would. A similar phenomenon may obtain within the JSP, precipitating the party to sever or at least weaken its ties with the leftism of *Sohyo* and the radical revolutionism of the Socialism Association, much in the same way that the CGP severed its ties with the Value Creation Society when those ties were judged to be more inhibitive than promotive of growth.

The ultimate shape parliamentary opposition would take is difficult to fathom. If what we have just said about the JCP and the CGP turns out to be generally accurate, however, certain modification of party distribution seems bound to take place, such as reorganization of opposition or even some kind of "conservative-progressive" coalition or realignment. Neither of these scenarios is entirely outlandish; both have been either advocated or quietly attempted off and on in recent years by certain sectors of different parties. Neither has thus far materialized primarily because of the persistence of the very kinds of party-constituency alignment, interparty difference and conflict, and distributive orientation that have characterized factions and parties in the politics of industrial society. Now, however, there are forces that are beginning to exert increasingly powerful pressures upon parties, ruling and opposition alike, to reexamine their respective orientations and roles and to adapt themselves to the emergent postindustrial environment. The Communists are one such force. The CGP might become another. Singly or in combination, they would help compel the LDP, and even the JSP, to change in attitude, organization, and policy direction. Other forces, however, forces that are emerging, not from the top (i.e., parliamentary parties and their pressures), but from the bottom, seem to be causing certain significant alteration in the character of politics in an ascertainable fashion and are challenging the parties to modify their aspects so they may be more consonant with the problems and requirements of the new society. We address ourselves to these forces in the next two chapters.

Part **III**
CHANGING PATTERNS
OF POPULAR
INVOLVEMENT
IN POLITICS

6

The New Mode of
Citizen Participation

POLITICAL ECOLOGY

Every political act is purposive, regardless of its apparent rationality or irrationality. Its purpose may be innovative or destructive, redressive or mediative, preventive or consolidative, depending upon the character of perception of the environment on the part of the actor. Put differently, a political act is in a very crucial sense the function of the actor's perception of his environment. The environment as he perceives it constitutes what we will call "political ecology." The political participation of citizens, be it in the form of casting a ballot, campaigning for a candidate, or otherwise acting individually or in group, violently or non-violently, constitutes a broad genre of political act. As such, it is a consequence of political ecology. The present chapter and the next examine the relationship between the change in political ecology as Japan moves from the industrial period to the emerging postindustrial era on the one hand and the shift in patterns of popular political involvement on the other.

As we indicated in chapter 1 and have reiterated repeatedly since, Japan is in transition to postindustrialism. She is yet to become fully postindustrial. She is in a transitional period in which the forces for change and those resisting change are in conflict. In short, she manifests at once many features that are characteristic of industrial society and those that are germane to the emerging postindustrial period.

During the industrial period, Japanese politics manifested varying degrees of difference in character, style, value, and mode of participation between the rural and the urban sectors. In short, the rural-urban dichotomy constituted a dimension of great significance and interest for any extensive inquiry into the politics in Japan. By and large, urban politics was viewed as modern and competitive, while rural politics was still parochial and noncompetitive. In the urban sector the "conservative" LDP was challenged by opposition parties with varying degrees of significance, but in the rural sector the LDP and its conservative allies virtually monopolized power both electorally and in policy making. With emerging postindustrialism, however, this conventional rural-urban political dichotomy seems to be increasingly overshadowed in salience by a new political dichotomy: local vs. national. The conventional rural-urban dichotomy has come to be eroded steadily by the material leveling effects of economic growth and prosperity and all that they entail, as we discussed in chapters 2 and 3. As one of the consequences of these leveling effects, the "conservative" domination of the rural sector is, as we discuss in some detail in the next chapter, ascertainably declining. The new local-national political dichotomy, instead, is gaining in salience precisely because of the rising relevance of certain differences in political ecology between the two levels. These differences are causing significant variations in patterns of citizen participation in the political arena between the local and the national levels.

We posit ten specific dimensions to political ecology. They are: (1) material dimension, (2) demographic dimension, (3) social cleavage, (4) constitutional arrangement, (5) participatory logistics, (6) institutional constraints, (7) role of parties, (8) role of organized interests, (9) ideological dimensions, and (10) cultural and attitudinal dimensions. These dimensions are conceptually separable, though they variously converge and overlap with one another in reality. These dimensions vary from the local to the national level, and, even at the local level, there is a considerable variation among areas, reflecting uneven paces of change from industrialism to postindustrialism. Since we are concerned about salient changes in Japanese politics, we shall focus on those areas of the political map at the local level where the type of ecology that more clearly suggests Japan's transition from industrialism to postindustrialism is readily ascertainable.

POSTINDUSTRIAL POLITICAL ECOLOGY

Material Dimension

The reader can infer from our preceding discussions that novelty of political ecology in Japan is the result of the cumulative effects of modern industrialism. The singleminded, entirely suprapartisan national pursuit of economic recovery, growth, and prosperity of the postwar era produced a range of quite unintended consequences while catapulting the nation into economic superstardom. Achievement of profuse affluence was accompanied by widespread environmental pollution and destruction, acute urban congestion, and many other ills of advanced industrial society; in short, the politicization of the costs of modern industrialism. These costs are significant in themselves, but within the context of our discussion their importance lies in their political ramifications. These costs had existed before, as we noted in chapter 3, but had produced little political impact. During the industrial period, people were entirely concerned with acquisition of material benefits of industrialism, and viewed those costs of industrialism largely as "inevitable." Their perception has changed considerably since. These costs of modern industrialism came to be regarded as "unacceptable." Hence their politicization.

Acute visibility of these costs was one cause for their politicization. There was another: their cross-stratal impact. The material leveling effect brought about by rising economic growth, prosperity, and affluence gradually led to an equalization of susceptibility of various groups of the population to negative externalities represented by those costs. The impact of these costs became less and less differential. Hence the popular perception that these costs are "unacceptable" cuts across conventional socioeconomic and ideological cleavages.

The level of politicization of the costs of modern industrialism differs from area to area, but even where it is high, the desire for more benefits from modern industrialism persists. The conventional distributive politics of industrial society therefore continues, but is now increasingly challenged by the rising redressive and preventive politics of postindustrial society. There is a pervasive air of popular ambivalence regarding the benefits and costs of industrialism, for these two issues—one old and the other new—often seem to call for mutually exclusive or contradictory means of resolution.

Demographic Dimension

One of the more significant demographic features of Japan today is that she is, as we noted in chapter 2, in many ways not merely an urban but a metropolitan society. Her population density is six times that of Holland. In many parts of the nation, population mobility is very high, affecting the traditional fabric of community. A majority of labor is absorbed by tertiary economy. And the increasing dominance of the tertiary sector suggests that the Japanese economy is becoming both white-collar and knowledge-intensive, where the number as well as the importance of well-educated professionals rise. Reflecting this trend, university enrollment nearly quadrupled in the twenty-five years since 1950, and the better-educated are found in more urban and metropolitan areas because of greater job opportunities and more varied cultural activities there. One-half of the population is within the 15–44 range in age, suggesting an increasing prevalence of "postwar," more democratic and egalitarian, and as we observed in chapter 2, less acquisitive value orientation.

Social Cleavage

Japan is free from regional, cultural, linguistic, racial, or religious cleavages. The fact that today 90 percent of the people consider themselves middle class seems to suggest general lack of social or class antagonism as well. This perceptual trend, of course, was greatly enhanced by the material leveling effects that advanced industrialism brought about in postwar decades. There are few very rich and few very poor in the nation. Revolutionary ideologies never had a significant popular appeal in Japan, and whatever level of public appeal Marxism once had, it has since declined ascertainably, even among labor.[1] At least in

1. See, for example, Robert E. Cole, "Japanese Workers, Unions, and the Marxist Appeal," *Japan Interpreter* 6 (Summer 1970); Koichiro Kuwata, "Political Parties in the Next Decade," *Japan Quarterly* 17 (April–June

the conventional sense of the term, therefore, Japan is a very stable society. New cleavages may be emerging, however, as in many other advanced industrial societies, e.g., involving the status of women, welfare recipients, senior citizens; and the rise in intensity of status politics (see pp. 51–53) tends to bear this suspicion out. Their salience, however, seems relatively delimited.

Constitutional Arrangement

Inasmuch as government in Japan is representative and not direct, the ordinary citizen's most permanent and consistent form of participation in policy making is indirect and formal: voting. Voting, while having its own normative value, tends, however, to be ritualistic insofar as actual policy making is concerned. Whether it expresses an expectation of policy making or approval of it after the fact, it has somewhat remote impact at the point of decision making. In order to have an effective and ascertainable bearing upon the point of policy making, that is, upon what policy is made and how, what we call effective or substantive participation is warranted. This is not to say that citizens or groups of citizens should sit where policy is being made and watch what policy makers say and how they behave. All it means is that voters, in order to exert an effective and ascertainable influence upon policy making, should not only know who or which of the policy makers is accountable for a given policy or a given set of policies, but also possess effective means to hold him accountable. The policy maker's accountability is the electorate's power.

There are some constitutionally prescribed methods by which citizens may engage themselves in substantive participation at different levels and in different directions. For example, the chief executive (mayor or governor) is popularly elected, not selected by the assembly. This enables voters, if sufficient numbers of them so desire and demonstrate their desire effectively, to link their electoral votes for the chief executive with what he does by way of policy making. If he does not deliver as he is expected, popular support may be withdrawn in the next election. He thus can be held popularly accountable with clarity, while the same cannot be said of individual assemblymen because of their number involved in legislative enactment where accountability is

1970); and Gerald L. Curtis, "The 1969 General Election in Japan," *Asian Survey* 10 (October 1970).

dispersed. Actual payoffs for determined popular action are direct and ascertainable.

Then, too, the constitutional arrangement permits voters to engage in substantive participation in policy making both at the administration and at the legislation. They are allowed to do so by way of "direct demands," i.e., (1) demand for legislation or legislative revision, (2) demand for investigation of conduct of the administration or any part thereof, (3) demand for the dissolution of the assembly, and (4) demand for recall of elected officials or other high-level government officials. When sufficient numbers of voters are aroused, they are constitutionally permitted to take the matter in their own hands, and exert direct impact upon policy making. In short, if they so choose, citizens are legally provided with recourse to substantive participation.

Participatory Logistics

The constitutional arrangement, however open or benign, would be of little value if citizens are not afforded appropriate logistical correlates. Do citizens enjoy an adequate degree of physical and psychological ease of access to the arena of relevant political action? Do they have available appropriate tools and methods for such action? A citizen cannot take his grievance to an appropriate authority if that authority is beyond his reach, for example. At the local level, however, there is considerable logistical ease and facility for popular participation, and the past economic advance has much to do with it. People are no longer living from hand to mouth, from hard day to hard day of the struggle for livelihood. They have more leisure, more money, better transportation, be it private or public, better communication, and constant flows of pertinent information. The arena of effective participation, say the mayor's office, an assemblyman's home, the city hall, or as has become quite common, the street, is within easy reach. Not only is there ease of communication between citizens and officials, there is also ease of mutual understanding, an essential ingredient of effective communication. Officials, elected or appointed, are residents of the locality and thus are more sensitive toward and understanding of citizens' concerns and problems than if they lived elsewhere.

At this level, it is also relatively easy for concerned citizens to seek out others with a similar or identical concern, and inasmuch as they are residents, neighbors, of the same locality, a sense of solidarity and an identity of interest are easy to engender. Their mutual physical proximity enables effective cooperation and coordination of their activities. Additionally, the kind of substantive participation concerned citizens want to engage in can often be undertaken within the range of financial costs that is manageable without dependence upon the self-interested generosity of special interests.

Thus, combined with the constitutional arrangement that is promotive of citizen involvement in effective political action, logistical ease at the local level tends to enhance the capacity for substantive popular participation.

Institutional Constraints

Political institutions such as assembly and bureaucracy are designed to process popular demands and societal needs for purposes of rational policy making. Their existence is functional and not intrinsic. Yet, as we noted in chapter 1, they tend to develop their own institutional imperatives and organizational inertia which militate against their original function and inhibit their adaptive capability. In short, they become insensitive and unresponsive to their fundamental task.

The government bureaucracy at the local level depends for its operation very much upon the financial support and guidance of the national government, the principle of local autonomy notwithstanding. It has often been said that local government is only one-third autonomous because it relies on national government for two-thirds of its funds. This phenomenon has resulted in a collusion of institutional self-interests between the national and local government bureaucracies whereby intra- as well as interbureaucratic politics tends to take precedence over the local bureaucracy's adaptation to the changing environment and effective management of issues and problems of popular concern. Local administrators are eager to stay in the good graces of national bureaucrats upon whose discretion hinges much of their funds. Bureaucratic secrecy is one of the inevitable concomitants. Another is the local administrators' sensitivity to preferences and priorities at the national level rather than to issues and problems that concern local citizens. Under the circumstances, the influence of those few powerful special interests whose preference coincides with policy and program priorities of the national and/or local bureaucrats rises at the expense of public interest.

All this suggests two critical phenomena: dominance of

national preferences over local, and a growing distance between the citizenry and their local government. Conventional popular political input activities such as voting and petition designed to protect popular sovereignty over local government and meant to be effective under normal circumstances become less and less efficacious, and the public begins to perceive them as such. Frustration and subsequent alienation reduce people's willingness to use those normal means and increase their willingness to resort to unconventional methods as well as constitutionally permitted means of substantive participation.

Role of Parties

Here we are concerned about the degree to which parties are developed and effective in terms of organizational infrastructure and integrative and mobilization capacities. Political parties should exist as major vehicles for mobilizing and organizing voters for electoral purpose and aggregating their interests for rational policy making. Their ability at the local level, however, seems rather low in this regard. Their development has been asymmetric: they are relatively developed and organized at the national level for electoral purposes, but are much less developed at the local level. The major reason for this, as noted in the preceding two chapters, is that they were formed at the national level by notables, strictly for electoral ends. None of the parties is a mass party or mass-based. While these parties maintain some semblances of local branches, their growth, as we noted in chapters 4 and 5, is variously inhibited. Briefly summarized:

The LDP at the local level is in effect a congeries of individual MPs' respective personal support clubs with intense mutual rivalry, with the result that party branches exist only in name. Members of these support clubs are loyal not to the LDP but to their respective patron MPs. Moreover, they belong to these clubs, not necessarily because of ideological conviction or policy preference, but rather because of their personal ties, connections, or relations with the MPs concerned or with other club members.

The JSP is just as intensely factionalized at the local as at the national level. Its branches are dominated by local members of contending *Sohyo* unions who constantly engage in internecine rivalry among themselves and by activists of the Socialism Society who are viewed with dislike and fear by many unionists.

These people are more concerned about their mutual internal factional political struggle than about developing effective grass-roots organizations.

The JCP and the CGP are showing some important signs of adaptation to the changing environment, as we discussed in chapter 5. In the past, however, both parties suffered from a number of strategic and tactical mistakes as well as residual popular antipathy and mistrust, which in combination kept them from posing serious challenge to the ruling LDP.

The DSP, the now minuscule remnant of the grouping of moderate socialists that seceded from the JSP in 1960, is too small and too closely tied to *Domei* to develop grass-roots strength.

Role of Organized Interests

This dimension focuses on the extent to which organized groups are capable of dominating or monopolizing substantive participation, while leaving the citizenry with only formal participation. Where participatory logistics are unfavorable to ordinary people, special interests dominate substantive participation and have greater direct impact upon policy making. Where they are favorable to ordinary citizens, organized interests' ability for substantive participation will be correspondingly reduced. Thus, special interests (e.g., corporate interests, *Sohyo*, the Socialism Association, to cite but a few) are very powerful at the national level where popular participatory logistics are inadequate apart from formal participation. At the local level, their influence is considerably weakened when voters resort to substantive participation. Insofar as citizens do in fact engage in substantive participation, special interests become "minorities." Because of the politicization of costs of modern industrialism, moreover, special interests with their inevitable roots in industrialism are prima facie suspect in the eyes of concerned citizens, and their attempt to exert influence over policy making in the face of challenge from citizens' substantive participation tends to energize the latter even more, thus further weakening their own influence.

Ideological Dimensions

Patterns of perception of issues as well as of participation are significantly influenced by whether and to what extent ideological conflict plays a role in the political arena. Intensity of ideological conflict tends to repress or inhibit instrumental orientation of popular participation, formal or substantive. Conversely, a decline in such intensity or salience encourages instrumental orientation on the part of political actors. They become problem-oriented. Also, if salience of ideological struggle is great, popular participation is likely to be channeled or mobilized through or by competing parties. Such participation when instrumentally oriented, however, may bypass parties if they insist on ideological politics.

In our discussion of opposition parties, we noted the decline in ideological politics in Japan. Perhaps the most important cause for the decline is certain cumulative consequences of modern industrialism. Apart from the economic leveling effect produced by advancing industrial growth and prosperity, which in itself would tend to reduce the level of ideological intensity, the politicization of the costs of industrialism played a very significant role in the decline of ideological politics. As mentioned, the costs became increasingly cross-stratal in impact, that is, they are indifferent to ideological distinction of victims. As these costs become more politicized, citizens develop a community of interest across conventional socioeconomic and ideological cleavages that separated them from one another and that used to be the motive for partisan ideological conflict. Instead, they seek concrete and effective solutions to the problems by which they are commonly disturbed. Ideological politics is being replaced by instrumental politics. People now seek, not ideological distinction or authenticity, but rather pragmatic options and solutions. Parties that insist on ideological politics (e.g., the JSP) further weaken their position because concerned citizens bypass them as meaningful and effective vehicles for popular mobilization and participation, and attempt to devise their own mobilizational and participatory means.

Cultural and Attitudinal Dimensions

How and to what extent citizens engage in formal or substantive political participation is determined in a significant sense by the pattern of expectation regarding the role of government and the distribution of salient political referents and behavioral inhibitions among them. Again, there is a significant shift in Japan in this dimension.

We briefly referred in chapter 3 to the revolution of rising expectations among citizens regarding what and how much government ought to do for them, and explored some causes for the phenomenon. It has indeed produced some interesting ramifications to the problem of popular participation. Since people demand more, they naturally participate more actively. And there is more.

Rapid urbanization and rising mobility in the 1950s and 1960s undermined many traditional political referents and behavioral inhibitions. The impersonality of urban life and subsequent decline in the sense of community among neighbors, and the growing instrumental orientation induced by the politicization of the costs of industrialism, among others, combined to reduce the efficacy of such traditional properties of interpersonal and social relations (as discussed toward the end of chapter 2) that used to determine the political behavior of citizens. Simultaneously, generational metabolism in value and attitude began to manifest itself, whereby more and more citizens are said to be egalitarian, less trusting toward formal authority. As a consequence, people are less awed by such traditional authority referents as age, lineage, wealth, institutional credentials (e.g., a Tokyo University diploma, a career in government service), and social standing. Conversely, they are more willing to voice their views and grievances and are more inclined toward voluntary political participation.

Then, too, there is an important change in the general outlook or psychological propensity of the Japanese people. We are not proposing to engage in any kind of "national character" study here, but it was often suggested in the past by competent authorities that the Japanese tended to rely on some "trend" or "tendency" that was presumed to be somehow natural or inevitable. Haga, in this connection, spoke of a typical Japanese expression, *nariyuki* (a matter running its own natural course, or a situation developing itself in its own way), and suggested that the Japanese really did not accept the thesis that the course of development of a matter or a situation was determined by human will and intervention.[2] Shinohara cited a number of examples of this "reliance on trends" orientation even among political leaders. For instance, when the late Premier Hayato

2. Yasushi Haga, *Gendai Seiji no Choryu* (Tokyo: Ningen no Kagaku Sha, 1975), pp. 130–31. We may suggest that another typical Japanese expression, *shikata ga nai* (it cannot be helped, or, there is nothing we can do about it) is consistent with the above observation.

Ikeda was promoting the famous "income-doubling" idea early in the 1960s, he was not saying, "We will double our income," but rather, "Our income will double." Leaders of opposition parties, in their statements during election campaigns, also indicated their habitual reliance, at once unwarranted, passive, and wishful, upon certain unclarified "trends" or "tendencies" (*nariyuki*), which they would invariably interpret in their favor.[3] Perhaps leaders of opposition parties are still hopeful that their parties will win the next election, and the LDP members still think that the "trend" (*nariyuki*) is in their favor. Citizens, however, seem increasingly less passive and less wishful in their thinking. Consider, for instance, the shift in their perception of pollution from "inevitable" to "intolerable." This shift is very significant, and has some important implications to patterns of political participation.

VOTING AS POPULAR PARTICIPATION

There are two general types of political participation for citizens: formal and substantive. Voting is a formal act, performed as a means of expressing either an expectation of policy making or an approval of such policy making after the fact, insofar as it is, however vaguely, purposive. It is difficult to tell the quality of this mode of participation; that is, this mode of formal participation generates little more than statistical information: what proportion of the electorate voted; how many votes this candidate or that party received; what percentage of which group of voters voted for what party; and so forth. Election statistics, of course, normally reinforce our common-sense understanding of the politics of industrial society, which is largely distributive: those people who do not like higher taxes and more spending on welfare and social services generally vote conservative; those whose views are opposite tend to vote progressive or left. And then there are groups in between. Which party any given group or aggregate of voters tends to support can easily be told even before the voting if we understand the pattern of the politics in industrial society and voter motivations in it. As for nonvoters, we are given to assume that they are more likely to be either apolitical or generally satisfied with things as they are.

3. Hajime Shinohara, *Nihon no Seiji Fudo* (Tokyo: Iwanami, 1971), pp. 34–35.

That makes sense in industrial society. But would the same view hold in postindustrial society? Throughout the preceding chapters, we have suggested that people in Japan are becoming frustrated with things as they are and disaffected with parties and politics because of their obvious lack of adaptability to the changing environment. Yet, when we look at election statistics, people vote much as they did. There is little difference in this sense between Japan today and Japan yesterday. The rates of electoral participation in recent national elections were as high as those in earlier years held during the era of rising economic growth and of national agreement on the desirability of continuous material advances.

Moreover, voter participation in local elections has increased sharply, especially in metropolitan and urban districts and prefectures. A most dramatic example of such rise in voter participation was seen in Tokyo's gubernatorial election in the spring of 1971[4]; since then, a majority of prefectures experienced significant and continued increase in electoral participation in local elections. How, then, do we explain the voter disaffection we have so often referred to?

The "Disengaged-from-Parties"

In an interesting contrast to the steady or even rising rates of voting is a continuous rise in the size of what came to be called *datsu seito* ("the disengaged-from-parties" or "disengaged from party identification") within the electorate. These are, as the term suggests, voters who no longer identify themselves with any party. The "disengaged" are not comparable to what we have in the past understood as "independent" voters in the United States. Of course, one reason for this is the difference in party system in general and in the nature of party competition in particular between the two nations. And this can be explained only by reference to divergent patterns of political development and growth of parties and party competition between the two. We shall, however, not engage in any historical recounting of the different patterns of development in Japan and in America in this volume. Suffice it, for our current purpose, to observe that independent voters in America remain neutral between the

---

4. For this trend, see Taketsugu Tsurutani, "A New Era of Japanese Politics: Tokyo's Gubernatorial Election," *Asian Survey* 12 (May 1972).

two major parties, not because they are dissatisfied with or alienated from either, but rather because the parties are so much alike (unlike in Japan) and because the independents wish to retain options of supporting one or the other of the parties inasmuch as the only difference between the two concerns the matter of *how* rather than *what*. Independents in America, therefore, are more or less problem-oriented. In Japan, however, "disengaged" voters are disgruntled with and alienated from existing political parties. They see no positive choice between one party and another, between the ruling Liberal Democratic party on the one hand and opposition parties on the other. If they see any choice, it is in a negative sense of "which party is less undesirable than others?" A considerable proportion of these "disengaged" voters obviously vote for a variety of reasons, some of which we shall explain in the next paragraph. Thus, the attitude of the "disengaged" voters in Japan today is considerably different from that of the independent voters in the United States as we have understood them in the past.

From table 6.1, we can readily see that the voter turnout in general elections in Japan is higher than that in the United States. In local elections, it is still higher (75–95 percent). This should not be too puzzling. Voters in Japan, as many students of Japanese politics and society have noted, have traditionally been

TABLE 6.1 RATES OF VOTER PARTICIPATION

Lower House Elections		Upper House Elections	
Year	Percentage	Year	Percentage
1946	72.08	1947	60.93
1947	67.95	1950	72.10
1949	74.04	1953	63.18
1952	76.43	1956	62.10
1953	74.22	1959	58.74
1955	75.84	1962	68.21
1958	76.99	1965	67.02
1960	73.51	1968	68.94
1963	71.14	1971	59.30
1967	73.99	1974	73.20
1969	68.51		
1972	71.76		

Source: *Nihon Tokei Nenkan Showa 48–49 Nen* (Tokyo: Sorifu Tokei Kyoku, 1974), p. 754; *Asahi Shimbun*, 28 June 1971, p. 2; and *Asahi Janaru*, 19 July 1974, p. 12.

imbued with a strong sense of duty to vote[5] (in a sense, we might say that they are not quite as blasé about politics as Americans because democracy is relatively new in Japan), and this sense was in the past enhanced and strengthened by social pressure of their groups and communities. "Communities," noted Kyogoku and Ike, "often compete to see which one can achieve the highest voting rate."[6] They make sure that even the sick and the infirm cast their ballot. There is also the consideration of residual behavior discussed earlier (see pp. 37–38). People are so accustomed to voting regularly that they continue to do so, albeit with a declining sense of efficacy and expectation. This is what Touraine calls "dependent participation,"[7] that is, performing a participatory ritual, though increasingly irrelevant, precisely because the continuity of the existing arrangement and its myths require it. This can be inferred from a variety of survey reports.

A survey conducted by the Ministry of Autonomy (*Jichi Sho*) and the semigovernmental Fair Elections Commission (*Komei Senkyo Renmei*) shortly before the general election of November 1972 indicated that 45 percent of respondents aged 20 and older and 79 percent of those aged 16–19 did not support any party.[8] Yet 72 percent of the electorate voted in that election. And, naturally, all the parties received more votes than they deserved, as it were, according to opinion polls. Another study showed that, long before 1972, "disengaged" voters as a proportion of the electorate had increased drastically between 1960 and 1972 in all relevant age groups: from 19 to 38 percent for the 20–29 group; 12 to 30 percent for the 30–39 group; 11 to 26 percent for the 40–49 group; and 17 to 29 percent for those 50 years of age and older.[9] These are rather drastic changes by any reckoning. Figures, of course, vary from survey to survey, but

5. Hajime Shinohara, *Nihon no Seiji Fudo* (Tokyo: Iwanami, 1971), pp. 52–53.

6. Jun'ichi Kyogoku and Nobutaka Ike, *Urban-Rural Differences in Voting Behavior in Postwar Japan* (Stanford University Political Science Series No. 66, 1959), p. 12.

7. Alain Touraine, *The Post-Industrial Society: Tomorrow's Social History*, trans. Leonard F. X. Mayhew (New York: Random House, 1971), p. 9.

8. *Asahi Shimbun*, 10 September 1973, p. 2.

9. Joji Watanuki, "Japanese Politics in Flux," *Prologue to the Future: The United States and Japan in the Postindustrial Age* (Lexington, Mass.: Heath, 1974), p. 74. Also see *Shimin Ishiki no Kenkyu: Suri Kenkyu Ripoto 31* (Tokyo: Tokei Suri Kenkyu Jo, 1973), p. 56.

considerable consistency prevails through surveys. Today, the "disengaged" account for more than one-third of the electorate by the most conservative estimates, thus surpassing in size the supporters of the ruling LDP, or of all opposition parties combined. This sector of the electorate consists of two subcategories, explicitly antiparty and nonparty, and it is significant that the increase in the "disengaged" sector has been caused by a radical growth in the explicitly antiparty voters. The size of this subcategory nearly doubled between 1967 and 1972.[10] And, as the reader by now probably expects, the phenomenon of the "disengagement" is more pronounced in urban and metropolitan areas that are more seriously affected by ill consequences of modern industrialism. It is noteworthy, also, that this phenomenon is manifesting itself simultaneously with the rise in electoral participation in these same areas.

In connection with the "disengagement" phenomenon, we might mention briefly that even partisan voters have developed less positive views of the parties they claim to support, clearly reflecting a tendency that gave rise to the "disengagement." A recent nationwide voter survey showed that the largest proportion of the LDP supporters said they supported the party because "other parties are no good." An essentially identical phenomenon was observed among the supporters of the opposition JSP ("the LDP is no good"). The second largest proportions of both the LDP and the JSP supporters could cite *no specific reasons* for their party support, thus giving credence to the ideas of dependent participation and residual behavior.[11] In an important sense, the "disengagement" phenomenon seems only the tip of a large iceberg of voter disenchantment and frustration with the political parties.

The "disengagement" phenomenon, especially when viewed in combination with the clear lack of positive reasons for party support among partisan voters, seems to suggest that, while election statistics as such have not manifested any significant divergence from the past, voting behavior today is quite different from the 1950s and most of the 1960s in motivation and in dynamics. This observation will be corroborated by an inquiry into changes in the second type of popular political participation in Japan today: substantive popular participation.

10. *Asahi Shimbun*, 26 June 1971, and 8 and 9 December 1972.

11. *Japan Opinion Poll January 1975* (Delray Beach, Fla.: Ross Snyder & Son, January 1975), n.d.

SUBSTANTIVE POPULAR PARTICIPATION: A CHANGING PATTERN

The typical activity in the area of substantive participation in modern industrial society is interest-group activity, with "interest" conventionally defined as economic and occupational (though other types also exist, such as ideological, avocational, and the like, but they are not the major kinds), and such activity is indeed the most highlighted input function performed in modern industrial society on the basis largely of economic cleavages and interests and competition among them. This input activity is presumed to be crucial to policy making. Groups articulate their respective interests and demands, to enhance their respective material and associated well-being. In an important sense, it is mostly these groups that engage in effective and substantive participation in policy making in industrial society. It is no exaggeration, in fact, to say that they monopolize the arena of substantive participation. The pattern of interaction we observed between the LDP and the corporate interests in chapter 4 is the paradigmatic example of substantive participation by organized interests in policy making. Groups lobby legislators and parties; they also lobby bureaucrats, for both legislation and implementation are highly discretionary, discriminate, and selective. The role of interest groups is therefore crucial for the ways in which the benefits of industrialism—in the forms of subsidies, tax policies, regulations of business and industrial activities, welfare programs, and a whole spectrum of fiscal, monetary, and income policies—are to be distributed through legislation (by the parliament) and implementation (by the bureaucracy). Ordinary citizens as such cannot really compete with these groups in the arena of substantive participation. Or at least they could not in Japan during the period of industrialism. Interest groups thus conceptually constitute a vital stratum in the whole structure of the policy-making process. And both political actors and political scientists have long felt that such patterns of interaction between government and society are appropriate and functional to a modern industrial state's rational decision making and generative of maximum benefits for all concerned as well as of political stability and order. In comparative politics, especially, the input function performed by the groups and the presumably smooth interaction between the groups and government have long been regarded as one important indicator of maturity and modernity of political systems, which less modern, less mature nations would be well advised to emulate. The rise of postindustrialism, however, may compel some serious questioning of this conventional notion.

One of the major features of postindustrial society is the politicization of the costs of modern industrialism. These costs include not only environmental pollution and urban congestion, but also a variety of distributive distortions during the period of rapid growth, such as the neglect of the matter of social capital. The politics of industrial society is dominated by organized interests that are economic in character and objective with all that it implies in terms of attitude and values. Existing institutions, public or private, are capable of acting only when their particular interests and preferences are involved and resistant to action in matters that are outside the purview of their material considerations or basic organizational imperatives. Thus, issues and problems for which organized interests have no inherent concern remain untended. Those interests that are substantive participants in policy making in industrial society want the government to do only what would maintain or increase their shares of the benefits of industrialism. In short, the pattern of substantive popular participation characteristic of industrial society is incapable of dealing with postindustrial problems.

Political parties, in the meantime, demonstrate an equally industrialism-bound inability effectively to mobilize citizens to cope with those postindustrial problems precisely because of their industrial origin, hence character, and their ties with those interest groups, as we observed in chapters 4 and 5. Ordinary citizens, when they become sufficiently aroused by new issues and problems, find themselves having to devise their own ways and means to seek effective participation so as to compel policy makers and policy-making organs to deal with those issues and problems. In short, there emerges an increasingly impatient urge among citizens to bypass parties in their expression of concern with things as they are.

Citizens' Movements

The lack of sufficient adaptive capability on the part of political parties in general and the monopoly of the arena of substantive popular participation by conventional interest groups eventually prompted ordinary citizens concerned with postindustrial problems to devise methods that would effectively generate popular participation and induce meaningful change in the status quo. The most widespread and, in more senses than one, novel and dramatic method thus devised came to be commonly called "citizens' movements" (*jumin undo*).[12] In the words of the authoritative *Chuokoron*, "the heightening of citizens' desire for political participation [through citizens' movements] . . . was precipitated by a lowering of their expectations toward political parties."[13] This novel mode of participation was compelled by the rising popular awareness of, to quote one Japanese expert on citizens' movements, "certain of the consequences of the rapid postwar industrialization and urbanization, and distortions created by various measures regarding those consequences."[14] The citizens' movement, in short, arose to fill a structural and processual vacuum created by the lack of adaptive capability on the part of the very instruments—parties to mobilize, organize, and represent concerned citizens in the formal arena of policy making in postindustrial society.

Participants in the Citizens' Movement

The very nature of the problems and the character of circumstances that gave rise to the citizens' movement had

12. *Jumin undo* is alternatively called *shimin undo*. These two terms, however, denote two generically distinct genres of popular political movement. *Shimin undo* emerged in the mid-1950s as a broad protest movement against the American nuclear experiments on the Bikini atoll of 1954 and therefrom developed into a generalized antinuclear-arms movement. Similar *shimin undo* were also organized to promote certain ideological concerns such as defense of democracy (against the latently antidemocratic tendencies of the LDP and other reactionary forces in society), the protection of fundamental human rights such as freedoms of speech and assembly (again, against certain vague "fascistic tendencies" in government and society). In the latter half of the 1960s, the escalation of the Vietnam war prompted another *shimin undo* protesting the war and giving aid and comfort to GI deserters. Thus, *shimin undo* as a genre of political movement was by and large motivated by conventional right-left, conservative-progressive, pro-American-anti-American ideological divisions. *Jumin undo,* which is the citizens' movement discussed in this volume, is supraideological, suprapartisan, local, areal, and concerned with concrete problems and issues that affect citizens daily, hence instrumentally oriented.

13. "Shakaito ron wa naze fumo ka," *Chuokoron*, November 1970, p. 39.

14. Ritsuo Akimoto, "Jumin Undo no Shokeitai," in *Jumin Sanka to Jichi no Kakushin*, ed Haruo Matsubara (Tokyo: Gakuyo Shobo, 1975), p. 138.

significant influences upon the organizational, operational, and behavioral features of the movement. In a typical case, the movement is formed in a specific locale and composed of volunteer activists from among its residents, with a wide-ranging occupational and socioeconomic spectrum, many of whom would never before have associated or worked together. In other words, movement membership is cross-stratal, reflecting the cross-stratal nature of the impact of issues and problems that gave rise to the movement. The particular nature of a given type of problems peculiar to a particular set of circumstances (e.g., industrial society or postindustrial society) calls for a particular kind of response appropriate to its solution. The cross-stratal nature of postindustrial problems calls for cross-stratal approaches to their solution. This combination of the specific set of circumstances (postindustrial society) and the particular nature of problems (cross-stratal) or popular perception thereof erode traditional barriers among various social groups and strata that have in the past inhibited the rise of mutuality of interest among them. The citizens' movement provides entirely novel milieus in which members of those hitherto or still largely "closed components," motivated by an increasingly acute common concern and objective, attempt to cooperate on terms of mutual equality. These people are finding that they can indeed work together and that the degree of their mutual cooperation and common effort is ascertainably related to the extent of their common effectiveness in the political arena.

Volunteer activists of the movement are mainly "middle Japanese" both in socioeconomic status and age, and not members of fringe groups who are historically and developmentally known to engage in unconventional political activities. (For details on these activists, see pp. 196–97.) Of particular interest, women (housewives, mothers of school-age children) participate in noticeable numbers—a phenomenon unknown in organized interests characteristic of industrial society. Another significant aspect of the movement is that it enjoys wide support and considerable participation of another traditionally apolitical or politically less active group: the young. Indeed, opinion surveys suggest that the young view the citizens' movement much more favorably as an effective form of political input activity than their elders; this possibly indicates a trend toward further growth of the movement in the future.[15]

15. See, for example, *Shimin Ishiki no Kenkyu*, pp. 63–65.

Estimates of the number of citizens' movements range from 1,400 to over 3,000. The size of membership differs from one situation to another. One recent survey indicated that approximately 54 percent of such movements had memberships of fewer than 500.[16] The relative smallness of the membership is obviously owing to the fact that most citizens' movements are locally organized, as mentioned. Many of these movements seek support from one another as well as from other nonmainstream groups such as senior citizens, nurses' associations, medical student groups, and scientists for purposes of exchange of information, mutual support, and so forth. Another common feature of these movements is what one recent investigator called "rejective response to established organizations."[17] This relates back to the problem of institutional constraints and distributive self-interests of organized groups formed along lines of conventional socioeconomic and occupational differentiation.

Activists and Leaders of the Citizens' Movement

Changes in political ecology, hence changes in the pattern of political participation, bring about change in the character or type of political participants, especially core activists and leaders. Among activists of the citizens' movement, we find noticeable numbers of people who would conventionally be regarded as politically quiescent or nonactive: housewives, mothers of schoolchildren, retirees, the young, newcomers, and middle-class professionals. These are people who would not be strongly or centrally involved in the distributive politics of industrial society. This is not to say, of course, that they are not interested in it or have no stake in it. What we mean is simply that they are not the direct or central participants in the politics of industrial society in which organized economic interests are the major actors. Members of the citizens' movement are actors in a new kind of politics: the preventive and redressive politics of postindustrial society; and their concern cuts across lines of economic and occupational differentiation along which those special interests of industrial politics are formed.

Core activists and leaders of the movement tend to be highly educated, white-collar, professional—lawyers, teachers, engineers, sometimes even local civil servants—in short, members

16. *Asahi Shimbun*, 21 May 1973, p. 4.

17. Akimoto, "Jumin Undo no Sho-keitai," p. 141.

of the tertiary economic sector. They are in their thirties and early forties. Those over forty-five years of age are relatively small in number and frequently play certain "symbolic roles"; those under thirty generally serve as subleaders.[18] One very surprising phenomenon: core activists and leaders of the citizens' movement are relative newcomers to the locality.

In conventional Japanese politics, activists and leaders in the locality are long-term residents, well known in the area by virtue of their lineage or wealth, their community status established over time, and with social and economic influence. And they form leader-follower relations with other residents of the locality in the manner discussed in chapter 4. Why the change, then?

The change has been brought about by certain consequences of the years of rapid demographic mobility and transformation precipitated by the policy of high economic growth. It was once estimated that the city of Yokohama, for example, experienced an annual gross population movement of 400,000 (250,000 in and 150,000 out), signifying, at least as a theoretical probability, a complete renewal of its population every six years. In one sense, therefore, it is out of sheer metabolic necessity that political activism gradually shifts to newcomers.

Second, because of the phenomenon of residual behavior combined with the potency of conventional political referents and behavioral inhibitions, long-term residents tend to continue to act according to those referents and inhibitions. They have difficulties adapting themselves to the changing environment with ease and dispatch. Their behavior is largely influenced by the existing, that is, conventional patterns of interpersonal and social relationships in the community. In contrast, newcomers, especially better-educated and more sophisticated newcomers, could not be politically active if they were to honor those conventional referents and inhibitions that would require them to be deferential to the local elders and notables and to local mores and the power structure. They are, however, too politicized and concerned to be restrained by those referents and inhibitions. In short, they are not bound by those constraints.

Newcomers who engage in political activism are professional, well-educated, and in their thirties, which means they

18. Hiroshi Satake, "Elections and Citizens' Movements in Japan," *Annals of the Japanese Political Science Association 1974* (Tokyo: Iwanami, 1975), p. 192.

have young children and are therefore sensitized to the problems of education, environment, traffic congestion, and other issues. They are just settling down in their permanent homes, which they have chosen for educational, professional, and cultural reasons. They get more easily aroused by local inequities, institutional irrationalities, and environmental and other problems than the locals because they are neither accustomed to them nor acquiescent toward conditions that they find much less to their expectation. Voter surveys show that newcomers are highly critical of the performance of local government, for example, while long-term residents are likely to be satisfied with or acquiescent in it.[19] In both concern and behavior, therefore, newcomers are far more attuned and adaptable to the new political ecology than long-time residents, and they are less hesitant to engage in the new mode of political participation than the others.

The new mode of political participation exemplified by the citizens' movement is more pronounced in areas where tertiary-sector employees are more numerous. This kind of activism is seldom found, especially as to the activist and leadership stratum, among primary-sector employees. Tertiary-sector employees, especially professionals and intellectuals, not only take active parts in the citizens' movement but also add to the movement's much needed professional and scientific expertise and knowledge as well as intellectual and organizational sophistication.[20] And by their uninhibited activism, they help politicize long-term residents and energize many of them into the citizens' movement.

Activities of the Citizens' Movement

In strategic and tactical dimensions, features of the citizens' movement should perhaps be discussed in two interrelated but conceptually distinct contexts: electoral and extraelectoral. In both dimensions, the citizens' movement, inasmuch as it is local in origin and areal in organization, its activities are perforce local, though its cumulative effects across the country produce, as we shall see in chapter 7, significant long-range impact upon

19. See Komei Senkyo Renmei, ed., *Toitsu Chiho Senkyo to Yukensha 1967–1971* (Tokyo: Komei Senkyo Renmai, 1972), 2: 265–74.

20. Michihiro Okuda et al., *Toshika Shakai to Ningen* (Tokyo: Nihon Hoso Shuppan Kyokai, 1975), p. 85.

the national politics. It is in any event significant that, while the most important mobilizational and organizing activities in Japan during its period of industrialism originated at the national level through political parties, the most dramatic and novel efforts at political mobilization and activities in her emergent postindustrial era are being generated at the grass-roots level, not by parties formed by national-level notables and influentials, but by ordinary citizens.

Electoral Activities.   The citizens' movement may opt for one or the other of two general strategies. One is an attempt to elect both the assembly and the chief executive (mayor, governor) from among the movement's members or others who could be genuinely representative of and responsive to concerned citizens. In short, the aim is to take over government from conventional politicians. For obvious reasons, this is a very difficult proposition to implement. No instance of success has yet been observed. The other option is both more feasible and more pragmatic: concentration of the movement's energy and resources upon electing to the office of chief executive a person of its choice. The movement, in choosing this electoral strategy, aims to change the status quo through active and sustained substantive popular participation after the election on the side of the chief executive in policy making. This strategy in the past produced results of varying magnitude in such postindustrial areas on the Japanese political map as Tokyo, Osaka, Kawasaki, and Nagoya.

These two electoral strategies produce what we call "movement-led elections." They obtain where parties are weak, for reasons discussed in chapters 4 and 5. In these instances, parties, if they want to get any political mileage out of elections (and they invariably do), are reduced to playing second fiddle to the citizens' movement. This is especially true in mayoral and gubernatorial elections and, by jumping on the citizens' movement bandwagon, parties, especially opposition parties (which never fail to try to generate the impression that the movement's candidate is their ally, if not their progeny), attempt to get their own partisan assembly candidates elected on the mayoral or gubernatorial candidate's coattail.

Where parties are relatively well organized, especially if opposition parties have significant relative levels of voter support and, conversely, the movement is less developed in contrast, these parties may take effective initiative in electoral politics, thus producing "party-led elections." The gubernatorial or mayoral candidate may be genuinely suprapartisan, but is more likely selected or recruited by the party or parties concerned. Even in this case, the citizens' movement is frequently consulted about his selection, even though it cannot dictate its terms to the party or parties because of their superiority in electoral logistics and resources. Still, the movement can exert significant influences upon the selection of candidates and conduct of electoral campaigns because it has the option of withdrawing its support from the "party-led" campaign. One example, which seems to be increasing in frequency, of such movement influence upon candidate selection and conduct of campaign is that the movement, if sufficiently cohesive and determined, can in effect force warring parties or factions to cease the unproductive bickering and mud-slinging and to rally to the support of one candidate (or one platform) on whose selection the movement itself would have much to say. The movement, in this case, acts as a combination of catalyst, balancer, and mediator among the warring parties, and in so doing, mobilizes available resources in the direction that it deems desirable. Thus, "party-led" electoral campaigns are often "movement-induced."

Whether a given electoral campaign is party-led or movement-led, the relationship between party and movement is ambivalent at best. To begin with, inasmuch as the citizens' movement arose partly in response to the ineptitude and hidebound partisanship of parties, its activists are naturally inclined toward mistrust of those parties. Second, they are aware that parties, in their desperate desire to survive and, if possible, to aggrandize themselves, will take advantage of the movement in any way that they think will enhance their narrow partisan objectives.[21] They also fear, and their fear has more than once been vindicated, that when parties logistically and organizationally lead a movement-induced electoral campaign, their (parties') mutual competition for partisan political mileage may undermine the effectiveness of the campaign and lead to its failure.[22] The relationship between party and movement remains very tenuous indeed.

21. For the movement's distrust of parties, see, for example, Yuichi Yoshikawa, "Shakyo wa Shimin Undo o riyo dekinai," *Chuokoron*, June 1973, esp. p. 210.

22. Keiji Yokoyama, "Uragirareta Jumin Undo," *Asahi Janaru*, 7 May 1971; and *Asahi Shimbun*, 29 April 1975, p. 4.

Extraelectoral Activities. Electoral campaigns are inter-mittent. Elections are, moreover, a matter of formal participation. One of the novel features of the citizens' movement, however, is that its activities are sustained and aim at exertion of substantive impact on the point of policy making after the election, regardless of its outcome. In this respect, the movement operates "in the sphere of pressure politics rather than party politics."[23] It bypasses parties and concentrates on individual assemblymen, the mayor, the governor, city hall, government agencies, or corporate organizations. It tries to combat the influence of special interests at the levels where those interests normally monopolize substantive participation in policy making. Contrary to the contention assiduously promoted by opposition parties, therefore, the movement actively solicits the understanding, cooperation, and support of LDP or "conservative" legislators (and the chief executive if he is not from or of the movement) as well, pressuring them to enact appropriate legislation and modify existing laws and regulations. The movement attempts to educate them and other government officials by inviting them to its meetings as well as to joint onsite inspections of problem areas and by otherwise impressing upon them its concern and cross-stratal appeal.

If gentle persuasion proves ineffective, as it often does, the movement resorts to more aggressive tactics, such as a sit-in at city hall, public rallies and street demonstrations and marches, thus mobilizing wider ranges of citizens in direct political action. If the legislature or the chief executive or certain officials continue to be recalcitrant, the movement, especially if it has succeeded in arousing sufficient public interest and support, may exercise its recourse to one or more of the constitutionally prescribed acts of extraordinary popular expression such as recall, a demand for legislation, and so forth. Conventional petition and lobbying as major methods of substantive participation are being overshadowed by public demonstration of cross-stratal concern in the open, in the street, if you like. It is aggressive, not a bit deferential toward formal authority, disdainful of bargaining and compromise, altogether uninhibited by conventional referents and behavioral inhibitions, and quite willing to step on the toes of established groups and institutions. Confrontation, not secret bargaining and quiet compromise, seems to be the preference

23. Michitoshi Takabatake, "Citizens' Movements: Organizing the Spontaneous," *Japan Interpreter* 9 (Winter 1975): 315.

of the citizens' movement. This is the preventive and redressive politics of open and relentless public pressure.

It may not be out of order to provide here a few specific examples, in very brief form, of extraelectoral activities of the citizens' movement.

Fujinomiya, southwest of Tokyo, is a beautiful semirural city at the southeastern foot of Mount Fuji. With the rise of the so-called leisure boom as a result of increasing prosperity and affluence and introduction of a five-day work week, land speculators and developers (most of them corporate giants in the field) began to converge on this city and its environs, as they did on other parts of the country, to buy up land in and around the city, in order to sell at higher prices later or to develop golf courses and other amusement and recreational facilities, hotels, and support industries. Many parcels of land were sold by local residents who naturally did not mind the sudden acquisition of wealth. As this process continued, however, a serious apprehension among local citizens emerged about the imminent danger of the city and its environs becoming a vast recreational and amusement area for urban weekenders, full of concrete, steel, aluminum, glass, car roads, with their original natural surroundings totally destroyed. In the end, this rising concern led to the formation of a citizens' movement. Supported by the sympathetic and concerned mayor, this movement applied successful pressure upon the city assembly to legislate an arrangement whereby the local farmers' cooperative would buy land, if its owner must sell it for financial or other pressing reasons, at 80 percent of prevailing market value, so as to retain the land in the hands of the local community. The owner, according to the movement-induced arrangement, was allowed to buy back the land five years after sale for the original sales price plus a small interest. In addition, the citizens' movement persuaded the local authority to enact legislation to prevent the land already purchased by outsiders from commercial exploitation.[24]

Kita Kyushu is the largest industrial center on the southern island of Kyushu, famous especially for its steel industry. Air pollution was a major problem for the local citizenry. Finally, in the absence of appropriate official concern of elected representatives and government agencies despite the worsening problem, a citizens' movement was organized (housewives were especially

24. *Asahi Shimbun,* 5 February 1974, p. 4.

active), not only to protest to authorities and the corporate culprits about the deplorable condition, but also to gather specific data by daily monitoring the amount of pollutants spewed out by industrial plants. When the movement had compiled sufficient amounts of these concrete data, it confronted local authorities with them and successfully forced them to enact certain antipollution measures.[25]

The town of Uchinada on the Japan Sea was governed by a mayor who, in support of interested industrial concerns, planned a construction of a thermal power plant within his administrative domain. Fearing air pollution from such a plant, townspeople, recognizing the need to counter the influence of those industrial concerns, organized a citizens' movement to protest against the mayor's official plan. Finding him recalcitrant, the movement initiated a recall procedure and successfully forced the mayor's dismissal from office. They then proceeded to elect a new mayor who was opposed to the building of the thermal power plant.[26]

The intensity and effectiveness of the pressure politics by the citizens' movement as a means of substantive popular participation in policy making differ from area to area, from circumstance to circumstance. It is nevertheless significant that a great majority of citizens feel this pressure politics to promise more tangible returns than conventional popular input activities. For example, one large-scale survey conducted in Tokyo showed that 70 percent of the respondents contended that problems of environmental decay and pollution—problems that are eminently cross-stratal—should be resolved by popular pressure exerted directly upon local government, while only 18 percent felt that these problems should be left up to government for resolution.[27] The same survey also found 44 percent of the respondents had already participated in various citizens' movements and an additional 15 percent expressed their willingness to join them. The typical citizens' movement participant's view is: "Direct action in the form of the citizens' movement is far more effective than voting, and more and more problems are of the kind that could

---

25. See, for example, "Shohisha undo wa kitai dekiruka," *Sekai*, April 1971.

26. *Asahi Shimbun*, 21 May 1973, p. 4.

27. *Ashai Shimbun*, 15 June 1973, p. 21.

be remedied only through direct action."[28] Indeed, far more citizens view the citizens' movement as more productive than elections, and only one out of ten voters expresses conventional cynicism regarding the utility of direct citizen participation.[29] It is significant, especially in view of the conventional understanding of Japanese politics that still persists, that an increasing number of ordinary citizens actually participate in direct political action. Equally important is the fact that such participation elicits not only a sense of efficacy for those who in fact participate, but also a vicarious sense of participation, hence a sense of potential efficacy, on the part of those who do not.

Impact of the Citizens' Movement as a New Pattern of Popular Participation

The conduct of government is perceptively influenced by patterns of popular political participation. The citizens' movement as the new form of substantive popular participation in efforts to bring about needed changes in the changing environment has already produced considerable impact upon the conduct of government at the local level in a number of ways.

One aspect of such impact is the perception of local officials of the pressure exerted by the citizens' movement for greater sensitivity and responsiveness in policy making to various problems that concern ordinary citizens. This has manifested itself, for example, in the establishment of local government offices and bureaus specifically designed to solicit and process citizen grievances, problems, and requests.[30] It is also apparent in new administrative slogans and catch-phrases such as "administration of kindness and thoughtfulness" and "administration on the basis of citizen requests." A recent study of a city government found that the proportion of administrators who felt that policy initiative lay in the citizens' movement and public opinion had in-

28. Ibid., 12 April 1971 (Evening), p. 10. Also see Rei Shiratori, *Nihon ni okeru Hoshu to Kakushin* (Tokyo: Nihon Keizai Shimbun Sha, 1973), p. 64, table I-11.

29. Yoshikawa, "Shakyo wa Shimin Undo o riyo dekinai," pp. 210–11.

30. See, for example, Taro Oshima, "Kakushin Jichitai to Kanryo-sei," in *Gendai Gyosei to Kanryo-sei,* ed. Ken Taniuchi et al. (Tokyo: Tokyo Daigaku Suppan Kai, 1974), 2:309–10.

creased twelvefold in ten years.[31] All these things suggest that government officials at the local level find themselves increasingly compelled to conduct their business in a manner that is different from business as usual.

The postindustrial political ecology has led citizens to express their preferences for a vastly enlarged set of political choices. This in turn generates a heightened level of pressure on local government for more and varied policies and services, not only for the prevention of further rises in the costs of modern industrialism, but also for the redress of distortions in social and economic well-being caused by the special-interests-dominated distributive politics of the past, especially regarding what many citizens regard as the minimum quality as well as level of socioeconomic well-being of those people in need of public assistance and corrective measures.

The citizens' movement also seems to be affecting the internal relations of local government. As we hinted earlier, there is this problem of institutional constraints, and one constraint is the entrenchment and subsequent resistance to change on the part of bureaucracy. With the growing complexity and volume of issues and problems to be dealt with in advanced industrial society, the role, hence power, of bureaucracy become increasingly dominant both at the national and local levels. The dominance and institutional self-interest of bureaucracy militate against adaptation to the changing environment and thus help give rise to the citizens' movement at the local level. The combination of the movement's electoral focus on the office of chief executive and its pressure politics after each election is causing a shift in administrative and political initiative and leadership from the bureaucracy to the chief executive. There is, of course, enormous bureaucratic resistance against this shift—in some cases so powerful that bureaucrats in effect ignore or sabotage the chief executive at the critical level of policy implementation.[32] And special interests that benefit from the politics as usual and political dominance of the bureaucracy aid and abet such resistance. If the chief executive is sufficiently committed and the

31. Mikio Muramatsu, "Political Participation and Administrative Process in Contemporary Japan," *Annals of the Japanese Political Science Association 1974*, p. 43.

32. Yomiuri Shimbun Seiji-bu, ed., *Nippon Kenryoku Chizu: Chiho Seijino So-tenken to Kaibo* (Tokyo: Saimaru, 1971), p. 96.

citizens' movement carries on sufficiently persistent pressure politics on the side of the chief executive, bureaucratic resistance can be overcome and in fact has been overcome in a number of instances.[33] Indeed, one of the most important contributions the citizens' movement can make to government at this level is to help force the bureaucracy to become more flexible, responsive, and responsible.

The impact of the citizens' movement and the dynamics it generates on politics and political participation, however, is not entirely without troubling aspects. The trivialization of politics we spoke of in chapter 3 is one such aspect. Recognizing that local government can be pressured into doing things that it did not do before, various groups of people become excessively eager to make demands, however trivial or contentious, on public authorities without regard to the limits or capacity of those authorities as well as of their communities. Bell calls this phenomenon the "revolution of rising entitlements,"[34] i.e., citizens demanding, as of right, not only a basic minimum income and other material dimensions of civilized living, but also access to higher education, employment, particular quality and quantity of public assistance, subsidy, and intervention in the treatment and care of a wide range of groups and problems. Thus a wholly new dimension is added to the conventional distributive politics, as well as to the new redressive and preventive politics. This phenomenon at least in part is clearly precipitated by the energy and success of the citizens' movement and its pressure politics, and aims at allocation of resources for an increasing number of items and problems that are frequently frivolous, trivial, even capricious for politicization, and at redress of petty grievances and other annoyances that should be resolved through voluntary and private acts and informal negotiations.

Thus, local government in the postindustrial political ecology is faced with both positive and troubling aspects of the impact of the rise in substantive popular participation and all that it implies and entails. With the politicization of the costs of industrialism and the trivialization of politics, the political arena now contains a much wider range of issues and problems precisely because the conventional issues of distributive politics remain. And these three major categories of issues and problems

33. Oshima, "Kakushin Jichitai to Kanryo-sei," pp. 315–17.

34. Daniel Bell, "The Public Household—On 'Fiscal Sociology' and the Liberal Society," *Public Interest* 37 (Fall 1974): 39.

in an important sense tend to compound one another because they seem, at least on the surface, to call for mutually exclusive or conflicting modes of management and resolution. Can the costs of industrialism be reduced without massive outlays of funds that could otherwise be expended to meet the resolution of rising entitlements? How could the existing distortions of the distributive politics be redressed without further economic development that, under the existing democratic system, alone would generate needed resources? What would be the additional costs of such development in terms of the quality of environment? These and other questions pose serious dilemmas for government, both local and national. There is a great danger, therefore, that the newly energetic rise in substantive popular participation might, as Huntington warned, "make postindustrial society extraordinarily difficult to govern."[35]

POLITICAL ECOLOGY AND CITIZEN INVOLVEMENT AT THE NATIONAL LEVEL

Political ecology in Japan seems bifurcated between the local and the national level, with the result that the pattern of citizen involvement in politics at the national level is ascertainably different from that at the local. The ecological variation between the two levels may be a matter of degree rather than a matter of difference in kind. In other words, ecology at the national level is less postindustrial (or more industrial) than at the local. The fact remains, however, that this variation in degree produces some ascertainably clear differences in the pattern of citizen involvement in politics.

Consider, for example, the material and demographic dimensions of political ecology. The degree, if not the nature, of their impact as well as content at the national level differs from the local. The costs of modern industrialism, which are specific at the postindustrial local level, are relatively dispersed and quite uneven in impact at the national level. To put the same thing a bit differently, what is acute at the postindustrial local level is a bit less so at the national level. In short, politicization of the costs of modern industrialism is differentially manifested at the national as compared to the local level. Demographically, too, spots of intensity are scattered from the national perspective,

---

35. Samuel P. Huntington, "Postindustrial Politics: How Benign Will It Be?," *Comparative Politics* 6 (January 1974): 177.

while locally they are concentrated. The national level also differs significantly from the local in the character of constitutional arrangement in some crucial aspects: The chief executive is selected by the Diet, not by popular vote. He is accountable, not to the electorate as his local counterpart is, nor even to the Diet when we consider the fact of the LDP parliamentary dominance and the particular pattern of intraparty factional politics, but, in effect, as noted in chapter 4, only to his rival faction leaders in the party. If the elected official's accountability is the electorate's power, then the voters have no power whatsoever over their chief executive at the national level.

Participatory logistics for substantive popular participation, too, varies greatly between national and local levels. At both levels, citizens are constitutionally guaranteed rights of petition for legislative enactment or amendment as well as for recall of officials; but at the national level, they effectively remain literal embellishments in the Constitution, for there are no meaningful logistical correlates. The seat of government is distant; like-minded citizens concerned about the status quo encounter virtually insurmountable difficulties in communication, organization, and coordination since their communities are widely dispersed. A meaningful sense of community or a compelling identity of interest is hard to engender. Elected representatives as well as government officials are remote, aloof, and far less understanding and appreciative of local problems than their local counterparts are, for obvious reasons. Popular pressure, even if it were possible to generate with any unified thrust, would most likely be dissipated through factional politics within major parties. In short, logistics are not manageable for the people. Citizens, when they need help from the national level, are, therefore, still forced to rely, à la clientelist politics as usual, upon the goodwill, political calculus, and intraparty clout of their distant representatives. All this naturally discourages the growth of new patterns of participation at the national level.

Institutional constraints are greater at the national than at the local level precisely because such vital national institutions as parliament and ministerial bureaucracies are more removed, more deeply entrenched, much vaster, more powerful and imperious and thus operate with more potent institutional imperatives and organizational inertia and greater imperviousness to the changing environment than their local counterparts. And the lack of adequate popular participatory logistics further enhances the rigidity and power of such institutional constraints.

Parties are much better organized and play a greater role at the national than at the local level precisely because they were formed as groupings of notables at the national level for electoral purposes. Because of the vastness of organizational, financial, and other resources required for election at this level, parties (and powerful special interests that support them) monopolize electoral efforts and campaigns. Parliamentary rules and the politics of the pork-barrel reduce nonpartisan MPs, especially in the lower house, to the role of mere spectators in the Diet proceedings; this would in effect render even a successful electoral campaign by citizens' movement candidates ultimately futile, assuming, of course, that such a campaign were indeed feasible. Since the role of parties is as secure at the national level as before, party competition in the manner of business as usual continues, with the ruling LDP in collusion with big business and industry and the national bureaucracy cranking out a patchwork of policies that are generally acceptable to powerful special interests that support it, while opposition parties more often than not engage in a more fierce mutual competition and struggle than their common challenge against the LDP.

Organized interests are powerful at the national level because they effectively monopolize substantive participation while citizens are reduced to formal, ritualistic participation. These interests are all organized along lines of economic and occupational differentiation, and as such are dedicated to stratal political competition over shares of material resources but are not capable of representing cross-stratal problems of postindustrial society. Then there are groups that are either in part or in toto devoted to the ideological disputation and struggle, and these groups persist in the ideological politics to the exclusion of more practical tasks such as innovating measures and policies to cope with problems and issues with which people are daily concerned. All this tends to repress the rise of effective instrumental orientation at this level.

The dimensions of political ecology at the national level sustain, and are sustained by, certain cultural and attitudinal predilections. The persistence of a combination of ideological politics and selective distributive politics help, and in turn are helped by, the persistence of conventional political referents and behavioral inhibitions. Citizens at this level manifest their residual tendency to cast their ballot in terms of party identification (present or past); many belong to MPs' personal support clubs where personal obligations, connections, and parochial loyalty are organizing principles. Conventional socioeconomic and ideological cleavages tend to assert themselves in influencing voter behavior, even though much less so now than before. And particularistic patron-client relations still obtain.

Thus, distance, both physical and psychological, the absence of a clearly ascertainable link between vote and policy, the total exclusion of the electorate from the selection of a chief executive, monopoly of substantive participation by organized special interests, the persistence of ideological and selective distributive politics, powerful institutional constraints, the control of electoral politics by parties, and the continued potency of conventional political referents and behavioral inhibitions all conspire to leave politics at the national level more or less as it has always been, and to discourage voluntary popular participatory and oppositional activities on the part of voters at the national level.

From our discussion in the chapter thus far, it appears that the citizens' movement as a new mode of substantive popular participation at the local level is replacing, not political parties as vehicles of electoral mobilization and direct participation in policy making, but the thrust, direction, and influence of organized special interests as actors in the arena of substantive participation in policy making. While the movement challenges the hidebound, industrial-politics orientation of parties and variously compels them, as we briefly saw earlier in this chapter and will see in our discussion of electoral politics in the next chapter, to modify many of their important aspects, the very existence of electoral politics and a representative form of government not only at the national but also at the local levels, combined with the fact of the areal nature of the movement and all that it implies, seem to suggest that the movement will not, unless parties allow themselves to disintegrate entirely, replace them. Except where parties are utterly disorganized or entirely feeble, in which case it may well play a dominant electoral as well as substantive role, the citizens' movement's primary significance seems to consist in its ability, by virtue of its motive, concern, energy, membership, and thrust, to challenge the conventional monopoly of substantive participation in policy making by organized special interests of industrial society in local politics. The nature of major issues and problems in an industrial society is segmental, and germane to socioeconomic and ideological cleavages. Hence the dominant role of special interests representing those segments reflecting those cleavages in the arena of substantive popular participation. The nature of major issues and problems more characteristic of the emerging postindustrial society is cross-stratal, and so there is this rising need for the force or mobilizational or organizing device that is capable of and committed to representing the cross-stratal interests that those issues and problems generate. As the segmental nature of political conflict over the distribution of income and wealth, hence the benefits of industrialism, determined the character of political parties and party competition, we can expect that the cross-stratal nature of the emerging postindustrial political concern would affect and eventually transform the character and operation of political parties. How this transformation or evolution of parties in Japan, formed as they were at the national level for electoral purposes in the first place, may be affected by the energy and dynamics generated by the citizens' movement at the local level, we shall see in the next chapter, through a discussion of changes in certain dimensions of electoral politics, both at the local and at the national level.

In an important sense, there is a dual political system in Japan today. Voters, it may be said, live in a kind of schizophrenic political world, and they frequently manifest this schizophrenia. In one context (postindustrial local), they are increasingly citizen-competent in their self-perception, cross-stratal and egalitarian in their participatory pattern, instrumental (and at times trivial) in their concern and orientation, and energetic in their political conduct. In the other (less postindustrial national) context, they still tend to be subject-competent, segmental and stratified, passive, dependent rather than assertive. In the past, the most noticeable, hence most talked-about political dichotomy was (and still is from a different perspective, i.e., in terms of variations in political ecology at the local level) rural vs. urban. This dichotomy today, however, is being overshadowed by a national-local dichotomy. The traditional rural-urban dichotomy has been considerably reduced, though by no means eliminated, in a number of contrasting dimensions, by the leveling effects brought about through economic growth, demographic change, and all that these entailed. What force, if any, would bridge the new local-national gap in political behavior? We shall attempt to answer this question at the conclusion of the next chapter.

7
Electoral Politics

Elections are the means by which people choose representatives to govern them. An obvious logical connection is that the elected representatives reflect the interests, needs, and concerns of the people and govern them accordingly. That, at any rate, is the theory behind elections in a democratic society. Clearly, of course, theory is quite a bit different from practice, and the quality of any democratic government should be measured according to the degree of the gap between the two. In Japan, as elsewhere, the gap between theory and practice appears to have widened in recent years, and the major reasons for this widening gap seems to be an increasingly apparent disjunction between the needs and problems of postindustrial society on the one hand and the political practices that were born of and are therefore deeply embedded in industrial society. Increasing numbers of citizens feel that elections are incapable of producing a government committed to coping with issues and problems that concern them and that parties are unresponsive to their needs and anxieties.

The phenomenon of "disengagement" and the rise of the citizens' movement are consequences of this widespread feeling within the electorate.

The Japanese people still support the parliamentary system of democracy. In fact, popular support for the system increased in the 1960s.[1] A number of observers have argued that many voters vote for opposition parties, especially the JSP, not because they support them, but in order to prevent the ruling LDP from becoming so powerful in its parliamentary strength that it could amend the Constitution to alter the existing parliamentary system.[2] In an important sense, Japanese voters have been anxious to protect their postwar form of government. Today, however, we notice an increasing degree of frustration within the electorate with the existing system. It remains no more than frustration because the voters are deeply committed to their Constitution and acutely fear what could be considered by some as an alternative to the existing political arrangement. In short, they are experiencing an inner tension between their commitment to democracy and their growing awareness that it is not working effectively with the variety of serious problems that they face. And they are engaged in a search for ways to make the system work without altering it. Significant and perceptible changes, therefore, are taking place in electoral politics in terms of its style, content, language, and tactics. It is to these problems that this chapter addresses itself. First, however, a few prefatory observations about electoral predicaments of major parties.

DECLINE OF THE LDP AND THE JSP

One of the politically relevant side effects of advanced industrialism in Japan is a noticeable shift in the pattern of party support in the two traditionally distinct areas of the political map: a drop in rural support for the ruling Liberal Democratic party and an equally manifest decline in urban-metropolitan support for the opposition Socialist party, and both without any

1. Hajime Shinohara, *Nihon no Seiji Fudo* (Tokyo: Iwanami, 1971), pp. 74–76.

2. See, for example, Tadashi Ishida, "Progressive Political Parties and Popular Movement," *Journal of Social and Political Ideas in Japan* 3 (April 1965): esp. 117; and Fukuji Taguchi, "The Japan Socialist Party," ibid., p. 101.

compensating growth in popular support elsewhere.[3] Between
1955 and 1972, electoral support for these two major parties
declined by 25 percent and 27 percent respectively.

The decline of voter support for the LDP in the more rural
and semiurban districts, on the basis of random samples, between
1955 and 1972 was approximately 18 percent, but by 1972 the
party had lost only 5 percent of the lower house seats it had held
in 1955 from those districts (still holding more than two-thirds
of those seats). In the more urban and metropolitan districts,
LDP electoral support dropped on the average by 33 percent
during the same period, and its share of those districts seats in
the lower house declined from 46 percent in 1955 to 29 percent
in 1972. Now, the JSP fortune in those same sets of sample
districts was equally downward. The Socialists' electoral support
by 1972 fell by an average of 48 percent over 1955 in large urban
and metropolitan districts, and their share of lower house seats
representing those districts changed from 52 percent in 1955 to
barely 21 percent in 1972. A rather interesting phenomenon is
the JSP vicissitude in rural and semirural districts. Using the
same set of those districts sampled for the LDP, we find that the
JSP fared relatively better in those districts than the LDP:
electoral support for Socialists dropped on the average by only
6 percent, and the JSP share of seats from those district showed
an equally small shift: from 28 percent in 1955 to 26 percent
in 1972.[4]

There is a close parallel in the pattern of decline in electoral
support between the LDP and the JSP, and table 7.1 indicates
that voters deserting the LDP and the JSP are voting for other
opposition parties. Yet the LDP retains its hegemony in the
House of Representatives. There are, of course, some good
reasons for this. One is that, while LDP support declined in the
rural and semirural districts, the party still managed to receive
a majority of votes in those areas. In those areas, many voters
who would, if opposition were not fragmented, support another
party, ended up voting for the LDP because they saw no con-

3. See, for example, Hajime Shinohara, "Bunkyoku-ka suru Seiji Ishiki,"
Asahi Janaru, 22 December 1972, esp. pp. 5–6; Naoki Komuro, "Kakushin
Jichitai no Tohyo Kozo," ibid., 29 December 1972, esp. pp. 102–3; Eiji
Yamamoto, "Hoshuto o hanarete yuku Nomin," ibid., 24 November 1972;
and Hajime Shinohara, "70 nen dai to Kakushin no Kanosei," *Sekai,*
March 1970.

4. These figures were computed from data in *Bessatsu Kokkai Binran:
Shiryo Soshu Hen* (Tokyo: Nihon Seikei Shimbun Shuppan Bu, 1975).

TABLE 7.1.   ELECTORAL SUPPORT

% of Votes for House of Representatives							
	1955	1958	1960	1963	1967	1969	1972
LDP	63.2	57.8	57.5	54.7	48.2	47.6	46.8
Opposition	32.2	35.5	39.2	40.4	46.5	46.9	47.9
(JSP only)	29.2	32.9	27.5	29.0	27.9	21.4	21.9
% Share of House of Representatives Seats							
LDP	63.6	61.5	63.6	60.6	57.0	59.3	55.4
Opposition	34.7	36.1	35.2	36.7	41.2	37.4	41.3
(JSP only)	33.4	35.5	31.0	30.8	28.8	18.5	24.0

structive alternative to it. Then, too, there is the matter of unequal representation. While the national average of the population per lower house seat was 210,000 for the latest general elections (1972), there was a wide disparity among the 124 multimember districts from the low of only 79,172 per seat in the Fifth District of Hyogo Prefecture to the high of 394,950 per seat for the Third District of Osaka. And districts with smaller numbers of population per seat are typically more rural or less urban than those with larger numbers of people per legislative seat. Rural Japan, then, is still overrepresented and urban Japan underrepresented. And the LDP is stronger in rural than in urban areas.

Table 7.2 shows the ten most overrepresented districts (which, not coincidentally, are all rural or semiurban) and the ten most underrepresented districts (which, by the same token, are all heavily urban or metropolitan) and compares the two sets of districts in terms of winners and percentage of votes received by the LDP and opposition candidates.

The contrast between the two sets of districts is very sharp indeed. First, the average ratio of voter support between the LDP and opposition is reversed between the overrepresented districts and underrepresented ones. The perfect symmetry, of course, is accidental, but the tendency has nevertheless been consistent in recent elections. Second, the LDP, in both sets of districts, won more seats than it won votes; conversely, the opposition won fewer seats than its share of popular votes indicated it should have. We shall discuss this problem later; suffice it at this point to suggest that opposition parties fight among themselves sometimes more fiercely than they struggle against their common adversary, the LDP. They frequently field more candidates than

TABLE 7.2. UNEQUAL REPRESENTATION IN ELECTORAL DISTRICTS

Ten Most Overrepresented Districts

District	Population per Seat	No. of Seats	Elected Candidates	LDP Votes (as % of total cast)	Opposition Votes (as % of total cast)
Fifth Hyogo	79,172	3	2 LDP, DSP	44.9	55.1
Third Kagoshima	81,670	3	3 LDP	78.4	21.6
Second Ishikawa	84,537	3	3 LDP	75.2	24.8
Second Akita	90,030	4	3 LDP, JSP	60.6	39.4
Third Ehime	90,276	3	3 LDP	80.7	19.3
Second Niigata	92,025	4	3 LDP, JSP	58.5	41.5
Second Miyazaki	93,226	3	2 LDP, JSP	71.5	28.5
Third Nagano	95,347	4	2 LDP, JCP, JSP	65.2	34.8
Second Yamagata	95,548	4	2 LDP, 2 JSP	58.2	41.8
Fourth Niigata	97,292	3	2 LDP, JSP	71.5	28.5
Average:	89,912			66.5	33.5

Total seats: 34. LDP, 25 (73.5%); opposition: 9 (26.5%). Opposition seats: JSP, 7; JCP, 1; DSP, 1.

Ten Most Underrepresented Districts

District	Population per Seat	No. of Seats	Elected Candidates	LDP Votes (as % of total cast)	Opposition Votes (as % of total cast)
Third Osaka	394,950	4	LDP, JSP, JCP, CGP	26.3	73.7
First Chiba	381,217	4	2 LDP, JSP, JCP	45.2	54.8
Seventh Tokyo	367,504	5	2 LDP, JSP, JCP, CGP	29.9	70.1
First Kanagawa	334,649	5	2 LDP, JSP, JCP, CGP	28.4	71.6
First Saitama	300,657	4	2 LDP, JCP, CGP	34.7	65.3
Second Kanagawa	280,543	4	2 LDP, JSP, JCP	35.8	64.2
Tenth Tokyo	257,280	4	2 LDP, JCP, CGP	37.0	63.0
Third Kanagawa	246,486	5	LDP, JSP, JCP, CGP, DSP	38.9	61.1
First Aichi	239,049	3	JSP, JCP, DSP	23.6	76.4
First Hyogo	230,951	4	LDP, JSP, JCP, GCP	35.0	65.0
Average:	303,329			33.5	66.5

Total seats: 42. LDP, 15 (35.7%); opposition: 27 (64.3%). Opposition seats: JSP, 8; JCP, 10; CGP, 7; DSP, 2.

Source: Computed from data in Takayoshi Miyagawa, *Seiji Handobukku* (Tokyo: Seiji Koho Senta, 1973), pp. 202–64.

are electorally sound and compete for anti-LDP votes, enabling lower-vote-getting LDP candidates to be elected. Third, the gap between the two sets of districts in terms of population per seat is extremely wide. The average size of population per seat for the underrepresented urban districts is 3.4 times that for the over-represented, LDP-dominated districts. The LDP is also in over-whelming control of the overrepresented rural and semiurban districts, but it has no absolute majority in terms of the number of seats held in any of the underrepresented urban or metro-politan districts, although it is tied with opposition in four of the ten such districts. The ruling LDP is still a rural party in its electoral strength. Its strength there, however, has been slowly eroding. Why?

Causes for the LDP decline in strength in rural or semiurban areas seem closely related to Japan's gradual transition from industrialism to postindustrialism. Among these causes are: (1) professionalization of agricultural cooperatives; (2) the leveling effects produced by economic growth, the spread of mass com-munication media, especially electronic media, and higher levels of education as well as generational changes; and (3) the general increase in instrumental orientation.

The countryside is politically more conservative during the industrial period than is the city. Urbanization as a concomitant of industrialization erodes parochial properties of interpersonal and social relations because of the phenomenon of a growing impersonalization of interactions. People act on the basis of different political and relational referents, such as ideology, policy preference, and economic calculus. In the countryside, however, traditional properties of interpersonal and social rela-tions persist, and members of parochial elites such as large landholders and other kinds of notables or their allies and progenies hold influence because of them. The very nature of rural communities discourages ideological debate and dispute and policy preferences are diffusely subsumed under those traditional properties of interpersonal and social relations. Po-litical organizations, such as politicians' personal support clubs (*koenkai*), therefore, are more personal than political, let alone programmatic.

In the countryside, the most extensive mass organization is the agricultural cooperative (*nogyo kyodo kumiai*, or *nokyo* for short). Each rural organization or activity was effectively con-trolled by local notables who were, again predictably, local political powers supported by their fellow citizens on the basis of those parochial properties of interpersonal and social relations. It was these local notables-politicians that used to see to it, through their positions in the agricultural cooperative, that the cooperative members (virtually all households) voted for LDP candidates. In short, the agricultural cooperative used to serve as the preeminent instrument through which rural votes were channeled in the direction of the LDP. Local politicians were very effective in this regard because they were in the position of encouraging the cooperative's members to vote for the LDP by virtue of the fact that they processed credit applications and requests for a variety of services that were provided by or through the cooperative.

This situation has changed in recent years. Consistent with the general trend toward amalgamation, consolidation, and rationalization of economic and other operations in advanced industrial society, agricultural cooperatives are now consolidated across village and township lines in structure and increasingly professionalized in personnel and operation. Farmers can now bypass local politicians and communicate directly with professionals in their substantive dealings with the cooperative. Local notables and politicos are processual underlings of the LDP. But now they have been deprived of an institutional instrument through which they could ensure delivery of rural votes to the party.

The leveling effect of advanced industrialism upon the countryside has many aspects. One such effect, of course, is the new consumption pattern and life style, which are virtually identical with those in cities. Perhaps one of the more pertinent aspects in this regard, however, is the change in occupational patterns. As noted in chapter 2, the major proportion of rural income is no longer derived from agriculture, but from employment in the secondary and tertiary economic sectors. Farmers spend a minority of their working time in the field; they hop into their Datsuns and Toyotas (sometimes even Fords and Opels), quickly transport themselves to a nearby city to work in factories and business establishments, where they are exposed to urban ethos in a variety of activities and interactions. In an important sense, they become increasingly urban in outlook and values, while physically residing in the rural sector. With such ready mobility and the spread of education and mass media, generational changes in values and attitudes come nearly as readily to the countryside as to cities.

Politicization of the costs of modern industrialism may be much less acute in the countryside as a geographical expression, but as a perceptual property, farmers are becoming increasingly concerned about it precisely because of what we described in the preceding paragraph. Their support for the LDP is basically a support for individual LDP MPs, as we noted in chapter 4; it has little to do with policies and programs as such. Value change as a consequence of daily mobility, growing attitudinal sophistication due to mass media, higher levels of education, and exposure to ethos of industrialism all combine to engender an instrumental orientation on the part of the rural population. And such instrumental concern runs counter to the diffuseness of whatever policy expectations there might be in the membership in personal support clubs for conservative politicians where the central organizing principles are those traditional properties of interpersonal and social relations that have no intrinsic relationship to policy and program. In short, farmers become disenchanted with their traditional mode of political behavior in general and with their conventional support for the LDP.

These three considerations, among others, seem to underlie the decline in rural electoral support for the LDP not only at the national but also at the local level in recent years. For example, in the first unified local elections of the decade of the 1970s, electoral support for LDP gubernatorial candidates in eight major rural prefectures declined between 5 percent and 58 percent over the previous election and in six other major rural prefectures, where voter support for LDP gubernatorial candidates increased slightly due to higher rates of voter turnout, opposition candidates gained far more votes over the previous election than the LDP candidates.[5] A similar downward trend in LDP voter support occurred in less urban prefectural and local legislative elections subsequently: a decline from over 30 percent to close to 60 percent in 1973 and a further drop in 1975.[6]

The major opposition party, the JSP, on the other hand has been losing electoral support in its traditional stronghold—large urban and metropolitan districts—much more rapidly than the LDP in rural areas. One observer noted that the JSP electoral support in those districts declined at an annual rate of nearly 2 percent since the 1960 election, while in the 1950s, it had shown an increase.[7] The party suffered a radical setback in the

5. *Seiji Handobukku*, pp. 289–300.

6. *Asahi Shimbun*, 19 July 1973, p. 4, and 2 May 1975, p. 4.

7. Koichiro Kuwata, "Political Parties in the Next Decade," *Japan Quarterly* 17 (April–June 1970): 144.

1969 general elections, losing 50 of its 140 lower house seats, and most of the seats lost were urban. In the 1972 general election the party managed to increase its lower house seats by 28 to 118, but the gains were made rather precariously, for they were not the result of any increase in voter support (voter support was only 0.5 percent over 1969). The major factor for the party's gain was the Socialists' attempt more carefully to limit the number of candidates in important districts so as not to dissipate votes for their party. Even then, however, the apparent increase in Socialist seats in the House of Representatives belied serious and continuing difficulties for the party in urban and metropolitan districts. In those districts the JSP was outshone and outvoted by the rapidly rising JCP, and many JSP winners barely squeaked in as lower vote-getters in those multimember districts.[8]

The general downward trend in voter support for the JSP has obtained in local elections as well. In the 1971 unified local elections, the JSP was the only party to experience a net decrease in voter support; all the other parties received a net increase in electoral support as a result of an increase in the number of eligible voters and a very high rate of voter turnout.[9] In the next local elections, held in 1973, the party did not experience any gain in voter support over 1971. In the latest (1975) local elections, the JSP suffered a further drop in electoral support, especially in metropolitan and large urban areas.[10]

Several factors collectively explain the decline of the JSP, and they all seem to be related to the emerging postindustrial politics. As we discussed in chapter 5, the JSP is burdened with ideological dogmatism, heavy dependence upon leftist *Sohyo* unions and the doctrinaire Socialism Association for financial, organizational, personnel, and other logistical support. All this is increasingly incongruous with the rising disposition of people, which is nonideological, instrumental, and distrustful toward established organizations of industrial society. We can see this

8. For analyses of the 1972 election and trends in voter support, see, for example, Hajime Shinohara, "Bukyokuka suru Seiji Ishiki," *Asahi Janaru*, 22 December 1972; Kazuo Endo, "Tenkan e no Shido," *Sekai*, February 1973; and Naoki Komuro, "Kakushin Jichitai no Tokuhyo Kozo," *Asahi Janaru*, 29 December 1972.

9. *Asahi Shimbun*, 22 May 1971, p. 2.

10. Ibid., 19 July 1973, p. 4, and 2 May 1975, p. 4.

incongruence even within organized labor itself, within *Sohyo.* While the JSP's tie with the labor council became closer, its appeal for rank-and-file unionists declined steadily. There is a serious practical discrepancy between labor leadership and union members whom the leadership presumably represents. As Cole pointed out, rank-and-file unionists elected leftist union leaders as a basically expressive act that would give "satisfying expression of a state of mind"[11] that is essentially residual of the times past when organized labor languished under authoritarian oppression. In the absence of a tradition of radicalism but recognizing the history of such tradition in other industrial nations, ordinary workers liked certain radical rhetoric, even revolutionary jargon and platitudes constantly chanted by their leadership, because those gave them a vicarious sense of modernity and a "progressive image," and they allowed their union leaders a free rein in ideological militancy and radical political posturing. But, then, that had little or nothing to do with their own practical choices and concrete preferences. As the ideological politics of the JSP supported by their leftist leadership continued to lose its relevance to the actual conditions of society, rank-and-file unionists began to abandon the party. The preponderance of those unionists in fact came to reject socialism as a means of improving society during the 1960s.[12] It is of particular significance, moreover, that the younger and the better educated among them reject socialism and the JSP even more strongly than the older and the less educated.[13]

POLITICAL ECOLOGY AND ELECTORAL POLITICS

For purposes of clarity in narrative, we shall look at electoral politics at the local and at the national level separately. Electoral

11. Robert E. Cole, *Japanese Blue Collar: The Changing Tradition* (Berkeley, Los Angeles and London: University of California Press, 1971), p. 267.

12. Robert E. Cole, "Japanese Workers, Unions, and the Marxist Appeal," *Japan Interpreter* 6 (Summer 1970); Kuwata, "Political Parties in the Next Decade"; and Gerald L. Curtis, "The 1969 General Election in Japan," *Asian Survey* 10 (October 1970).

13. Cole, "Japanese Workers," p. 115; and Masumi Ishikawa, "Datsu Seito So no Kiken kara no Tenkai," *Asahi Janaru*, 19 July 1974, esp. pp. 9–10.

politics, like patterns of substantive political participation, differs from one context to the other as the general character of relevant political ecology varies between the two levels.

Electoral Politics at the Local Level

Electoral politics at the local level, where postindustrial political ecology more explicitly obtains, shows some marked signs of change. Much of this change is the combined consequence of the weakness of parties and the rise of the citizens' movement to fill a certain political vacuum created by the parties' weaknesses. Perhaps the most significant sign of change, therefore, is the decline in the efficacy of parties as the vehicles of electoral politics. The politicization of the costs of modern industrialism, the subsequent rise in redressive and preventive politics and its concomitant, instrumental orientation all revealed a general lack of sufficient adaptability by political parties that are either ideologically or in economic interest aligned with vested interests of industrial society. These parties have variously demonstrated their organizational and programmatic shortcomings as instruments for integrating citizen concerns with new types of issues and problems and mobilizing voters for the purpose of dealing with those issues and problems. Citizens have been forced to devise their own unique method of mobilizing themselves so as to compel authoritative decision makers to attend to matters that concern them deeply. In electoral politics, in their disillusionment with parties, citizens have come to engage in organizing activities designed to elect or help elect the kinds of candidates who may be better able to represent their concern and who are free from partisan considerations and other constraints characteristic of conventional political candidates.

In chapter 6 we referred to the role the citizens' movement plays in elections at the local level and the distinction between "movement-led" and "party-led" elections. We also mentioned that many "party-led" elections were in fact "movement-induced." In those more postindustrial localities, citizens' movements are not only overshadowing the influence of conventional special interests, which used to play a significant part in electoral politics during the industrial period in alliance with parties, but also posing a challenge to parties as the primary vehicles of electoral politics and campaigns. This challenge seems very important especially where parties, because of their close ties with special interests (the LDP with business and industry, the

JSP with *Sohyo* unions), are no longer sufficiently capable of aggregating and representing the concerns and demands of citizens and are instead in danger of reducing themselves to the role of pressure groups tenaciously clinging to segmental interests and preferences that are more characteristic of industrial society.[14] This danger may, of course, be more apparent than real, since, for the purpose of sheer survival, parties are however belatedly and inadequately attempting, as we shall see shortly, to adapt themselves to the changing environment whose magnitude they have long neglected.

Elsewhere, the citizens' movement's challenge to parties differs only in degree and not in character. They are variously compelled to attempt to modify many of their electoral aspects and modes and tactics of campaigns, for the rise and spread of the citizens' movement precipitated a number of phenomena and forces in electoral politics that are both significant in themselves and suggestive of the character of postindustrial politics that is emerging to challenge industrial politics. Let us take a brief look at some of these phenomena and forces.

Voter Motivation. We referred in chapter 6 to the decline in party identification among voters and the rise of the "disengagement" phenomenon. These phenomena, suggesting as they do the decline in the efficacy of parties in electoral politics, are further corroborated by changes in voter motivation for supporting one candidate or another. In local elections in the 1970s, the number of voters casting their ballot on the basis of such traditional electoral referents as a candidate's party, political connections, and the like, decreased significantly; conversely, those casting their ballot on the basis of their personal assessments of a candidate's policy commitment and instrumental qualifications rose (double in 1971 over 1967, and a nearly 70 percent rise in 1975 over 1971).[15] Another closely related development is the decline in the number of party-endorsed candidates. In the 1975 case, the number of party-endorsed gubernatorial candidates was

14. One scholar in fact warns against the transformation of parties into pressure organizations *(seito no atsuryoku dantaika).* See Rei Shiratori, *Nihon ni okeru Hoshu to Kakushin* (Tokyo: Nihon Keizai Shimbun Sha, 1973), pp. 51–52.

15. See, for example, Komei Senkyo Renmei, ed., *Toitsu Chiho Senkyo to Yukensha: 1967–1971* (Tokyo: Komei Senkyo Renmei, 1972), 2:70–177; and *Tokyo Shimbun,* 5 January 1976, p. 2.

only 10, in contrast to 22 in the previous (1971) election, and party-endorsed mayoral candidates dropped by 22 percent over the previous election.[16] Local elections indeed became increasingly suprapartisan, "disengaged," nonideological, and problem-oriented, so much so, in fact, that more and more candidates came to view party support, which used to be indispensable, as counterproductive. Party labels turn voters off. Candidates with partisan background and record, especially of the LDP, now make strenuous efforts to "conceal . . . party ties," as one newspaper observed.[17] Gubernatorial and mayoral candidates are particularly anxious to project an image of "citizens' candidate";[18] for this purpose, they publicly secede from the party, especially when they face powerful candidates of other parties or are challenged by citizens'-movement-supported opponents and/or platforms. Even those candidates who do not withdraw from their parties try their hardest to play down party affiliation and, frequently in their campaign posters, the names of their parties are printed in such small print as to be virtually invisible to the naked eye.[19] These candidates, especially of the ruling LDP, even when they run publicly on the LDP ticket, seek to avoid any visible campaign assistance from national party leaders whose open support had in the past been eagerly coveted.[20] These tendencies are equally noticeable among legislative candidates, both LDP and JSP. More and more of them seek to run on the merit of their public concern with issues and problems that have given rise to the citizens' movement.

New Types of Candidates. Since partisan identification as well as support are increasingly in decline, and the kind of issues and concerns around which elections revolve generates "rejective response to established organizations," it is perhaps only natural that there is a noticeable change in the type of

16. See *Asahi Shimbun,* 29 April 1975, p. 2.

17. Ibid., 10 February 1975, p. 1.

18. Shigetaro Iizuka, "Kakushin wa Ikutsu Chiji o toru ka," *Chuokoron,* January 1975, p. 43.

19. Yasushi Haga, "Datsu Seito Jidai to yu Genso," *Jiyu,* December 1971, p. 36.

20. See, for example, "Jiminto ni kusuburu 'Hanran' no Hi no Te," *Sande Mainichi,* 30 April 1972, p. 131.

candidate in local politics. Traditionally, candidates for local office, especially governorship and mayoralty, who commanded the widest voter support were former high-level bureaucrats or party notables at or with close relations to the national level, LDP or Socialist. They were potent vote-getters because they had personal, political, administrative, or career ties with politicians and bureaucrats of the national government and business and industry, which could be translated into favored allocations of material resources—benefits of industrialism—by the national level for local benefits. Voters wanted those allocations, to generate industrial development, public works, and so forth, in their localities. Before the 1971 elections, for example, 70 percent of prefectural governors were former officials of the national government.[21] They were good and popular politicians in those days because they brought the benefits of industrialism to the community—highway construction, housing development, industrial expansion, more jobs, more people.

All this began to change, however, as Japan became increasingly postindustrial. What used to be the prime campaign asset (connections with the national bureaucracy and political influentials) in the industrial period is becoming a virtual stigma in the emerging postindustrial era. The voting public is rejecting candidates endowed with those conventional credentials that are at once partisan, industrial, and institutional. It is instead more attracted to candidates who are free from conventional career, partisan, bureaucratic, or special-interest ties. Two new types of candidates, especially for local office of chief executive, are scholars and younger local administrators with little or no partisan background. Of the seventeen prefectural governors elected (or reelected) in 1975, for example, five were university professors, six were local administrators, and only four were former higher civil servants at the national level. It is of some interest to note that those four former higher civil servants were elected governors in four decidedly rural prefectures. A similar trend is apparent in the mayoral field. Of the ten largest cities in the country, seven, including the six largest, are now governed by mayors of the new breed. These seven cities have a total population of 26 million, while the other three governed by mayors of traditional ilk have a combined total of only 3 million.

21. Ryuken Ohashi, *Nihon no Kaikyu Kozo* (Tokyo: Iwanami, 1972), p. 92.

Or 47 out of 163 cities with a population of 100,000 or more each are governed by members of this new mayoral breed. To put the same thing in a slightly different perspective, today, approximately 40 percent of the Japanese population is governed by the new breed of local chief executives. Understandably, this proportion of the population finds itself in urban and metropolitan areas that are more postindustrial in political ecology than others.

Academics and younger local administrators are viewed by the electorate as antipolitician—unfettered by conventional political referents, operational parameters, and other constraints that arise from conventional ties with special interests and the national government. In short, they are without political baggage.[22] The "amateurism" of academics is contrasted to the "political savvy" of special interest-tied politicians. And younger administrators are still untainted by corruption and not only familiar with local problems but also more genuinely concerned about them than their elders. In outlook, predisposition, and concern, therefore, academics and younger local administrators are quite similar to core activists of the citizens' movement.

Language of Electoral Politics. Consonant with the decline of ideological politics and conventional referents and behavioral inhibitions, as well as the change in the nature and character of issues and problems, we notice some interesting shifts in the language of electoral politics at the local level. In the past, there were two distinct languages, one employed by the LDP and its conservative allies, and the other by the opposition, especially the JSP. The former stressed the benefits of industrialism and the latter, ideological authenticity. One was a language of growth and prosperity, the other a language of ideological confrontation. It was no accident, therefore, that the LDP and its allies long continued to be favored by voters during the period of rapid growth because people were entirely preoccupied with material pursuits, not ideological disputation.

LDP candidates for local office, especially chief executive,

22. One study showed that the proportion of voters expressing this particular kind of antipolitician feeling increased from 38% in 1955 to 51% in 1973. Yoshinori Ide, "Konmei no naka no Hoshu Gyakuten Senkyo," *Asahi Janaru,* 19 July 1974, pp. 13–14. Another study reported an identical range of increase in antipolitician sentiment between 1953 and 1968. See Tokei Suri Kenkyu Jo Kokuminsei Chosa Iinkai, ed., *Dai 2 Nihon-jin no Kokuminsei* (Tokyo: Shiseido, 1973), pp. 146–47.

used to garner voter support by a claim of direct line of personal contact with the national government (*chuo chokketsu*, direct connection with the center), meaning they would be better able than their opponents to get more funds and developmental projects from the national government and to induce business investment and industrial development in the locality.[23] This was entirely consistent with citizen expectations for more benefits of industrialism and greater affluence, not to mention special interests that would benefit from growth and development. The opposition, and that meant mostly the JSP, with its inveterate addiction to ideological abstractions and rhetorical generalities removed from the reality of voter desires, had little chance of effectively challenging the LDP dominance. And the more remote its chance of replacing the incumbent conservative government, the more stridently ideological it became.

Politicization of the costs of modern industrialism and other novel problems of advanced industrial society, however, gradually came to alter the character of the language of politics at the local level. This new language may be characterized as a language of prevention and redress. It focuses on the need to prevent further deterioration in the quality of life and to redress tangible and intangible damages inflicted upon the locality by the mindless pursuit of economic growth and prosperity, by the insensitivity and unresponsiveness of self-centered institutional imperatives and organizational inertia of government both at the local and national levels. It also seeks to redress distributive distortions that were allowed to go unchecked during the period of feverish national pursuit of growth and prosperity.

Thus, in recent local elections, candidates began to stress such ideas as "priority attention to the needs of local residents," "improvement in the quality of life," "protection of daily life," "environmental improvement," "life in harmony with nature," "development without environmental pollution and destruction," "from economic development to community development." There is also an emerging emphasis on "human rights" and a corresponding decline in the conventional concern with "property rights." These are among the campaign phrases and slogans first used by citizens' movements early in the 1970s which, once proven effective, came quickly to be emulated by opposition

---

23. For effective LDP slogans in the past, see Hajime Shinohara, "Bunka Henyo to Chiho Jichi no Kadai," *Sekai*, April 1971, p. 41.

es and the LDP alike. "Direct connection with the center"
many other conventional winning slogans became virtual
oos, and the JSP began to make efforts to mute its customary
eological stridency.

Style of Electoral Politics. The rise of the citizens' movement and all that it signifies have produced a visible effect upon
the style of electoral politics at the local level. In chapter 6 we
distinguished between "movement-led elections" and "party-led
elections." "Movement-led" electoral campaigns are of course
limited largely to localities that are more clearly postindustrial in
political ecology; Tokyo's 1971 gubernatorial election was the
first major and successful instance of such campaigns,[24] and it
set a pattern for subsequent movement-led electoral campaigns
elsewhere. In areas where parties are organizationally relatively
strong, campaigns are usually "party-led," but as noted in the
preceding chapter, many of those campaigns are variously
"movement-induced." Citizens' movements, even where they are
organizationally and logistically inferior, often cause warring
parties or factions of a party to suspend their quarrels during the
campaign in support of, say, a single gubernatorial or mayoral
candidate who is a suprapartisan candidate of the new breed.
Parties tend to be induced to support him in part because partisan
candidates no longer have much voter appeal but also because
none of them really would support another party's candidate.
Successful mayoralty campaigns in such major cities as Nagoya,
Osaka, and Kobe are among the recent examples of this kind of
party-led but movement-induced elections.

In local assembly elections, citizens' movements are fielding
an increasing number of their own candidates in competition
against partisan candidates, LDP or opposition. Since these movements are areal in organization and cross-stratal in membership,
some large cities and prefectures with uneven patterns of political
ecology are not yet congenial to movement-led or even movement-
induced mayoral or gubernatorial campaigns. In these cities and
prefectures, therefore, citizens' movements do better to field
assembly candidates of their own in those districts where they
are strong and where political ecology is more compatible with
their activities. Information on citizens' movement efforts in this

24. For an account of this particular election, see Taketsugu Tsurutani,
"A New Era of Japanese Politics: Tokyo's Gubernatorial Election," *Asian
Survey* 12 (May 1972).

regard, however, is still sketchy; we have no extensive data by which to assess the extent of movement penetration into legislatures.

It does seem, however, that electoral campaigns are, apart from the matter of campaign logistics, which are still provided largely by parties, becoming in their character and style increasingly "disengaged from parties and party identification," reflecting the rising phenomenon, for example, of "disengagement" on the part of the electorate and the emerging postindustrial political ecology. Regardless of the background of candidates and which parties support them logistically, campaigns are more often than not suprapartisan or antipartisan, citizen-centered, problem-oriented, and rejective of established groups and organizations. We may even say that issues and problems of postindustrial society have now reached the level of salience in electoral politics that compels all contending candidates in local elections to compete in terms of who can provide the best practicable solutions to them or who can best champion the ordinary citizens' concerns and needs. In an important sense, politics at the local level is indeed becoming postindustrial.

Responses of Parties

Still endowed though it is with funds, patronage, and legislative and bureaucratic power which can readily be manipulated, the LDP is clearly in decline and it realizes that the mere manipulation of conventional ingredients of power can no longer ensure its survival as the most powerful party in the face of the emerging postindustrial politics at the local level. There are three major aspects to the LDP's attempt to adapt itself to the changing environment of local electoral politics: the type of candidate, the nature of platform, and electoral alliance.

Instead of recruiting and endorsing local party bosses or former high-level government officials for gubernatorial and mayoral candidacies, the LDP in recent years began to recruit younger men from local administration with a fresh public image who can appeal even to opposition voters and who can run on a platform that integrates the major concerns of citizens' movements. In short, the party began to attempt to provide the kind of platform that is more relevant to popular concerns within a given locality or prefecture and to field candidates who can project an image of authentic citizen orientation and independence from the party government and national party leadership.

The 1975 gubernatorial elections showed that, where the LDP managed to retain the governor's mansion, it was largely owing to its determined effort to provide fresh candidates and/or more authentically citizen-centered, problem-oriented platforms.[25]

Another method by which the LDP is attempting to meet the challenge to its power at the local electoral level is to seek the support of one or more of the opposition parties for its candidates. The four opposition parties war among themselves constantly and frequently more fiercely than they take a common stand against the LDP. Taking advantage of this fact of divided opposition, the LDP often endorses or supports a candidate who is, for a variety of reasons, acceptable to one or more opposition parties that cannot decide whether to field a candidate of their own or agree on a joint candidate to compete against the LDP candidate. The most frequent electoral partner of the LDP in this regard is the DSP, simply because the DSP is ideologically and in policy preference closest to the LDP among the opposition parties. (In these instances of joint support, the candidates concerned run as independents.) There have been instances, also, in which the LDP and the JSP supported the same candidates; most of these obtained in areas where JCP candidates or JCP-supported candidates were viewed as strong.

Opposition parties, but especially the JSP, try assiduously to cultivate a public impression that citizens' movements and movement-induced candidates are their allies, if not their progenies, in spite of the fact that those movements arose out of popular frustration and disillusionment with their ineptitude and lack of adaptability in the changing environment. Some of the gains these parties made in recent assembly elections were made on the coattails of citizens' movements and movement-supported candidates. Opposition parties are more often than not beneficiaries of citizens' movements rather than their political benefactors.

Opposition parties, much like the LDP, also recruit, often under pressure from citizens' movements, as gubernatorial and mayoral candidates persons from outside their own ranks and partisan affiliations, academics and younger local administrators prominent among them. Unlike the LDP, however, these parties, particularly when two or more of them attempt to promote a joint candidate, frequently encounter serious problems of cooperation and coordination because they quarrel among themselves

25. See *Asahi Shimbun*, 10 February 1975, p. 1.

over the platform more ardently than they provide support for the candidate's campaign in unity. Sometimes, the precarious electoral alliance thus formed breaks down even before serious campaigning begins (the period of campaign is limited by law). Then there is the problem of internal unity even within a single opposition party, in particular the JSP. The JSP, as we recall from chapter 5, is factionalized not only at the national level (the parliamentary party and the party convention) but also at the local level (contending *Sohyo* unions and Socialism Association activists), and there is considerable tension, as a result, between the national and local levels. It is not rare, therefore, that contending factions at the local level promote opposing candidates, or that the national leadership and the local branch support different candidates. Even when the difference is resolved by hard bargaining and negotiation, the disaffected faction or level would more often than not sit on its hands during the campaign, and greet the defeat of the officially supported candidate with ill-concealed glee and we-told-you-so.

We must briefly look at the JCP and the CGP in electoral politics at the local level. As we noted in chapter 5, they were the only parties to increase their legislative representations in recent local elections. Their growing electoral strength is the result of the fact that, in their grass-roots activities, they are the only two parties that have made vigorous and successful attempts at dealing with issues and problems that became the increasing public concern with the emergence of postindustrial society. As political parties, their actions and orientation are consistent with those of citizens' movements and the concerns of ordinary voters. Their residual fear or antipathy toward these parties notwithstanding, increasing numbers of voters are electorally supporting them. In short, the JCP and the CGP have demonstrated a considerable degree of adaptability to the changing environment and the postindustrial political ecology. The combination of their relative size as parties and the residual fear or uncertainty the public at large still feel, together with a combined opposition from other parties, have thus far prevented these two rising parties from electing their own (i.e., Communist or Clean Government) candidates for gubernatorial mansions and mayoralties of large cities. Inasmuch as they are thus far the only parties with ascertainable potentials for successfully coopting the citizens' movement or establishing a coherent alliance with it, any future rise in their electoral popularity may well enable them to elect their own candidates to the office of local chief executive.

Electoral Politics at the National Level

The variation in political ecology we noted in chapter 6 between the national and local levels produces different patterns of electoral politics. For example, the fact that the chief executive (prime minister) at the national level is *not* popularly elected (that is, the electorate is excluded from his selection) deprives the electorate of one major dimension of electoral politics that energizes popular participation at the local level as well as of many spinoff effects that it produces at the local level.

Participatory logistics at the national level are unfavorable to citizen involvement in electoral politics except for the formal act of voting. Consider, for example, the amount of campaign funds needed. In the 1969 general elections, it was widely estimated that it cost, on the average, 100 million yen (approximately $280,000 at the then exchange rate) to carry out a successful campaign for a lower house seat.[26] In the 1972 general elections, the average campaign cost per seat allegedly rose to 200 million yen.[27] In the House of Councilors election of 1974, per seat campaign costs for victory were said to be 500 million yen.[28] The level of campaign financing required at the national level can be generated only by parties; it is beyond the capability of citizens' movements that have no financial patrons and engage in no money-making enterprises. Diet laws require that a party hold 51 seats or more in the lower house in order to present a legislative proposal involving a budget,[29] and only a party with 20 or more members is accorded the right of representation in House committees. These considerations combine to perpetuate the monopoly of electoral politics by the parties, and whatever energy citizens' movements or their allies may be able to generate is dissipated through competition among parties as well as factional politics within major parties. Instead, organized interests, by virtue of their political entrenchment at the national level, their financial capabilities, and their monopoly of substantive

26. See, for example, Hans Baerwald, "Itto-Nanaraku: Japan's 1969 Elections," *Asian Survey* 10 (March 1970).

27. Takashi Tachibana, "Tanaka Kakuei Kenkyu—Sono Kinmyaku to Jinmyaku," *Bungei Shunju*, November 1974, p. 94.

28. *Asahi Shimbun*, 4 July 1974, p. 2.

29. Yomiuri Shimbun Sha Yoron Chosa Shitsu, ed., *Senkyo o tettei Bunseki suru: 70 nen-dai no Senkyo to Seiji* (Tokyo: Yomiuri Shimbun Sha, 1975), p. 37.

participation in policy making at the national level, play the role at this level that effective citizens' movements play at the local level.

As a consequence, there is little fundamental change in electoral politics at the national level in language, style, concern, and type of candidate. Voters, many of whom became problem-oriented, suprapartisan or antipartisan, and effectively participatory in local electoral politics, revert to conventional cleavages, preferences, and referents in their behavior in national electoral politics. In local politics, they are increasingly capable of acting in manners that are appropriate to postindustrial politics; at the national level, there is still this powerful tendency among them to act in conventional ways.

At the national level, therefore, parties, especially major parties (the LDP and JSP), are responding not to the rise of new patterns of political participation or to the emergence of issues and problems that are explicitly postindustrial in character, but rather to the changing statistics of electoral fortunes as such. Thus the pattern of response of the parties differs considerably between the national and local levels.

The LDP, since it is in power and its position seems unassailable given the fragmented opposition, still acts as if it is impervious to changing circumstances. Perhaps it can afford business as usual for the time being simply because, as the perennial government party, it has funds, patronage, influence, and legislative power at its disposal, although an increasing number of its members, especially younger ones, realize the serious need for the party's shift in policy direction, commitment, and image. Thus far, at any rate, the overall propensity of the party at the national level seems more energetically to capitalize on and maximize the use of its conventional political assets that in the past has ensured its supremacy, such as money (hence the so-called "money power politics" which even some of its own members decry).

There is a possibility that even in national electoral politics, certain effects of postindustrial ecology at the local level may be asserting themselves. For example, age and experience are important authority referents in politics in industrial Japan and, as we noted in chapter 5, the LDP is gerontocratic. In the 1972 general elections, however, there were rather interesting phenomena that might presage the future pattern of LDP response to the changing environment of society. We refer to the fact that younger LDP members were elected with more popular votes than their elders. Looking at nine most underrepresented (hence more urban) and nine most overrepresented (less urban) lower house districts for the 1972 general elections, in each of which the LDP elected at least two candidates, we find the following:[30]

1. Top LDP vote-getters in these districts, both under-represented and overrepresented, were significantly younger than the second LDP winners in those districts: on the average, 53 vs. 58 years of age in urban districts and 58 vs. 60 in rural.

2. If we eliminate from the two sets of districts the most unusual case in each (because of the unusual popularity/prestige of certain aged LDP MPs), we see an even sharper age difference between the top winner and the second vote-getter in each district: 51 vs. 60 in urban and 57 vs. 64 in rural districts.

3. In five of the urban and seven of the rural districts, top LDP winners were younger than second-LDP winners (by 16 years in urban and 9 years in rural).

4. Top LDP vote-getters in six of the nine urban districts and four of the nine rural districts had less parliamentary and party seniority than the second vote-getters. Among these top winners were two novices in each of the two sets of districts.

There were other interesting occurrences. For example, of the twenty most underrepresented districts, five each had at least two LDP candidates running, but only one was elected. In four of these cases, the lone LDP winners were younger than their partisan losers by an average of 22 years, and in the fifth case, where the older candidate won, the age difference was only 4 years. In addition, in those four cases where the much younger men won over the much older fellow partisans, the winners were invariably much junior men in terms of parliamentary career than their losing elders.

If the general tendency these observations suggest proves consistent in the near future, we might expect a gradual internal reform of the LDP in policy direction, hence in its pattern of response to postindustrial challenge that would be compatible with the changing environment of the nation. In an important

30. Computed from data in *Seiji Handobukku*.

sense, this indicates that the party's adaptation to postindustrial society would be involuntary, rather than a matter of deliberate act.

Opposition parties' responses to voter disaffection and their changing fortunes are varied. The JSP and DSP, much like the LDP, are responding, not to the emergent postindustrial politics, but rather to election statistics. And their main efforts to revitalize their respective electoral support seem, for all practical purposes, to be limited to strengthening their ties with their respective traditional institutional allies, i.e., labor organizations: *Sohyo* for the JSP and *Domei* for the DSP. (In case of the JSP, the Socialism Association as well.) For reasons discussed in chapter 5, these parties, with their respective manners of internal and electoral operations, seem incapable of unloading their industrial political baggages without tearing themselves asunder. Their close respective ties with those institutional allies have already deprived them of much of their aggregative abilities and virtually reduced them to the role of pressure groups rather than political parties.

That these parties are responding not to the rise of novel issues and problems but merely to shifts in election statistics can be further observed in their intermittent and rather less coherent attempts at "joint electoral struggle of the opposition parties" (*yato kyoto*) and "reorganization of the opposition" (*yato saihen*). These are both electoral gimmicks that their proponents think would produce election statistics favorable to them and unfavorable to the ruling LDP. And they are the kind of gimmicks that these parties are constitutionally incapable of working out.

The motive for joint electoral struggle of the opposition (in which the JSP, the DSP, and the CGP have in the past expressed varying degrees of interest) is quite simple: to maximize the number of opposition seats in the Diet. In practical campaign terms, this calls for reductions of opposition candidates in various districts to optimum numbers in order to ensure the most effective use of anti-LDP votes. Many LDP candidates in past elections won because opposition parties insisted on fielding their own respective partisan candidates who, because of their numbers, ended up reducing one another's election chances instead of reducing LDP votes. One of the consequences of this repeated phenomenon is that even partisan supporters of opposition parties, as Curtis noted in regard to the 1960 general elections, did not vote because they knew their candidates would lose anyway.[31] Even if we disregard these potential opposition supporters, we can still argue that effective "joint electoral struggle" of these parties would most likely have produced a significantly different electoral outcome in any of the recent elections. On the basis of the votes cast, for example, in the 1972 (latest as of this writing) general election, we note that, if opposition parties had fielded fewer candidates, they could have picked up to 52 additional lower house seats. My calculations show that the combined votes for the two losing opposition candidates in each of 52 (out of 125) districts exceeded the number of votes received by the lowest LDP winner by 3.3 percent to 87.8 percent. In 34 of those cases, the excess was by over 20 percent.[32] Of course, partisan hostility and mistrust among supporters of these opposition parties would in reality have influenced actual outcomes in these districts, but it nevertheless seems entirely plausible, especially in view of the fact that in the election under review, the LDP received fewer votes nationwide than the opposition parties combined, that effective "joint struggle" among the latter would have produced distribution of House of Representative seats considerably dissimilar to the actual distribution produced by that election.

The trouble is that opposition parties have proved themselves incapable of implementing the "joint electoral struggle" against the LDP, and the reasons for their incapacity are quite explicit. As one opposition leader observed, there are at least three areas of agreement needed for meaningful "joint struggle": (1) platform, (2) candidate, and (3) campaign logistics.[33] Where parties play second fiddle to citizens' movements in gubernatorial or mayoral elections, these areas of agreement have often been worked out precisely because the source of initiative or inducement is outside the parties and the postindustrial political ecology leaves opposition parties little choice, as we noted earlier. In electoral politics at the national level, however, parties (and their supporting industrial special interests) are not only the primary but the only actors. They are therefore exposed to one another directly without any intervening cushions, so to speak. There is nothing to mediate them in their direct interaction.

31. Curtis, "The 1969 General Election in Japan," p. 867.

32. Computed from *Seiji Handobukku*, pp. 203–64.

33. Junkichi Geji, "Kakushin Chiji no Jitsugen to Toitsu Sensen," *Zen'ei* (January 1973).

Each of those three areas of agreement more often than not aggravates the relations between or among the parties concerned. There is a deeply ingrained mutual mistrust among these parties, between the JCP and others, between the JSP and the DSP, and between the JSP and the CGP. And each opposition party wants to promote a platform that reflects its own preferences. One JSP leader who does not support the "joint struggle" thesis warned his party against the danger of losing, through platform compromise, its ideological autonomy and policy independence.[34] Even if a common platform were agreed upon by parties concerned at the national level, there would still remain this problem of having such an agreement accepted by local branches (with the exception of the JCP, which is highly disciplined internally). A party's branch in a district may be more radical than its national leadership, or more conservative. Resistance from the local level could wreck the agreement at the national level.

Agreeing on a joint candidate in any district is no easier task for the parties concerned. For a party to agree to support another party's candidate means an actual or potential loss of one Diet seat for itself. Besides, the joint candidate might lose in the election. Every party wants its own candidate(s) jointly supported by other parties, and no party is willing to be deprived of its own candidate(s), regardless of objective assessments of their respective strengths. Again, even if an agreement were possible at the national leadership level, we would still face the problem at the local level.

Campaign logistics would present no less taxing problem, for even if agreement were possible on the foregoing two areas of "joint struggle," it could meet considerable difficulties at the critical level of implementation in the day-to-day business of campaign activities. Local organizations of the parties concerned are mistrustful toward one another. Maybe there are some old scores to settle.

All in all, therefore, the three areas of agreement necessary for effective joint struggle turn out to be, not mutually complementary, but instead mutually aggravating. In fact, mere suggestion of joint struggle often sensitizes and compounds mutual mistrust between the parties concerned and, by the same token, stirs up conflict among factions within them.

---

34. Toshiaki Yokoyama, "Senkyo Kyoto ni tsuite no Shomondai," *Gekkan Shakaito*, April 1971, p. 25.

"Reorganization of the opposition" (*yato saihen*), too, arises out of an equally optimistic assumption on the part of its proponents regarding its practical feasibility and, perhaps more significant, its adequacy as a response to rising popular concerns in the changing society. The idea of two major parties as viable alternatives to each other is of course attractive, but the proponents of reorganization of the opposition parties (presumably excluding the JCP) into one unified party effectively to compete with the LDP both underestimate serious practical obstacles in their path and miss the point about the character of voter disaffection in an increasingly postindustrial society. The obstacles encountered by efforts for "joint electoral struggle" we referred to above in essence would confront any attempt at a reorganization of the opposition with magnified intensity. If these obstacles prevent opposition parties from "joint struggle" in some electoral districts, then surely they would render "opposition reorganization" wholly impossible. The only way in which these parties could merge to form a single opposition party would be for them, first, to unburden themselves of the respective political baggage which fetters them in many crucial dimensions of their behavior. And this leads to our other point, that is, the proponents of opposition reorganization are not sufficiently taking into account the character of citizen concerns in this increasingly postindustrial society. Voters are concerned, not about the mere putting together of opposition parties into a larger party (which is essentially a matter of parliamentary arithmetic), but rather about the management and resolution of issues and problems that are characteristic of postindustrial society. Arithmetic would not solve those issues and problems; only a meaningful change in attitudes, values, and policy directions of those elected representatives and parties would. Arithmetic would be meaningful only when it was used to count appropriate properties. Mere juggling of the structure of the opposition would not constitute a proper response to the problems of society.

THE FUTURE OF POLITICS AND POLITICAL ECOLOGY AT THE NATIONAL LEVEL

At the end of the preceding chapter, we asked a question and deferred our answer to it: What force, if any, would bridge the local-national gap in political behavior in general and participation in particular? We should answer this question against the issue of political ecology, inasmuch as political behavior in general and political participation in particular are consequences of political ecology.

The fact that the national political ecology differs from the local suggests that patterns of political participation, formal or substantive, at the national level can never be the same as that at the local level, at least in the foreseeable future. Political ecology at the national level can change in some of its dimensions; in others, however, it most likely will not. Consider, for example, the dimensions of constitutional arrangement and participatory logistics. Barring constitutional amendments and a physical restructuring of society, they are likely to remain as they are. On the other hand, material, demographic, ideological, and cultural and attitudinal dimensions could change and, in consequence or in concert, institutional constraints, roles of parties and organized groups would be variously affected.

From our discussion in the present chapter and in chapter 6, it seems quite clear a serious conflict is developing between the national and the local levels. Local government in the new postindustrial political ecology is ceasing to be a passive, subservient tool of national government and bureaucracy, as the result of an ascertainable change in the character of electoral politics and the rise of substantive popular political participation at this level. In this rising conflict (some have already began to view it as confrontation), local government has at its disposal considerable means to discomfit and frustrate national government and bureaucracy: e.g., united public opposition at the stage of policy making and resistance and sabotage at the critical level of implementation. Potential effectiveness of these means of local resistance against the national level would be in part enhanced by the propensity of opposition parties and the internal vulnerability of the ruling party at the national level. Opposition parties, which all claim to be "progressive," in the Diet would do anything to embarrass, disturb, or encumber the LDP government in hopes of gaining whatever political mileage could be gained, and they would seek every opportunity to do so. They are constantly looking for issues that could be exploited for this purpose. The LDP government, on the other hand, is, as we noted in chapter 4, extremely loathe to create or confront serious public controversies because of its internal factional considerations, particularly at a time when governance of the nation is becoming increasingly difficult in the face of a drastic decline in the rate of economic growth and a general decline in its popular support. All this suggests, then, that the national government and bureaucracy may prove to be more amenable in the future to a rising pressure from local government for some meaningful change in policies and priorities. In short, local governments, prodded, energized, and supported by citizens' movements, might well come to challenge the power of conventional special interests at the national level much in the same way as citizens' movements at the local level have come to challenge and overshadow the power and influence of special interests.

Apart from this "bottom-upward" pressure emanating from the local level, another source of pressure could be directly exerted at the national level upon the conduct of government. Here we refer, not to the JSP or the DSP, but specifically to the JCP and, possibly, the CGP. That these two parties are enjoying a rising electoral support not only at the local but at the national level is significant in itself. More important, however, are some fundamental political aspects of these parties that, as we discussed in chapter 5, distinguish them from other parties. The LDP and the JSP are institutionally handicapped and weighed down by their seemingly inextricable political, financial, and/or organizational ties with powerfully entrenched special interests of industrial society. In contrast, the JCP and, *mutatis mutandis*, the CGP seem quite independent of such burdensome political baggage. They are institutionally, financially, hence politically free from the imperatives and constraints of the politics of industrial society.

The JCP was once on the verge of electoral extinction and was without support from any organized groups, including labor. This eventually turned out to be a blessing in disguise inasmuch as the party was compelled to cultivate support from ordinary citizens at the grass-roots level by focusing on and tending their immediate problems, toward which the LDP and the JSP alike demonstrated a remarkable lack of sensitivity. The CGP, on the other hand, even while it was still tied to the Value Creation Society, had been engaged in energetic grassroots efforts to foster popular electoral support beyond that which could be generated from the religious movement's membership and, since its formal severance of ties with the movement in 1970, has redoubled its efforts. As a consequence, its electoral strength has radically increased at the local level and shown signs of growth at the national level since the setback suffered in the 1972 general elections. There seems to be a remarkable degree of similarity between these two parties in the character of their grass-roots efforts and their rising electoral popularity. They both address

themselves, not to ideological abstractions or political disputation, but to the kinds of issues and problems that gave rise to
the citizens' movement: pollution, congestion, high prices, inequity in taxes, the insensitivity and unresponsiveness of government agencies and officials, arrogance and impertinence of
special interests, inadequacy of social capital, difficulty of getting
welfare benefits, among others. Unlike their LDP and JSP counterparts, members of the JCP and the CGP plunge themselves
into what citizens' movement activists call "sustained daily activities" (*nichijo katsudo*), e.g., actively soliciting grievances of
ordinary citizens, taking them through their (JCP or CGP) legislators or directly to relevant officials and agencies, and persisting
in their efforts until they get results; taking active part in, or
sometimes taking the initiative in, organizing citizens' movements at the local level; in short, doing what citizens' movement
activists do. And they maintain close coordination and communication with their elected representatives at the local as well as
the national level. The JCP and the CGP can do all this precisely
because they are not constrained by ties and alliances with any
major forces of industrial society. They are not afraid of stepping
on the toes of powerful special interests.

It is not surprising, therefore, that the JCP and the CGP are
the only parties to experience any significant rise in voter support
in recent years. In contrast, both the LDP and the JSP have
suffered consistent decline in electoral support both nationally
and locally, and their respective traditional strongholds are being
seriously weakened without any compensating growth in popularity elsewhere. They have lost voters to the JCP and the CGP.

The JCP and the CGP, their newly discovered strength
arising from their vigorous championing of postindustrial problems and issues of ordinary citizens, would be able to exert
critical pressure upon the national government and help alter
the character of politics at the national level, especially when
they respectively capture 51 or more seats in the more important
House of Representatives (currently they hold 39 and 29 seats
respectively). As we observed before, Diet laws require a party
to hold 51 seats or more in order for it to present a legislative
proposal involving a budget. When the JCP and/or the CGP
have met this requirement for more effective legislative activity
and participation, their voice in the Diet will be vastly increased
and will help generate contingencies that would precipitate some
important modification in government policies and even a new
alignment of forces in the legislative arena.

This potential further growth in the power and popularity of the JCP and the CGP is significant, not in terms of conventional electoral and parliamentary arithmetic (which, in itself, have nothing to do with the character of politics), but because it is based on the same set of forces that have given rise to new patterns of substantive popular participation at the grass-roots level as exemplified by the citizens' movement. In other words, the growth of the JCP and the CGP is entirely consistent with and reflective of some of the critical phenomena of the emerging postindustrial society.

A combination of a continuing increase in the number of local governments responsive to and/or precipitated by citizens' movements on the one hand and a further rise in parliamentary strength of the JCP and the CGP on the other would promise a significant modification of the character of politics at the national level in the direction of reducing the national-local dichotomy discussed earlier. Logistical correlates for popular participation at the national level are largely absent, and processual features of parties as major vehicles of electoral participation would therefore remain largely unchanged. The modification of the character of politics at the national level, modification that would reduce the gap between the national and local level, would be in the nature of its thrust, language, concern, style, and objective; and in this process of modification, the character of politics at the national and that at the local level would become mutually complementary, reinforcing, and reflective.

Part IV
CONCLUSION

8

Political Change in Japan

We began this volume with a hope that Japanese politics could be usefully studied from a perspective of industrial-postindustrial contrast. Our treatment of the subject in the preceding chapters is limited in scope; it is not, nor is it meant to be, exhaustive or comprehensive, for we focused our attention on those dimensions and aspects that are more elucidative of the kind of political change that is taking place in the country. It nevertheless seems that certain ascertainable and/or incipiently distinct features have emerged from our study. These features, moreover, may well be suggestive of a direction or directions in which future studies of Japanese politics can be conducted. In addition, we hope, though it is not our intention in this volume as such, that with further conceptual refinement some of the features that have emerged from our study of Japanese politics may be applicable to inquiries into other postindustrial societies.

Perhaps the most significant feature of political change in Japan that emerges from our investigation is a certain transition from the industrial to the postindustrial period in the character and thrust of politics. This transition, of course, is extremely difficult to conceptualize. But, let us try. The emerging postindustrial politics may be defined as "a community-centered, problem-oriented redressive politics" in contrast to the conventional, industrial-age politics which may, in turn, be viewed as "a special-interests-centered, growth-oriented distributive politics." By community-centered, problem-oriented redressive politics, we mean a politics that focuses its primary thrust upon the daily well-being of the citizenry without stratal or sectoral distinction, upon correcting distributive and ecological distortions brought about or left unresolved by industrial politics, and upon safeguarding and promoting the collective citizen welfare even at the expense of sectoral private interests. Private interests or special interests should after all be regarded as only instrumental to the collective well-being rather than paramount in themselves. This postindustrial politics in addition is indifferent to ideological distinctions regarding problems and solutions. In short, the redressive politics is one that addresses itself to the fundamental postindustrial issues and problems and views their management and resolution as subsuming stratal and sectoral problems and preferences.

The special-interests-centered, growth-oriented distributive politics of industrial society, on the other hand, concerns itself primarily with the allocation of resources (benefits of industrialism) on the basis of differential potencies of inputs by special and sectoral interests concerned. This politics views the primacy of special interests as functional to the well-being of the collectivity since, in its perspective, the well-being of those interests generates trickle-down effects of benefits to society at large. The well-being of any such interest rests on constant economic growth and that of society at large rests upon receipts of portions of net growth enjoyed by that interest. In short, what is good for special interests is regarded as good (though perhaps not nearly as good as it is for them) for society at large. In the nature of things and phenomena in the political arena and policy making, special interests characteristic of industrialism are operationally superior to the collectivity, for they monopolize substantive participation in policy making while the collectivity —citizenry—as such is largely confined to the arena of formal participation. It is precisely for this reason that special interests are accorded the topmost priority by authoritative policy makers. In contrast, in postindustrial redressive politics, the rise of substantive popular participation in policy making, either directly through the citizens' movement at the local level or through the growth in influence of parties and local government that reflect this phenomenon at the national level either in legislative politics or pressure politics, subordinates special interests to the collectivity and accords them the level and quality of consideration that is commensurate with the level and quality of the positive net contribution they are capable of making toward the collective well-being.

This distinction, while clear verbally or conceptually, is very difficult to demonstrate in actuality because, in the real world, each type of politics is not that pure and authentic. In reality, the distinction is not absolute; in an important sense, the difference is in degree. The difference in degree, however, does make a difference in character when it is superimposed upon circumstances that are sufficiently different in terms of historical evolution and development of society. Conventional industrial politics, especially as industrialism reaches more advanced stages, contains considerable elements of what we here describe as postindustrial politics and the latter, in turn, contains much that is found in the former. The distribution of the benefits of industrialism—income and wealth—is an indispensable aspect of redressive politics, for, without it, existing distributive and ecological distortions cannot be redressed. In the process, various interests cannot but be differentially treated, albeit on a different set of operational criteria. Redress or correction of glaring inequity in the distribution of income and wealth is clearly an element of the conventional industrial politics, for it is the reduction in that inequity that brings about the integration of potentially revolutionary have-nots into the total social fabric and the decline in the intensity of political conflict in industrial society. Policy making in industrial politics is clearly concerned about the well-being of the collectivity as opposed to that of special interests. There are certain features in each of these two types of politics, however, that nonetheless distinguish it from the other. And each places different emphasis upon different kinds of issues and problems.

The crucial distinction between industrial and postindustrial political decision making has to do with differing perceptions of the relationship between special interests and the collectivity as well as with differing levels of intensity or urgency with which these two distinct spheres are treated. The industrial perception of the relationship between private interests and the collectivity subordinates the latter to the former, while the postindustrial perception reverses the relationship between the two. In one, what is good for special interests cannot but be good for the collectivity as well; in the other, what is good for the collectivity is also good for special interests, and, if not, there is obviously something wrong with those special interests. The difference between these two distinct perceptions is not a mere matter of emphasis. In fact, there is a very critical disjunction between them. For there is a sense in which we can strongly argue that, in industrial society, the most potent, hence authoritative collective endeavor, i.e., public governmental policy-making process, is appropriated for the enhancement of private special interests; in postindustrial society, such effort is mobilized for collective, as opposed to private, benefits.

This distinction is very important for us to understand and bear in mind. Else we would be unable to see much important difference between industrial politics and postindustrial politics Consider, for example, the matter of instrumental orientation, as opposed to ideological orientation. Instrumentalism or instrumental orientation suggests that problems are dealt with pragmatically, by such methods or techniques as would most expeditiously manage or resolve them. In this sense, both industrial and postindustrial politics are instrumentally oriented, at least in open democratic societies. But the concept of instrumentalism cannot be profitably employed in the discussion of postindustrial politics unless we understand the distinction we have indicated in the preceding paragraph, for, in an ordinary sense, industrial politics is just as nonideological as postindustrial politics. Neither is concerned about ideological distinctions of a given problem or a given method (though, residually, that still can be resuscitated, albeit increasingly peripherally). Both are concerned primarily about pragmatic functionality or instrumental efficacy of a problem or a method. Does that mean, then, that there is no difference between the politics of industrial society and that of postindustrial society? If we understand the distinction stated in the preceding paragraph, we should be able to recognize a very crucial difference. This difference concerns itself with the object and thrust of instrumentalism. Instrumentalism in industrial politics accommodates itself into demands of special interests and imperatives of economic growth and expansion. In postindustrial politics, instrumentalism has to do with the focus on welfare, the quality of life and environment, redress of distributive distortions that have accumulated, and the resolution of the cross-stratal issue of costs of modern industrialism. It attempts to assimilate private interests into the necessary change in favor of collective well-being. In industrial politics, instrumentalism is stratal, sectoral, and geared to growth and expansion; in postindustrial politics, it is cross-stratal, collectivist, and redressive in orientation.

Another dimension of this distinction in character and thrust between industrial politics and postindustrial politics has to do with the role of politics in the area of prescription and responsiveness. As discussed in chapter 3 and in the Introduction to part 2, the issue of who gets what in industrial politics is determined by relative extents of power and influence competing claimants (organized groups) in the political arena can exert upon policy makers and the entire decision-making processes. All participating groups and interests in the relevant and effective arena are treated as intrinsically equal in value and legitimacy, and whether or not one group or one alignment of groups gets more than another depends entirely upon the extent to which it can outperform the others in influencing policy making and policy makers. There are basically no other standards. Power, and not need, determines who gets how big a slice of the expanding pie. To this extent, it is clear that government in industrial politics is highly responsive—responsive, that is, to the powerful and the influential. In an important sense, therefore, industrialism has deprived politics of its fundamental prescriptive role and reduced it to a selective arena of the free-for-all (those who are influential enough to engage in substantive participation) where power is operationally right (hence, the more powerful, the more right, i.e., the more needful in terms of the distribution of benefits of industrialism). Government moves in any direction that the more powerful among those interests steer it to move. In the classical sense of the term, political debate in industrial society is not political at all.

In postindustrial politics, government would have to cultivate (or, in a normative sense, restore) its fundamental prescriptive capability if it is effectively to meet the challenge of the new historical period. Prescription necessarily implies an act of will, a projective capacity, and bold innovation. It defies convention and conventional constraints; it disdains vested interests; and it necessarily focuses upon the fortune and well-being of the collectivity. Its responsiveness is not directed toward the powerful and the privileged but rather toward the needs of citizenry and the requirements of collective interests. This is the challenge both parties and government in Japan face today.

The prevailing condition in Japan today is extremely ambivalent in these regards. There is a growing recognition that the conventional politics of industrial society is no longer adequate and that there is a critical necessity for a wholly new direction for government and a radically innovative thrust for policy making. This recognition is widespread among citizens at the local level where political ecology is more postindustrial, and widely shared by a growing number of politicians and political leaders. At the national level, however, where certain dimensions of political ecology inhibit the pace of transition from industrialism to postindustrialism, the same recognition has not yet been sufficiently translated into any extensive behavioral or electoral manifestation. The power and resistance of conventional industrial politics are still enormous, especially at the national level where the arena of substantive participation is largely monopolized by special interests. This conflict of fundamental values and requirements between industrialism and postindustrialism takes place within the individual as well as within society at large. Hence the ambivalence. But the plain fact that such conflict is taking place clearly suggests that the politics of postindustrialism has already emerged to challenge the conventional politics of industrial society.

A second significant feature of political change in Japan pertains to popular political participation. Here it has to do not only with the pattern of participation but also with the quality of participation. In industrial Japan, rates of electoral participation were high, but only in terms that neither suggested a high citizen competence nor were concerned with collective well-being. In essence, the type of popular participation characteristic of the industrial period was largely formal or ritualistic. It was symbolic participation without power. This is not to say, of course, that such participation was devoid of significance, for it was clearly functional for the purpose of maintaining the general political arrangement and status quo regarding the national commitment to economic growth and prosperity, which people at large either fully supported or willingly acquiesced in. That was the reason for the remarkable degree of sociopolitical stability and the phenomenal economic growth that the country enjoyed in the past two decades. Symbolic participation, however, is meaningful only as long as the general status quo of society, including the goal that society pursues, is acceptable to the citizenry. Once the status quo becomes unacceptable, symbolic participation, too, becomes devoid of positive political meaning. And, clearly in

Japan today, symbolic popular political participation has ceased to be very useful.

In response to the emergence of novel issues and problems of postindustrial character, there has arisen an increasingly pronounced trend away from merely symbolic participation and toward what we have been calling substantive participation, especially at the local level where political ecology is more post-industrial. During the industrial period, substantive participation was restricted largely to special interests (and at the national level where political ecology differs in some of its dimensions from the local, this is still the case), for it was they, and not ordinary citizens, that engaged in effective input activities. Citizens were largely content with the symbolic input activity— voting. Today, however, increasing numbers of ordinary citizens have become aware that the conventional pattern of voter participation that they took for granted as the appropriate democratic popular input activity is really neither an effective way to assert popular sovereignty nor a meaningful method of influencing policy making. They recognize the need for an instrumental focus, sustained action, cross-stratal thrust and organization, and pressure politics as indispensable ingredients of effective popular participation. This recognition has resulted in politically energizing many voters, especially those who were traditionally regarded as either acquiescent or apolitical, indifferent or cynical, particularly in areas where political ecology is clearly more postindustrial. As exemplified by the citizens' movement, the new pattern of popular participation is action-oriented, focuses on issues and problems that need no contrived articulation, attempts to mobilize community energy outside parties and established organizations and groups, rejects conventional political referents and behavioral inhibitions, and is sustained by a sense of commitment and urgency.

In electoral politics, the new mode of popular participation has variously demonstrated its energy at the subnational level where chief executives—governors and mayors—are elected by direct popular vote and therefore can be held directly and visibly accountable to citizens, and in areas where the particular level of electoral logistics required for effective campaign enables the citizens' movement to field their own legislative candidates. And the dynamic forces that the movement generates are compelling parties to modify many of their aspects in order to retain their role and influence in electoral politics. At the national level, however, variations in certain dimensions of political ecology inhibit direct penetration of the new mode of participation, with the result that electoral politics at this level is still monopolized by parties that are resistant to change, although some of the parties (the JCP and the CGP) are increasing their electoral strength by vigorously attempting to adapt themselves to the changing environment. While the external behavior of the major parties has not shown any clear sign of modification, internally there are certain indications, especially within the ruling LDP, of involuntarily accelerated generational metabolism both in age and in outlook. How soon this metabolism will translate itself into external behavior, however, remains to be seen.

Perhaps the most significant impact of the new mode of popular political participation exemplified by the citizens' movement is seen in the area of substantive participation at the post-industrial local level and of influence upon the conduct of local government. Local government agencies, for long dependent upon national government and bureaucracy financially, hence politically, had become increasingly insensitive and unresponsive to citizen concerns as society began to undergo the transition from industrialism to postindustrialism. This disjunction between a rising citizens' concern with postindustrial problems and local government's continued industrial orientation (which favored special interests of industrial society) ultimately resulted in the rise and spread of citizens' movements which, aided by participatory logistics available to them, began effectively to challenge special interests in the arena of substantive participation in policy making and, concomitantly, to exert increasing pressures upon policy-making organs and officials of local government through sustained direct activities and confrontation tactics, bypassing parties that are, owing to their ties with special interests of industrial societies, incapable of meaningfully aggregating and intergrating citizens' concerns in the formal political arena. Local chief executives who are more blatantly supportive of special interests and resistant to citizens' demands are being subjected to more critical popular scrutiny and recalcitrant ones among them are frequently thrown out of office by movement-initiated recall.

In more clearly postindustrial localities, the mode, as well as the mood, of popular political participation exemplified by the citizens' movement are producing ascertainable changes in the behavior of local government. New offices and bureaus are set up to deal exclusively with issues and problems of ordinary citizens; officials are demonstrating greater responsiveness to citizen demands and grievances; and they are finding themselves in an increasing conflict with directives, preferences, and orientation of national government and bureaucracy.

The energy and mood generated by the new pattern of substantive popular participation at the local level has, in the meantime, also produced some unintended consequences. Petty grievances and trivial annoyances that should be resolved by voluntary private action and negotiation as well as contentious demands are pressed upon local government together with issues and problems of genuine importance. This invariably tends to strain the capability of public agencies and create new areas of tension and conflict between government and citizenry that should be avoided. The integrity of both the new pattern of popular participation and government is in danger of being seriously compromised to the benefit of neither. This is the concrete danger that the new pattern of popular participation faces. And the danger has arisen precisely because the new pattern of participation has proven effective.

At the national level, the new pattern of substantive popular participation has produced little or no direct impact, due, clearly, to the particular nature of the constitutional arrangement and participatory logistics obtaining at this level. The impact of substantive popular participation on this level is likely to be indirect, through local government. Citizens' movements, where successful, are compelling local government to engage in pressure politics in its relationship with national government and bureaucracy and to challenge the dominance of special interests in the arena of substantive participation at the national level. In this respect, the new pattern of popular substantive participation, if it can sustain itself over time, will have a very significant, albeit indirect, influence upon the character and orientation of the politics at the national level as well.

The unprecedented, direct action-oriented pattern of popular political participation is enhanced by, and in turn enhancing, a decline in potency of conventional political referents and behavioral inhibition that have in the past dominated Japanese society and determined the character of political participation. Various kinds of personal ties and connections (*kankei*) as potent political referents, for example, have in the past played a crucial role as the primary organizing principle for electoral politics, but as we observed in chapter 6, they show signs of considerable erosion, thus enabling voters to gravitate, especially at the level of local politics, toward one another across conventional socioeconomic or ideological cleavages on the basis of acutely felt common concerns. Traditional authority referents such as age and institutional credentials are also declining in popular appeal. Conventional conservative-progressive ideological dichotomy, too, is losing its political relevance. Traditional socioeconomic and ideological cleavages that have in the past prevented meaningful horizontal interaction and political co-operation are gradually overcome by increasing numbers of citizens who engage themselves in citizens' movements. The relationship between the new pattern of popular participation and the erosion of conventional political referents and behavioral inhibitions, therefore, seems definitely to be mutually reinforcing.

A third feature of change in Japanese politics that is clearly ascertainable is the rise of new types of political activists and leaders, as well as candidates. Activists emerging from the new pattern of popular participation are relatively young, well-educated professionals, and newcomers to the locality. They are also more often than not "disengaged from partisan identification." They manifest postwar generational attitudes and values that are much less deferential toward conventional authority referents, more problem-oriented, more citizen-competent, more open and egalitarian. In short, new breeds of activists are free from the constraints of traditional political referents and behavioral inhibitions by which conventional kinds of political activists (partisan, industrial politics-oriented, older, locally in-fluential by virtue of conventional properties of interpersonal and social relations) are still influenced. The 1970s are the first decade in which values and attitudes of the postindustrial gen-eration are beginning to assert themselves in the political arena. Then, too, political candidates, especially at the local level, show certain marked differences from candidates in the industrial era or the industrial political ecology. In political origin, they are increasingly suprapartisan rather than partisan; in career back-ground, they are amateurs such as academics, or relatively junior local administrators, and not former high-level government officials or local politicos; their popular image suggests no political ties, and independence from party politicians and influentials and special interests, instead of political "savvy" and experience, and good connections with political influentials and special interests. In terms of base of support, new candidates are suprapartisan, and anti-special interests, and appeal to voters who participate in or are sympathetic toward the citizens' move-ment; while conventional candidates are partisan, supported by party and special interests. These comparative characteristics of candidates are quite distinct between the new and the conventional types. In these dimensions of comparison, the new type of candidate is decidedly unconventional. Parties, ruling and opposition alike, now acknowledge the significance of the change in popularity regarding the type of candidates, and they are assiduously attempting to cultivate candidates whose characteristics accord with the new public appeal and popular expectation.

Statistically observable ups and downs in electoral support for parties seem to have little to do with conventional economic-ideological differences among these parties as such at the local level. Fluctuations in voter support are increasingly the function of public perceptions of candidates regardless of these men's former or present party affiliation/support or absence thereof. Voters are concerned about whether or not these candidates, regardless of their past political inclination or partisan reference, are sufficiently independent of parties, partisan considerations, and special interests to be problem-oriented and citizen-centered. Without this understanding of voter perception and the distinction between the old and the new types of political candidate, local election results would be very confusing, for candidates who are reported by mass media to be supported by the LDP do win, and those who are supported by opposition parties but not always accurately identified with the new trend toward substantive popular participation do lose. Almost invariably, however, where LDP-supported candidates have won, closer examinations suggest that they won not so much because they received support from the LDP as because they were successful in persuading voters of their commitment to and concern about the new issues and problems and their independence from special interests and even the party that supported them. In short, they won because they were publicly identified with the postindustrial, community-centered, problem-oriented redressive politics. As a consequence, in more and more local elections, opposing candidates, whether they receive support from one party or another, are becoming more alike in that they are increasingly demonstrating those common features of the new type of political activists and candidates. This, of course, creates a difficulty of choice for voters, but it can be argued that the phenomenon of Tweedledum and Tweedledee in this context is preferable to that in the context of industrial politics.

Fourth, the conventional rural-urban political dichotomy seems definitely in decline, increasingly overshadowed by a novel

local-national dichotomy. The decline of the conventional dichotomy, of course, is inevitable according to the dynamics and logic
of industrialization, economic growth, and prosperity. Advanced
industrialism hastens the process of reducing the rural-urban
differences in a number of politically relevant dimensions, e.g.,
the life style, consumption patterns, penetration of mass communications media, a rising level of education, intergenerational
value and attitude changes, virtual "urbanization" of rural occupations as manifest in the rapid decline of agricultural income as
proportion of the total rural income, and, not least important, the
onslaught of certain ill consequences of advanced industrialism
which affect the rural sector in Japan much more rapidly and
extensively than in other industrial states because of the geographical compactness and population density of the nation. The
decline of the conventional rural-urban political dichotomy is
gradually expressed in the drop in electoral support for the LDP,
an erosion in the efficacy of traditional political referents and
behavioral inhibitions, and the rise of issue-centered activist
orientation. In value, attitude, occupation, political sophistication, and impact of postindustrialism, if not in physical setting,
rural Japan seems to be becoming increasingly less distinguishable from urban Japan.

The decline in the rural-urban political dichotomy as a
result of the nation's gradual transition toward postindustrial
society is accompanied by the rise of a local-national political
dichotomy. The new dichotomy, too, is a consequence of certain
dynamics of postindustrialism, and it can be explained, as we
attempted to explain, by certain differences in the character of
political ecology between the two levels that have become salient
with the rise of postindustrialism. Political behavior at the local
level is more ascertainably postindustrial in a variety of its
dimensions, e.g., electoral politics, substantive citizen participation, the language and style of politics, the character of issues
and problems, and responses of parties and government; at the
national level, it lags far behind in the degree and character of
change. This divergence in the rate and nature of political change
between the local and the national levels is creating considerable
amounts of stress and strain in the political and administrative
relationships between the two levels. The local level, especially
where political ecology is more clearly postindustrial, is increasingly postindustrial in political behavior and manifestation; in
contrast, the national level in these regards is still more
ascertainably industrial. Two emergent forces, however, could

in combination help change the character of political ecology at the national level and thus reduce the gap between the two levels in the character of politics. They are local government, and the two political parties that are institutionally and operationally more adaptable to postindustrialism than the other parties: the JCP and the CGP.

Local government is absorbing and integrating much of the dynamics generated by the postindustrial political ecology and the concomitant rise in popular political activism, both electoral and substantive. In so doing, local government is becoming an increasingly potent organization to challenge the conventional special interests in the arena of substantive participation in policy making at the national level. National government and bureaucracy, to which local government has long been subservient, are being increasingly compelled to heed the demands of local government if they are to avoid serious contingencies of confrontation and subsequent political controversies and instability. At the same time, the JCP and the CGP are showing positive signs of growth in electoral popularity both at the local and at the national level by virtue of their championing of issues and problems of postindustrial society, and the political energy emanating from their relative freedom and independence from the politics of industrial society, especially when they achieve the level of representation in the Diet that would afford them the power of effective policy initiation, would perforce cause significant changes in the character, concern, orientation, and thrust of politics at the national level. At that point, the bottom-upward pressure from local government and the impact of the influence of the JCP and the CGP would become mutually reinforcing in narrowing the existing local-national political dichotomy.

Fifth, as the result of features of political changes summarized above, Japan's political culture is also undergoing a significant transformation. The well-stated paradox of the country being an open society made up of closed components is becoming less descriptive, especially at the local level. The new pattern of popular political participation and the concomitant decline in efficacy of traditional political referents and behavioral inhibitions, precipitated as they have initially been by the emergence of critical cross-stratal and redressive problems of advanced industrialism, are slowly but surely eroding the social and psychological walls that have in the past persistently separated one sector of the population from another and that have thus far prevented genuine social and political integration of the vertically and horizontally stratified society. Citizens from those heretofore closed components are joining forces on the basis of mutual equality in order to combat issues and problems that afflict or concern them without the neat and precise discrimination with which they have in the past been socially compartmentalized. Catholicity of affliction and concern tends to eliminate behavioral selectivity of class distinction. Thus, the kind of mutuality of interest that has never existed before is emerging among people from mutually exclusive social groups. Moreover, the discovery that they can have an ascertainable impact on politics, albeit still largely limited to the local level, when they cooperate with one another across conventional cleavages on the basis of the mutuality of interest is engendering among these citizens an increasing awareness of their inherent political competence and efficacy. Subject competence that has characterized Japan's political culture in the past is gradually being replaced by citizen competence. Traditional Japanese political culture has been segmentally exclusive, authoritarian, subject-competent, materialist-oriented, and ideologically bifurcated. The emerging political culture seems to be cross-stratally open, egalitarian, citizen-competent, less materially oriented, and supraideological. Gradual and hesitant though it may be, the transformation in the character of political culture is bound to be of great historic import for the future of Japanese politics and society.

Japanese politics has in the past and in the existing literature been regarded as variously deficient in modernity, as we discussed in the opening chapter of this volume. Somehow, it has been widely felt by both Japanese and foreign observers that Japan has a lot to catch up with in order to be legitimately certified as fully modern and developed in her politics. This view, of course, has been the product of a particular comparative perspective that has dominated and, in more senses than one, still dominates the discipline of comparative politics. Every analytical perspective dictates certain types of criteria, and criteria that underlie this conventional perspective of political change and development are generically Western or, perhaps more accurately, Anglo-American. Since Japan is generically different—neither American nor British—she is perforce short of the requisite conditions that would fully satisfy the criteria inherent in this conventional perspective.

Viewed from a different analytical perspective, as we have attempted to view in the present volume, however, our perception of Japan and her politics differs considerably from the picture of Japan and her politics that would emerge from an investigation from the conventional perspective. We have attempted to study Japanese politics on its own ecological terms. These ecological terms, not incidentally, are not unique to Japan. They are generated by certain dynamics of modern industrialism that Japan shares with other advanced industrial nations. In an important sense, therefore, they could provide a basis upon which not only Japan but also any other advanced industrial society may be studied and, hence, a comparative study of any number of such nations may be feasible. In any event, this perspective, arising as it does from certain elements of transition from industrial to postindustrial societies, has led us to a tentative conclusion that, in many of her political dimensions, Japan is manifesting certain phenomena of political change that go beyond those known within the modern, open industrial world. The question of what causes Japan to manifest such change much more readily or sooner than some other advanced industrial states is not central to the present volume, though some considerations regarding it have been implicit in various parts of the volume. This question, which is indeed not only germane but also crucial to a comparative inquiry, would warrant an entirely separate and more rigorous treatment.

There is always a possibility that the process of political change gets perverted or distorted. Any society in transition, be it from preindustrial to industrial or from industrial to postindustrial society, faces this danger. The kind of direction in which our study suggests Japanese politics seems to be moving could be seriously hampered, even reversed, by the emergence of contingencies whose destabilizing effects are of great magnitude. War (however unlikely it may be), depression (due to any number of causes both domestic and external), or even a prolonged period of serious resource shortage (as ominously hinted at by the Arab oil embargo a few years ago) could repress impulses toward postindustrial politics and reinvigorate forces of industrial politics. Even without such serious contingencies, the course of political change in Japan in her transition from the industrial to the postindustrial era will most likely be less than certain, consistent, and smooth. Such, however, is the inherent nature of any historically significant transitional travail.

Bibliography

Akimoto, Ritsuo. "Jumin Undo no Shokeitai." In *Jumin Sanka to Jichi no Kakushin*, edited by Haruo Matsubara. Tokyo: Gakuyo Shobo, 1975.

Almond, Gabriel A., and Verba, Sidney. *The Civic Culture: Political Attitudes and Democracy in Five Nations*. Boston and Toronto: Little, Brown, 1965.

Arendt, Hannah. *On Revolution*. New York: Viking, 1965.

Aron, Raymond. *The Industrial Society*. New York: Simon & Schuster, 1967.

———. *Progress and Disillusion*. New York: Praeger, 1968.

Asahi Janaru.

Asahi Shimbun.

Asahi Shimbun Sha. *Asahi Nenkan 1973*. Tokyo: Asahi Shimbun Sha, 1973.

———. *Asahi Nenkan 1975*. Tokyo: Asahi Shimbun Sha, 1975.

———. *Nihon Kyosanto*. Tokyo: Asahi Shimbun Sha, 1973.

Baerwald, Hans H. "Factional Politics in Japan." *Current History* 46 (April 1964).

————. "Itto-Nanaraku: Japan's 1969 Elections." *Asian Survey* 10 (March 1970).

————. "Japan: New Diplomatic Horizons, Old-Style Domestic Politics." *Asian Survey* 8 (January 1968).

————. *Japan's Parliament: An Introduction.* New York: Cambridge University Press, 1974.

Beardsley, Richard, et al. *Village Japan.* Chicago: University of Chicago Press, 1959.

Bell, Daniel. *The Coming of Post-Industrial Society: A Venture in Social Forecasting.* New York: Basic Books, 1973.

————. *The End of Ideology.* Glencoe, Ill.: Free Press, 1960.

————. "Notes on the Post-Industrial Society I." *Public Interest* 6 (Winter 1967).

————. "Notes on the Post-Industrial Society II." *Public Interest* 7 (Spring 1967).

————. "The Public Household—On 'Fiscal Sociology' and the Liberal Society." *Public Interest* 37 (Fall 1974).

Benedict, Ruth. *The Chrysanthemum and the Sword.* Boston: Houghton Mifflin, 1946.

Bennis, Warren G., and Slater, Philip. *The Temporary Society.* New York: Harper & Row, 1968.

Bieda, K. *The Structure and Operation of the Japanese Economy.* Sydney: John Wiley & Sons Australia Pty., 1970.

Birnbaum, Norman. *The Crisis of Industrial Society.* New York: Oxford University Press, 1969.

————. *Toward A Critical Sociology.* New York: Oxford University Press, 1971.

Boguslaw, Robert. *The New Utopians: A Study of System Design and Social Change.* Englewood Cliffs, N.J.: Prentice-Hall, 1965.

Brzezinski, Zbigniew. *Between Two Ages: America's Role in the Technetronic Era.* New York: Viking, 1970.

Cheng, Peter P. "The Japanese Cabinets 1885–1973: An Elite Analysis." *Asian Survey* 14 (December 1974).

Chuokoron.

Cole, Allan B., et al. *Socialist Parties in Postwar Japan.* New Haven and London: Yale University Press, 1966.

Cole, Robert E. *Japanese Blue Collar: The Changing Tradition.* Berkeley, Los Angeles, and London: University of California Press, 1971.

————. "Japanese Workers, Unions, and the Marxist Appeal." *Japan Interpreter* 6 (Summer 1970).

Collingwood, Robin G. *The Idea of History.* New York: Oxford University Press, 1967.

Curtis, Gerald L. *Election Campaigning Japanese Style.* New York and London: Columbia University Press, 1971.

———. "The 1969 General Election in Japan." *Asian Survey* 10 (October 1970).

DeVos, George A. "Japan's Outcast: The Problem of the Burakumin." In *The Fourth World: Victims of Group Oppression,* edited by Ben Whitaker. New York: Schocken Books, 1973.

Dimock, Marshall E. *The Japanese Technocracy: Management and Government in Japan.* New York and Tokyo: Walker/ Weatherhill, 1968.

DiPalma, Giuseppe. *The Study of Conflict in Western Society: A Critique of the End of Ideology.* Morristown, N.J.: General Learning Press, 1973.

Dixon, Karl. "The Growth of a 'Popular' Japanese Communist Party." *Pacific Affairs* 45 (Fall 1972).

Doi, Takeo. *Amae no Kozo.* Tokyo: Kobundo, 1971.

Duverger, Maurice. *Political Parties.* New York: Wiley, 1963. Translated by Barbara and Robert North.

Eda, Saburo, "Kakushin Seiken wa toreru ka." *Jiyu* 14 (February 1972).

———. "A New Vision for Socialism," *Journal of Social and Political Ideas in Japan* 1 (August 1963).

Ellul, Jacques. *The Technological Society.* New York: Vintage Books, 1964.

Endo, Kazuo. "Tenkan e no Shido." *Sekai,* February 1973.

Epstein, Leon D. *Political Parties in Western Democracies.* New York: Praeger, 1967.

Etzioni, Amitai. *The Active Society.* New York: Free Press, 1968.

Fukui, Haruhiro. *Party in Power: The Japanese Liberal Democrats and Policymaking.* Berkeley, Los Angeles: University of California Press, 1970.

Galbraith, John K. *The New Industrial State.* Boston: Houghton Mifflin, 1967.

Gallagher, Charles F. *Prosperity, Pollution, Prestige.* American Universities Field Staff Report, Asia 17, no. 3 (July 1971).

Gibney, Frank. *Japan: The Fragile Superpower.* New York: Norton, 1975.

Gomi, Kosuke. "Tanaka Kakuei Shi ni miru Gakureki Yuyo Ron." *Chuokoron,* January 1975.

Guillain, Robert. *The Japanese Challenge.* Philadelphia and New York: Lippincott, 1970. Translated by Patrick O'Brian.

Gusfield, Joseph R. *Symbolic Crusade: Status Politics and the American Temperance Movement.* Urbana and London: University of Illinois Press, 1966.

Haga, Yasushi. "Datsu Seito-ka Jidai to yu Genso." *Jiyu*, December 1971.

————. *Gendai Seiji no Choryu.* Tokyo: Ningen no Kagaku Sha, 1975.

Hagiwara, Nobutoshi. "Some Doubts about the Japan Socialist Party." *Journal of Social and Political Ideas in Japan* 3 (August 1965).

Hancock, M. Donald, and Sjoberg, Gideon, eds. *Politics in the Postwelfare State: Responses to the New Individualism.* New York and London: Columbia University Press, 1972.

Hani, Goro. *Toshi no Ronri.* Tokyo: Keiso Shobo, 1969.

Hartman, Heinz. "Institutional Immobility and Attitudinal Change in West Germany." *Comparative Politics* 2 (July 1970).

Heaphy, James J. *Spatial Dimensions of Developmental Administration.* Durham, N.C.: Duke University Press, 1971.

Heilbroner, Robert L. *The Making of Economic Society.* Englewood Cliffs, N.J.: Prentice-Hall, 1962.

Heisler, Martin O., ed. *Politics in Europe: Structures and Processes in Some Postindustrial Democracies.* New York: McKay, 1974.

Himmelstrand, Ulf. "Depoliticization and Political Involvement: A Theoretical and Empirical Approach." In *Mass Politics: Studies in Political Sociology*, edited by Eric Allardt and Stein Rokkan. New York: Free Press, 1970.

Hori, Yukio. *Komeito Ron: Sono Kodo to Taishitsu.* Tokyo: Aoki Shoten, 1973.

Huntington, Samuel P. "Political Development and Political Decay." *World Politics* 16 (April 1975).

————. "Postindustrial Politics: How Benign Will It Be?" *Comparative Politics* 6 (January 1974).

Ide, Yoshinori. "Konmei no naka no Hoshu Gyakuten Senkyo." *Asahi Janaru*, 19 July 1974.

Iizuka, Shigetaro. "Kakushin wa ikutsu Chiji o toru ka." *Chuokoron*, January 1975.

Ike, Nobutaka. "Economic Growth and Intergenerational Change in Japan." *American Political Science Review* 67 (December 1973).

————. *Japan: The New Superstate.* San Francisco: Freeman, 1974.

————. *Japanese Politics: Patron-Client Democracy.* New York: Knopf, 1972.

Inglehart, Ronald. "The Silent Revolution in Europe: Intergenerational Change in Post-Industrial Societies." *American Political Science Review* 65 (December 1971).

Irie, Tokuro. "Nichijo Katsudo to wa nani ka." *Chuokoron,* March 1970.

Ishida, Tadashi. "Progressive Political Parties and Popular Movement." *Journal of Social and Political Ideas in Japan* 3 (April 1965).

Ishikawa, Masumi, "Datsu Seito so no Kiken kara no Tenkai." *Asahi Janaru,* 9 July 1974.

Japan: Environment Agency. *Quality of the Environment in Japan 1973.*

————. Keizai Kikaku Cho: *Kokumin Seikatsu Hakusho 1970.* Tokyo, 1971.

————. Ministry of Health and Welfare: *Showa 48 Nen Ban Kosei Hakusho.* 1973.

————. Ministry of Foreign Affairs: *Information Bulletin 1973.*

————. Sorifu Tokei Kyoku: *Nihon Tokei Nenkan Showa 48–49 Nen.* Tokyo, 1974.

————. Sorifu Tokei Kyoku: *Kokusai Tokei Yoran 1975.* Tokyo 1975.

Japan Interpreter.

Japan Quarterly.

Japan Times Weekly.

Japan Society, Inc. (New York). *Social Change in the United States and Japan.* Report on a Wingspread Conference sponsored by Japan Society, Inc. and the Johnson Foundation, November 1972.

The Japanese Political Science Association, ed. *Political Participation: Theory and Practice: The Annals of the Japanese Political Science Association 1974.* Tokyo: Iwamani, 1974.

Johnson, Chalmers. "The Reemployment of Retired Government Bureaucrats in Japanese Big Business." *Asian Survey* 14 (November 1974).

Kahn, Herman. *The Emerging Japanese Superstate.* Englewood Cliffs, N.J.: Prentice-Hall, 1970.

————, and Wiener, Anthony. *The Year 2000: A Framework for Speculation for the Next Thirty-Three Years.* New York: Macmillan, 1967.

Kaminogo, Toshiaki. "Shakaito: Soso Koshin Kyoku." *Bungei Shunju*, September 1975.

Kataoka, Hiromitsu. "Koka 100% no Seito Senryaku." *Jiyu*, June 1971.

Kawai, Hidekazu. "Parliamentary Democracy in Crisis: An Analysis of the Weakness of the Socialist Party." *Japan Interpreter* 6 (Autumn 1970).

Kesselman, Mark. "Overinstitutionalization and Political Constraint: The Case of France." *Comparative Politics* 3 (October 1970).

Komei Senkyo Renmei, ed. *Toitsu Chiho Senkyo to Yukensha 1967–1971*. 2 vols. Tokyo: Komei Senkyo Renmei, 1972.

Kokumin no Seiji Kenkyu Kai, ed. *Kutabare Jiminto*. Tokyo: Eru Shuppan Sha, 1970.

Komuro, Naoki. "Kakushin Jichitai no Tohyo Kozo." *Asahi Janaru*, 29 December 1972.

Koyama, Hirotake. *Sengo Nihon Kyosanto Shi*. Tokyo: Mitsuki Shobo, 1968.

Krauss, Ellis S. *Japanese Radicals Revisited: Student Protest in Postwar Japan*. Berkeley, Los Angeles, London: University of California Press, 1974.

Kubota, Akira. *Higher Civil Servants in Postwar Japan*. Princeton, N.J.: Princeton University Press, 1969.

Kusayanagi, Daizo. "Kanryo Okoku Ron: Okura Sho." *Bungei Shunju*, June 1974.

Kuwata, Koichiro. "Political Parties in the Next Decade." *Japan Quarterly* 17 (April–June 1970).

Kyogoku, Jun'ichi, and Ike, Nobutaka. *Urban-Rural Differences in Voting Behavior in Postwar Japan*. Stanford, Calif.: Stanford University Press, 1959.

Langer, Paul F. *Communism in Japan: A Case of Political Neutralization*. Stanford, Calif.: Hoover Institution Press, 1972.

Lee, Chae-lin, "Factional Politics in the Japanese Socialist Party: The Chinese Cultural Revolution Case." *Asian Survey* 10 (March 1970).

Lee, Joo-in. "Komeito: Sokagakkai-ism in Japanese Politics." *Asian Survey* 10 (June 1970).

Leiserson, Michael. "Factions and Coalitions in One-Party Japan: An Interpretation Based on The Theory of Games." *American Political Science Review* 62 (September 1968).

Levine, Solomon B. *Industrial Relations in Postwar Japan*. Urbana, Ill.: University of Illinois Press, 1960.

Lindberg, Leon N., ed. *Politics and the Future of Industrial Society.* New York: McKay, 1976.

————. *Stress and Contradiction in Modern Capitalism: Public Policy and the Theory of State.* Lexington, Mass.: Lexington Press, 1976.

Lipset, Seymour M. *Political Man: The Social Bases of Politics.* Garden City, N.Y.: Doubleday, 1963.

Lowi, Theodore. *The Politics of Disorder.* New York and London: Basic Books, 1971.

Macrae, Norman. "Pacific Century, 1975–2075?" *Economist,* 4–10 January 1975.

Mainichi Shimbun.

Massey, Joseph A. "The Missing Leader: Japanese Youth's View of Political Authority." *American Political Science Review* 69 (March 1975).

Masujima, Hiroshi. "The Japan Socialist Party: How to Break the Present Stalemate." *Journal of Social and Political Ideas in Japan* 3 (April 1965).

Matsubara, Haruo, ed. *Jumin Sanka to Jichi no Kakushin.* Tokyo: Okubo Shobo, 1975.

Meadows, Donella H., et al. *The Limits to Growth: A Report for the Club of Rome's Project on the Predicament of Mankind.* New York: New American Library, 1972.

Miyakawa, Takayoshi, ed. *Seiji Hando Bukku.* Tokyo: Seiji Koho Senta, 1973.

Morley, James, W., ed. *Prologue to the Future: The United States and Japan in the Postindustrial Age.* Lexington, Toronto, London: Heath, 1974.

Murakami, Shigeyoshi. *Komeito.* Tokyo: Shin Nihon Shuppan Sha, 1970.

Muramatsu, Mikio. "Political Participation and Administrative Process in Contemporary Japan." *Annals of the Japanese Political Science Association 1974.* Tokyo: Iwanami, 1974.

Nakane, Chie. *Japanese Society.* Berkeley and Los Angeles: University of California Press, 1970.

Nihon Seikei Shimbun Sha. *Bessatsu Kokkai Binran: Shiryo Soshu Hen.* Tokyo: Nihon Seikei Shimbun Shuppan Bu, 1975.

Oberdorfer, Don. "Japan: The Risen Sun." *Washington Post,* 3–7 August 1975.

Ohara Institute for Social Research. *Nihon Rodo Nenkan 1974.* Tokyo: Hosei University Press, 1974.

Ohashi, Ryuken. *Nihon no Kaikyu Kosei*. Tokyo: Iwanami, 1972.

Okimoti, Daniel I. "LDP in Transition: Birth of the Miki Cabinet." *Japan Interpreter* 9 (Spring 1975).

Okubo, Sadayoshi. *Nihon-jin no Tohyo Kodo*. Tokyo. Shiseido, 1974.

Okuda, Michihiro, et al. *Toshika Shakai to Ningen*. Tokyo: Nihon Hoso Shuppan Kyokai, 1975.

Oshima, Kiyoshi. "Nihon Nogyo wa korede yoinoka." *Sekai*, November 1971.

Oshima, Taro. "Kakushin Jichitai to Kanryosei." In *Gendai Gyosei to Kanryosei*, edited by Ken Taniuchi et al. 2 vols. Tokyo: Tokyo University Press, 1974.

Packard, George R. "Living with the Real Japan." *Foreign Affairs* 46 (October 1967).

————. *Protest in Tokyo: The Security Treaty Crisis of 1960*. Princeton, N.J.: Princeton University Press, 1966.

Passin, Herbert. "The Sources of Protest in Japan." *American Political Science Review* 56 (June 1962).

Reich, Charles. *The Greening of America*. New York: Random House, 1971.

Richardson, Bradley M. *The Political Culture of Japan*. Berkeley, Los Angeles, London: University of California Press, 1974.

————. "Urbanization and Political Participation: The Case of Japan." *American Political Science Review* 67 (June 1973).

Roszak, Theodore. *Where the Wasteland Ends: Politics and Transcendence in Postindustrial Society*. New York: Doubleday, 1972.

Ryang, Key Sun. "Postwar Japanese Political Leadership: A Study of Prime Ministers." *Asian Survey* 13 (November 1973).

Sakisaka, Itsuro. "A Correct Platform and a Proper Organization." *Journal of Social and Political Ideas in Japan* 3 (April 1965).

Sande Mainichi.

Sankei Shimbun, ed. *Nihon Kyosanto no Subete*. Tokyo: Sankei Shimbun Shuppan Kyoku, 1973.

Satake, Hiroshi. "Elections and Citizens' Movements in Japan." *Annals of the Japanese Political Science Association 1974*. Tokyo: Iwanami, 1974.

Scalapino, Robert A. *The Japanese Communist Movement 1920–1966*. Berkeley and Los Angeles: University of California Press, 1967.

———. "Japanese Socialism in Crisis." *Foreign Affairs* 38 (January 1960).

———, and Masumi, Junnosuke. *Parties and Politics in Contemporary Japan*. Berkeley and Los Angeles: University of California Press, 1962.

Segal, Ronald. *The Struggle Against History*. London: Weidenfeld & Nicolson, 1971.

Sekai.

Seki, Yoshihiko. "The Socialist Party and 'Structural Reform.'" *Journal of Social and Political Ideas in Japan* 1 (August 1963).

Sengoku, Tamotsu, and Toyama, Atsuko. *Hikaku Nihonjin Ron*. Tokyo: Shogakukan, 1973.

Shaplen, Robert. "Letter from Tokyo." *New Yorker*, 20 May 1974.

———. "A Reporter at Large: From MacArthur to Miki—II." *New Yorker*, 11 August 1975.

Sheldon, Eleanor, and Moore, Wilbert, eds. *Indicators of Social Change*. New York: Russell Sage Foundation, 1968.

Shimizu, Shinzo. *Nihon no Shakai-Minshushugi*. Tokyo: Iwanami, 1972.

Shinohara, Hajime. "Bunka Henyo to Chiho Jichi no Kadai." *Sekai*, April 1971.

———. "Bunkyokuka suru Seiji Ishiki." *Asahi Janaru*, 22 December 1972.

———. *Nihon no Seiji Fudo*. Tokyo: Iwanami, 1971.

———. "70 nen dai to Kakushin no Kanosei." *Sekai*, March 1970.

Shiratori, Rei. *Nihon ni okeru Hoshu to Kakushin*. Tokyo: Nihon Keizai Shimbun Sha, 1973.

———. "Seiji no Kakushin o motomete." *Jiyu*, November 1970.

Shon, Donald A. *Beyond the Stable State: Public and Private Learning in a Changing Society*. London: Temple Smith, 1971.

Smith, Robert, and Beardsley, Richard, eds. *Japanese Culture: Its Development and Characteristics*. Chicago: Aldine, 1962.

Stockwin, J. A. A. *The Japanese Socialist Party and Neutralism*. Melbourne: Melbourne University Press, 1968.

———. "The Japanese Socialist Party Under New Leadership." *Asian Survey* 6 (April 1966).

Sunada, Ichiro. "The Thought and Behavior of Zengakuren:

Japanese Student Movement." *Asian Survey*
69).

o. "Kyosanto dai 12 kai Taikai o kaibo suru." *Jiyu*,
ry 1974.

ia, Takashi. "Tanaka Kakuei Kenkyu: Sono Kinmyaku
o Jinmyaku." *Bungei Shunju*, November 1974.

guchi, Fukuji. "The Japan Socialist Party." *Journal of Social
and Political Ideas in Japan* 3 (April 1965).

———. *Nihon Seiji no Doko to Tembo*. Tokyo: Miraisha, 1964.

Takabatake, Michitoshi. "Citizens' Movements: Organizing the
Spontaneous." *Japan Interpreter* 9 (Winter 1975).

Takada, Yoshitoshi. "Mezameru howaito kara." *Asahi Janaru*,
6 September 1974.

Takahashi, Masao. *Modern Japanese Economy*. Tokyo: Kokusai
Bunka Shinko Kai, 1968.

Taniuchi, Ken, et al. *Gendai Gyosei to Kanryosei*. 2 vols. Tokyo:
Tokyo University Press, 1974.

Thayer, Nathaniel B. *How the Conservatives Rule Japan*. Princeton, N.J.: Princeton University Press, 1969.

Thurston, Donald R. "Aftermath in Minamata." *Japan Interpreter* 9 (Spring 1974).

Toffler, Alvin. *Future Shock*. New York: Bantam Books, 1970.

Tokei Suri Kenkyu Jo. *Shimin Ishiki no Kenkyu: Suri Kenkyu
Ripoto 31*. Tokyo: Tokei Suri Kenkyu Jo, 1973.

———. *Nihonjin no Kokuminsei*. 2 vols. Tokyo: Shiseido, 1973.

Tokyo Shimbun.

Totten, George O. "The People's Parliamentary Path of the Japanese Communist Party—Part I and Part II." *Pacific Affairs* 46 (Summer 1973 and Fall 1973).

Touraine, Alain. *The Post-Industrial Society: Tomorrow's Social
History*. New York: Random House, 1971. Translated by
Leonard F. X. Mayhew.

Tsuneishi, Warren M. *Japanese Political Style*. New York:
Harper & Row, 1968.

Tsurutani, Taketsugu. "Causes of Paralysis." *Foreign Policy* 14
(Spring 1974).

———. "A New Era of Japanese Politics: Tokyo's Gubernatorial
Election." *Asian Survey* 12 (May 1972).

———. "Political Leadership: Tentative Thoughts from Early
Meiji Japan." *Journal of Political and Military Sociology* 1
(Fall 1973).

———. "Japan as a Postindustrial Society." In *Politics and the*

Future of Industrial Society, edited by Leon N. Lindberg. New York: McKay, 1976.

Uchida, Kenzo. *Sengo Nihon no Hoshu Seiji.* Tokyo: Iwanami, 1972.

Uehara, Shumpei, ed. *Nihon no Nashonarizumu.* Tokyo: Tokuma Shoten, 1966.

Van Zandt, Howard. "Japanese Culture and the Business Boom." *Foreign Affairs* 48 (January 1970).

Vogel, Ezra F. "Beyond Salary: Mamachi Revisited." *Japan Interpreter* 6 (Summer 1970).

Ward, Robert E. *Japan's Political System.* Englewood Cliffs, N.J.: Prentice-Hall, 1967.

Watanabe, Tsuneo. *Habatsu: Hoshuto no Kaibo.* Tokyo: Kobundo, 1958.

Watanuki, Joji. *Gendai Seiji to Shakai Hendo.* Tokyo: Tokyo University Press, 1967.

————. "Japanese Politics in Flux." In *Prologue to the Future: The United States and Japan in the Post-Industrial Age,* edited by James W. Morley. Lexington, Mass.: Heath, 1974.

White, James W. *The Sokagakkai and Mass Society.* Stanford, Calif.: Stanford University Press, 1970.

Yamaguchi, Toshio. "Jiminto Dai-ni-to Ron." *Jiyu,* May 1971.

Yamamoto, Eiji. "Hoshuto o hanarete yuku Nomin." *Asahi Janaru,* 11 November 1972.

Yanaga, Chitoshi. *Big Business in Japanese Politics.* New Haven and London: Yale University Press, 1968.

Yokoyama, Keiji. "Uragirareta Jumin Undo." *Asahi Janaru,* 7 May 1971.

Yomiuri Shimbun.

Yomiuri Shimbun Seiji Bu. *Nihon Kenryoku Chizu: Chiho Seiji no Sotenken to Kaibo.* Tokyo: Saimaru, 1971.

————. *Sori Daijin.* Tokyo: Yomiuri Shimbun Sha, 1972.

Yomiuro Shimbun Sha Yoron Chosa Shitsu. *Senkyo o Tettei Bunseki suru.* Tokyo: Yomiuri Shimbun Sha, 1975.

Yoshikawa, Yuichi. "Shakyo wa Shimin Undo o Riyo dekinai." *Chuokoron,* June 1973.

Yui, Tsunehiko. "The Japanese Propensity for Saving." *Japan Interpreter* 8 (Winter 1974).

Index